SMITHSONIAN INSTITUTION
BUREAU OF AMERICAN ETHNOLOGY
BULLETIN 90

PAPAGO MUSIC

BY

FRANCES DENSMORE

UNITED STATES
GOVERNMENT PRINTING OFFICE
WASHINGTON : 1929

Printing Statement:

Due to the very old age and scarcity of this book,
many of the pages may be hard to read due to the
blurring of the original text, possible missing pages,
missing text and other issues beyond our control.

Because this is such an important and rare work, we
believe it is best to reproduce this book regardless of
its original condition.

Thank you for your understanding.

LETTER OF TRANSMITTAL

SMITHSONIAN INSTITUTION,
BUREAU OF AMERICAN ETHNOLOGY,
Washington, D. C., May 8, 1928.

SIR: I have the honor to transmit the accompanying manuscript, entitled "Papago Music," by Miss Frances Densmore, and to recommend its publication as a bulletin of the Bureau of American Ethnology.

Very respectfully yours,

H. W. DORSEY,
Chief Clerk, Smithsonian Institution.

Dr. CHARLES G. ABBOT,
Secretary of the Smithsonian Institution.

FOREWORD

The songs of a desert people are here presented, and will be found to contain interesting contrasts to the songs of the woodland, prairie, and high plateau tribes previously considered.[1] The Papago are a gentle, agricultural tribe living in Sonora, Mexico, and southern Arizona. Their songs were recorded at San Xavier, Sells, and Vomari, on the Papago Reservation in Arizona, during the spring of 1920 and the following winter.

The writer desires to acknowledge the assistance of her principal interpreters, Harry Encinas of San Xavier, who was formerly a student at the United States Indian School, Carlisle, Pa., and Hugh Norris, of Sells, the official interpreter of the Indian agency. Without the interest and cooperation of these interpreters it would have been impossible to win the confidence of the Papago and make so intimate a study of their music.

---

[1] Chippewa Music, Bull. 45; Chippewa Music II, Bull. 53; Teton Sioux Music, Bull. 61; Northern Ute Music, Bull. 75, and Mandan and Hidatsa Music, Bull. 80, Bur. Amer. Ethn.; Music of the Tule Indians of Panama, Smithsonian Misc. Colls., vol. 77, no. 11.

CONTENTS

ILLUSTRATIONS

LIST OF SONGS

1. ARRANGED IN ORDER OF SERIAL NUMBERS

SONGS CONNECTED WITH LEGENDS

XI

Songs Used in the Treatment of the Sick

SONGS CONNECTED WITH CEREMONIES

2. ARRANGED IN ORDER OF CATALOGUE NUMBERS

2. ARRANGED IN ORDER OF CATALOGUE NUMBERS—Continued

2. Arranged in Order of Catalogue Numbers—Continued

Catalogue No.	Title of song	Name of singer	Serial No.	Page
993	Song for success in a race_____	Mattias Hendricks_	149	202
994	"My wings make a noise as I fly"____	_____do_____	151	204
995	Song concerning the lost children_____	_____do_____	105	152
996	Song of Elder Brother after he created the spirits of men.	_____do_____	3	20
997	Song of Elder Brother after he created the wind and the clouds.	_____do_____	4	20
998	Song after the inhabitants of Casa Grande were killed.	Jose Manuel_____	16	31
999	Song that gave woman the strength to carry the burden basket.	_____do_____	17	32
1000	Song of Coyote after the flood_____	_____do_____	1	18
1001	Song of Elder Brother after the flood_	_____do_____	2	19
1002	"Sing louder"_____	_____do_____	138	190
1003	"I am dancing"_____	_____do_____	139	191
1004	"I have gone through this before you."	_____do_____	137	189
1005	"You beg for food like a woman" ___	_____do_____	136	189
1006	"We are making wonderful things"__	_____do_____	101	146
1007	"Each singer wears a white feather"_	_____do_____	102	147
1008	"A flaming light in the east"_____	_____do_____	103	148
1009	"We are singing in the night"_____	_____do_____	99	142
1010	Song before an expedition to obtain salt.	_____do_____	121	171
1011	"We will run around the salt bed"___	_____do_____	122	172
1012	"Cowaka, come and help us sing"_	do	120	169
1013	Song for success in hunting_____	_____do_____	160	211
1014	Song to cure an injury by a horse____	_____do_____	58	99
1015	"You tied me with a black hair rope"_	_____do_____	60	100
1016	"I came from the east"_____	_____do_____	59	100
1017	Song of a black horse_____	_____do_____	61	101
1018	Song of an unsuccessful hunter_____	_____do_____	161	211
1019	".A place of many springs"_____	Rafael Mendez____	140	192
1020	Song concerning a wounded Apache__	_____do_____	141	193
1021	"They covered me with sunshine"___	_____do_____	54	96
1022	"A painted snake comes out"_____	_____do_____	55	97
1023	Song to a little yellow wasp_____	_____do_____	56	98
1024	Song of the badger medicine_____	_____do_____	53	95
1025	Song after drinking the wine_____	_____do_____	111	160
1026	"A blue wind"_____	_____do_____	110	159
1027	Song of the dawn_____	_____do_____	70	112
1028	"The wind blows from the sea"_____	Jose Hendricks____	123	173
1029	"The rain on the corn and the squash"	_____do_____	124	174
1030	"The sun rises over the mountain"___	_____do_____	125	175
1031	Song of the watchers (b) _____	_____do_____	107	154
1032	Song during rain divination_____	_____do_____	108	156
1033	"The morning shines on Manasi Mountain."	_____do_____	46	87

2. Arranged in Order of Catalogue Numbers—Continued

Cata-logue No.	Title of song	Name of singer	Serial No.	Page
1034	"The pigeon and his tiswin lodge"___	Jose Hendricks____	167	217
1035	Song of Earth Magician when disappearing in the ground.	_____do_____	5	21
1036	"Sandy loam fields"_____	Jose Pancho_____	48	92
1037	"I will sit and sing"_____	_____do_____	49	93
1038	"Out of the mountains"_____	_____do_____	50	93
1039	"Singing to the leaves and flowers"__	_____do_____	51	94
1040	"Toward the mountains"_____	_____do_____	52	95
1041	Song when administering herb medicine.	_____do_____	47	89
1042	"Brown lizard"_____	_____do_____	57	98
1043	"I am running toward the edge of the world."	Jose Aseencio_____	114	165
1044	"White blossoms on Baboquivari Mountain."	_____do_____	115	166
1045	"Cottonwood leaves are falling"_____	_____do_____	116	166
1046	"The morning is shining upward"___	_____do_____	117	167
1047	"On top of the mountain the wind blows."	_____do_____	118	167
1048	Dream song of a captive woman_____	_____do_____	152	205
1049	Song of the watchers (a)_____	_____do_____	106	154
1050	"The corn on Frog Mountain"_____	_____do_____	100	145
1051	Opening song of the Bat dance_____	_____do_____	150	203
1052	"The squirrel and the mesquite beans"_	_____do_____	163	213
1053	"The robin brings the cold wind"____	_____do_____	164	214
1054	"I am going to the mountain"_____	Victoria_____	154	206
1055	"I wandered away"_____	_____do_____	153	206
1056	"The thunder sounds in the east"___	_____do_____	156	208
1057	"I went to the edge of the world"___	_____do_____	155	207
1058	Song while tiswin is distributed_____	_____do_____	109	157
1059	"White mountain birds were singing"_	_____do_____	157	209
1060	"A black crow"_____	_____do_____	158	209
1061	"I sat under Santa Rita Mountains"_	_____do_____	159	210
1062	"The little captive children"_____	_____	135	187
1063	"Clouds roll toward me"_____	Leonardo Rios____	95	135
1064	"Great white birds over the ocean"__	_____do_____	96	136
1065	"The dwelling place of the sun"_____	_____do_____	97	137
1066	"I will toss up the sticks"_____	_____do_____	43	79
1067	"The snow is falling"_____	_____do_____	165	215
1068	Lullaby_____	Juana Maria_____	162	212
1069	"The voice of the herald"_____	_____do_____	134	186
1070	"I met a Mexican"_____	_____do_____	166	216
1071	Song of the Limo_____	Harry Encinas____	143	196
1072	"A white wind from the west"_____	_____do_____	45	86
1073	"I draw the rain"_____	Jose Antoin_____	104	150
1074	"Clouds are approaching"_____	Mattias Encinas___	98	140
1075	"The sunrise"_____	Kiyatan_____	71	113
1076	Opening song of the Limo_____	Nuñez_____	142	194

SPECIAL SIGNS USED IN TRANSCRIPTIONS OF SONGS

These signs are intended simply as aids to the student in becoming acquainted with the songs. They should be understood as supplementary to the descriptive analysis rather than a part of the musical notation.

+ placed above a note shows that the tone was sung slightly higher than the indicated pitch. In many instances the tones designated by this and the following sign were "unfocused tones," or were tones the intonation of which varied in the several renditions of the song. The intonation of these tones was not such as to suggest the intentional use of "fractional intervals" by the singer.

− placed above a note shows that the tone was sung slightly lower than the indicated pitch.

(· placed above a note shows that the tone was prolonged slightly beyond the indicated time. This and the following sign are used only when the deviation from strict time is less than half the time unit of the song and appears to be unimportant. In many instances the duration of the tones thus marked is variable in the several renditions of the song.

·) placed above a note shows that the tone was given slightly less than the indicated time.

⌐⎯⎯⎯⎯⌐ placed above a series of notes indicates that these tones constitute a rhythmic unit.

NAMES OF SINGERS AND NUMBERS OF SONGS TRANSCRIBED

Sivariano Garcia	68	Juana Maria	3
Jose Manuel	21	Harry Encinas	2
Mattias Hendricks	20	Mattias Encinas	1
Jose Asceneio	11	Jose Antoin	1
Rafael Mendez	9	Kiyatan	1
Victoria	9	Nuñez	1
Jose Hendricks	8		
Jose Panco	7	Total	167
Leonardo Rios	5		

CHARACTERIZATION OF SINGERS

Sivariano Garcia, who recorded more songs than any other Papago, lives at San Xavier and is the singer with Owl Woman when she treats the sick. He is familiar with all the old tribal songs and has an excellent voice.

Jose Manuel of Sells is a carpenter by trade. He was one of the Papago who volunteered to go with the United States Cavalry on their quest of Geronimo and was with them when the famous Apache was captured.

Mattias Hendricks, whose songs are next in number, is chief at Vomari village and acted as interpreter during the writer's work in that locality. His father is said to have been chief of all the Papago.

Jose Ascencio, also of Vomari, is an energetic, industrious man with a particularly wide knowledge of old songs and customs.

Rafael Mendez lives at Vomari. His selection of songs shows a refinement and poetry that are interesting.

Victoria is an aged member of the tribe living at Sells. His voice is weak but he recalls many old songs.

Jose Hendricks, brother of Mattias Hendricks of Vomari, is almost totally blind. The light was so painful to his eyes that he was photographed with eyes downcast. In the words of his songs, like those of Mendez, we find particularly fine examples of native poetry.

Jose Panco, of San Xavier, was a doctor who treated those afflicted with "deer sickness." He died in 1928.

Leonardo Rios, who also lives at San Xavier, expressed a conviction that a machine could not record and reproduce the voices of Indians. His statement was brought to the writer's attention, when working at that place, and he was invited to come and hear the records made by his friends. Later he recorded several songs.

The only woman who recorded songs was Juana Maria of Sells, an aged woman living in the Papago village near the agency.

Harry Encinas, the interpreter at San Xavier, is not familiar with many old songs but recorded two which are of rather unusual interest.

Mattias Encinas, his father, is not considered a singer but recorded the songs of his dream, one of which is presented.

Jose Antoin is chief at Pisinimak village, northwest of Sells.

Kiyatan is an old medicine man living at San Xavier, a man of keen eye and quiet manner.

The only young man except Harry Encinas who was asked to record songs was Nuñez, who recorded one song.

PAPAGO MUSIC

By Frances Densmore

THE PAPAGO TRIBE [1]

The name of this tribe is derived from *papáh*, meaning "beans," and *óotam*, meaning "people." They are a Piman tribe, closely allied to the Pima, and their original home was the territory in the main and tributary valleys of the Santa Cruz River and in the territory south and southeast of the Gila River, especially south of Tucson, Ariz., and extending across the desert into Sonora, Mexico. They are an agricultural people, maize, beans, and cotton formerly being their principal crops, which they cultivated by irrigation. Many desert plants contributed to their food supply, especially the mesquite, the beans of which are eaten, and the saguaro or giant cactus (*Cereus giganteus*), from the fruit of which a ceremonial drink was formerly made. An extensive trade in salt was formerly conducted by the Papago, who obtained the salt from the great inland lagoons and sold it in Tucson and Tubac. At present their principal crops are wheat and barley, and they raise cattle to a considerable extent. They are by nature an industrious people and are now finding employment in various activities incidental to the coming of the white race. For instance, many are able to make a living by cutting mesquite wood on the desert and selling it in the neighboring towns. The skin of the Papago is reddish brown and they are gentle in their nature. Like the Pima, the Papago women are expert basket makers but their baskets are much coarser than those of the Pima. Their pottery is far inferior to that of the Pueblos, and the designs and patterns of both the baskets and the pottery are the same as those of the Pima. They were not lacking in bravery in old times, as shown by their expeditions against the Apache, from whose raids they suffered severely. Their typical dwelling was dome-shaped, consisting of a framework of saplings thatched with grass or leafy shrubs, with an adjacent shelter or ramada. At the present time they live chiefly in adobe houses. There are six subdivisions of the tribe living within the United States. The number of Papago in the United States as shown in the census last preceding this work was 4,465. There was no family of mixed blood (Papago and white) living on the reserva-

---

[1] See Handbook of American Indians, Bull. 30, part 2, Bur. Amer. Ethn., p. 200, from which this description of the tribe is quoted.

tion and it was the opinion that there was no mixture with Mexican or Spanish. The Government maintained four day schools on the reservation.

The study of Papago music was begun at San Xavier, near Tucson, Ariz., in February, 1920. The Papago village is near San Xavier Mission, which was established in 1692. At this mission the Franciscan Fathers minister to the Indians, who number about 700 in this locality. The Government agency was located here in 1915, but was moved two years later to Indian Oasis, now known as Sells, Ariz. The Papago at San Xavier live in adobe houses and still grind their own corn, but are adopting a general use of food supplies purchased in Tucson. (Pl. 2.) The country around San Xavier is desert with mesquite and cactus. There are rugged hills and deep gorges cut by rivers that are raging floods at some seasons and "dry runs" at other seasons. The principal varieties of cactus are the saguaro or giant cactus, and the cholla. (Pl. 3.)

On a hillside near San Xavier is an old burial place. (Pl. 4, a.) The burial spaces are formed by building a low stone parapet on the side of the hill and roofing it with heavy timbers thrust into the hillside. The bodies were placed in these spaces, or shelters, and all openings were closed with stones. After a suitable time the bodies were taken out and others were placed in the inclosure. There were compartments in these burial chambers and several bodies were placed in each compartment. They have not been used in recent times and some remain tightly closed, while in others it is possible to see parts of skeletons and fragments of various sorts. Plate 4, b, c, shows the same opening, one being at a distance and the other showing the interior, where a skull can be seen. Near it was a bone that appeared to be part of a leg or arm. Scattered about were bits of leather resembling parts of a saddle. This place is particularly sightly. It faces the south, with a magnificent sweep of view. The mountains in Mexico can be seen at a distance of about 40 miles, while in the foreground is an expanse of desert. The old and new are strangely mingled here, as it is in this desert that the Government is establishing (1921) an irrigation system by means of which the Indians will be able to irrigate their land.

A further study of Papago music was made in November and December, 1920, at Sells, more than 60 miles west of Tucson. Songs were also recorded at Vomari village, and information was obtained at Santa Rosa, the former being in the extreme southern and the latter in the extreme northern part of the reservation. The customs and songs differ somewhat in different localities, and numerous photographs were taken showing the geography of the country. Between Sells and Vomari the country is more mountainous than in the vicinity of San Xavier, the most prominent mountain being Baboquivari

SIVARIANO GARCIA PLAYING FLUTE

a, San Xavier village and mission

b, Well and water trough at San Xavier

c, Papago house at San Xavier

a, Desert near San Xavier

b, Hillside with saguaro cactus near San Xavier

c, Cholla cactus near San Xavier

SITES OF HILLSIDE BURIALS AT SAN XAVIER

a, Baboquivari Mountain, southeast of Sells, Ariz.

b, Foot of Baboquivari Mountain

c, Opposite Baboquivari Mountain

a, House in Santa Rosa village

b, Ramada in Santa Rosa village

c, Enclosure around water hole in Vomari village

a, Jose Panco using scraping sticks with basket resonator

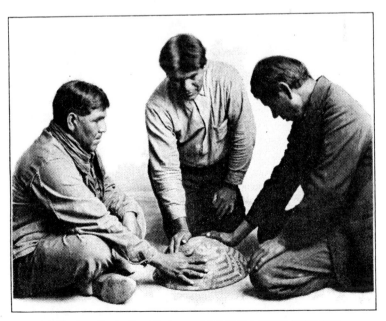

b, Sivariano Garcia, Harry Encinas, and Jose Panco pounding basket drum

a, Mattias Hendricks

b, Mother of Mattias Hendricks

TABULATED ANALYSES

COMPARISON OF CHIPPEWA, SIOUX, UTE, MANDAN, AND HIDATSA SONGS WITH PAPAGO SONGS

MELODIC ANALYSIS

TABLE 1.—TONALITY

	Chippewa, Sioux, Ute, Mandan, Hidatsa	Per cent	Papago	Per cent	Total	Per cent
Major tonality_____	442	*54*	78	*47*	520	*53*
Minor tonality_____	363	*44*	61	*36*	424	*42*
Both major and minor_____	3	------	2	*1*	5	------
Third lacking_____	10	*1*	16	*10*	26	*2*
Irregular_____	2	------	10	*6*	12	*1*
Total_____	820	------	167	------	987	------

TABLE 2.—FIRST NOTE OF SONG—ITS RELATION TO KEYNOTE

	Chippewa, Sioux, Ute, Mandan, Hidatsa	Per cent	Papago	Per cent	Total	Per cent
Beginning on the—						
Fourteenth_____	1	------	------	------	1	------
Thirteenth_____	4	------	------	------	4	------
Twelfth_____	143	*17*	------	------	143	*10*
Eleventh_____	14	*1*	------	------	14	*1*
Tenth_____	54	*7*	1	------	55	*6*
Ninth_____	28	*3*	------	------	28	*3*
Octave_____	188	*23*	11	*6*	199	*20*
Seventh_____	13	*1*	3	*1*	16	*2*
Sixth_____	19	*2*	15	*9*	34	*3*
Fifth_____	201	*24*	63	*37*	264	*30*
Fourth_____	14	*1*	3	*1*	17	*2*
Third_____	66	*8*	16	*10*	82	*8*
Second_____	17	*2*	5	*3*	22	*2*
Keynote_____	56	*7*	40	*24*	96	*10*
Irregular_____	2	------	10	*6*	12	*1*
Total_____	820	------	167	------	987	------

TABLE 3.—LAST NOTE OF SONG—ITS RELATION TO KEYNOTE

	Chippewa, Sioux, Ute, Mandan, Hidatsa	Per cent	Papago	Per cent	Total	Per cent
Ending on the—						
Sixth	1				1	
Fifth	253	30	74	44	327	33
Third	97	12	15	9	112	10
Keynote	467	57	68	41	535	54
Irregular	2		10	6	12	1
Total	820		167		987	

TABLE 4.—LAST NOTE OF SONG—ITS RELATION TO COMPASS OF SONG

	Chippewa, Sioux, Ute, Mandan, Hidatsa	Per cent	Papago	Per cent	Total	Per cent
Songs in which final note is—						
Lowest in song	715	87	18	10	733	74
Highest in song	1				1	
Immediately preceded by—						
Fifth below	1				1	
Fourth below	13	1	10	6	23	2
Major third below	4		3	2	7	
Minor third below	14	1	14	8	28	3
Whole tone below	17	2	2	1	19	2
Semitone below	7				7	
Immediately preceded by lower tones and containing tones lower than final tone	48	6	120	74	168	17
Total	820		167		987	

TABLE 5.—NUMBER OF TONES COMPRISED IN COMPASS OF SONG

	Chippewa, Sioux, Ute, Mandan, Hidatsa	Per cent	Papago	Per cent	Total	Per cent
Seventeen tones	3				3	
Fifteen tones	1				1	
Fourteen tones	15	2			15	2
Thirteen tones	54	6			54	5
Twelve tones	169	21	2	1	171	18
Eleven tones	78	9	4	2	82	8
Ten tones	105	13	6	3	111	10
Nine tones	76	9	27	13	103	10
Eight tones	217	26	67	40	284	30
Seven tones	33	4	29	18	62	6
Six tones	36	4	20	12	56	6
Five tones	26	3	10	6	36	4
Four tones	5		1		6	
Three tones	2		1		3	
Total	820		167		987	

TABLE 6.—TONE MATERIAL

	Chippewa, Sioux, Ute, Mandan, Hidatsa	Per cent	Papago	Per cent	Total	Per cent
First five-toned scale[1]	2	------	11	7	13	1
Second five-toned scale	86	10	13	8	99	10
Fourth five-toned scale	177	22	50	30	227	20
Fifth five-toned scale	2	------	------	------	2	------
Major triad	13	1	------	------	13	1
Major triad and one other tone	105	12	14	8	119	14
Minor triad	4	------	------	------	4	------
Minor triad and one other tone	86	10	------	------	86	9
Octave complete	51	6	7	4	58	6
Octave complete except seventh	75	9	18	10	93	9
Octave complete except seventh and one other tone	66	8	27	13	93	9
Octave complete except sixth	33	4	5	3	38	4
Octave complete except sixth and one other tone	15	2	------	------	15	1
Octave complete except fifth and one other tone	1	------	------	------	1	------
Octave complete except fourth	24	3	2	1	26	3
Octave complete except fourth and one other tone	8	------	2	1	10	1
Octave complete except third	2	------	3	1	5	------
Octave complete except second	26	3	1	------	27	3
Other combinations of tone	44	4	14	8	58	6
Total	820	------	167	------	987	------

[1] The 5-toned scales mentioned in this table are the 5 pentatonic scales according to Helmholtz, described by him as follows: "1. The first scale, without third or seventh . . . To the second scale, without second or sixth, belong most Scotch airs which have a minor character. . . The third scale, without third and sixth . . . To the fourth scale, without fourth or seventh, belong most Scotch airs which have the character of a major mode. The fifth scale, without second and fifth." (Helmholtz, H. L., The Sensations of Tone, London, 1885, pp. 260, 261.)

TABLE 7.—ACCIDENTALS

	Chippewa, Sioux, Ute, Mandan, Hidatsa	Per cent	Papago	Per cent	Total	Per cent
Songs containing—						
No accidentals	697	85	147	88	844	87
Sixth raised	14	1	3	2	17	1
Fourth raised	16	1	4	3	20	2
Third raised	2	------	1	------	3	------
Third lowered	------	------	2	------	2	------
Other accidentals	89	11	------	------	89	9
Irregular	2	------	10	6	12	1
Total	820	------	167	------	987	------

TABLE 8.—STRUCTURE

	Chippewa, Sioux, Ute, Mandan, Hidatsa	Per cent	Papago	Per cent	Total	Per cent
Melodic	482	59	112	67	594	60
Melodic with harmonic framework	161	19	36	21	197	20
Harmonic	175	21	9	6	184	19
Irregular	2	------	10	6	12	1
Total	820	------	167	------	987	------

TABLE 9.—FIRST PROGRESSION—DOWNWARD AND UPWARD

	Chippewa, Sioux, Ute, Mandan, Hidatsa	Per cent	Papago	Per cent	Total	Per cent
Downward	547	67	61	37	608	61
Upward	273	33	106	63	379	38
Total	820	------	167	------	987	------

TABLE 10.—TOTAL NUMBER OF PROGRESSIONS—DOWNWARD AND UPWARD

	Chippewa, Sioux, Ute, Mandan, Hidatsa	Per cent	Papago	Per cent	Total	Per cent
Downward	14, 039	64	2, 809	59	16, 848	63
Upward	8, 000	36	1, 929	41	9, 929	37
Total	22, 139	------	4, 738	------	26, 777	------

Table 11.—INTERVALS IN DOWNWARD PROGRESSION

	Chippewa, Sioux, Ute, Mandan, Hidatsa	Per cent	Papago	Per cent	Total	Per cent
Interval of a—						
Twelfth	1				1	
Ninth	1				1	
Octave	2				2	
Seventh	2				2	
Major sixth	13				13	
Minor sixth	20				20	
Fifth	128		10		138	
Fourth	1, 488	10	273	10	1, 761	10
Major third	1, 424	10	227	7	1, 651	10
Minor third	4, 347	31	752	27	5, 099	30
Augmented second	8				8	
Major second	6, 191	44	1, 362	48	7, 553	46
Minor second	414	3	185	6	599	3
Total	14, 039		2, 809		16, 848	

Table 12.—INTERVALS IN UPWARD PROGRESSION

	Chippewa, Sioux, Ute, Mandan, Hidatsa	Per cent	Papago	Per cent	Total	Per cent
Interval of a—						
Fourteenth	1				1	
Twelfth	17				17	
Eleventh	4				4	
Tenth	14				14	
Ninth	14		1		15	
Octave	134	1	2		136	1
Seventh	28		12		40	
Major sixth	90	1	32	2	122	1
Minor sixth	75		7		82	1
Fifth	497	6	148	7	645	6
Fourth	1, 272	16	414	22	1, 686	17
Major third	919	11	149	7	1, 068	10
Minor third	2, 088	26	401	21	2, 489	25
Major second	2, 607	33	660	35	3, 267	33
Minor second	240	3	103	5	343	3
Total	8, 000		1, 929		9, 929	

TABLE 13.—AVERAGE NUMBER OF SEMITONES IN AN INTERVAL

	Chippewa, Sioux, Ute, Mandan, Hidatsa	Per cent	Papago	Per cent	Total	Per cent
Number of songs	820		167		987	
Number of intervals	22, 039		4, 738		26, 777	
Number of semitones	67, 662		14, 222		81, 884	
Average number of semitones in an interval	3. 07		3		3. 05	

RHYTHMIC ANALYSIS

TABLE 14.—PART OF MEASURE ON WHICH SONG BEGINS

	Chippewa, Sioux, Ute, Mandan, Hidatsa	Per cent	Papago	Per cent	Total	Per cent
Beginning on unaccented part of measure	289	37	65	39	354	36
Beginning on accented part of measure	489	63	102	61	591	60
Transcribed in outline	42				42	4
Total	820		167		987	

TABLE 15.—RHYTHM (METER) OF FIRST MEASURE

	Chippewa, Sioux, Ute, Mandan, Hidatsa	Per cent	Papago	Per cent	Total	Per cent
First measure in—						
2–4 time	429	55	110	66	539	54
3–4 time	305	39	51	30	356	36
4–4 time	9	1			9	1
5–4 time	13	1			13	1
6–4 time	1				1	
7–4 time	2				2	
3–8 time	5		2	1	7	
4–8 time	5		1		6	
5–8 time	6		2	1	8	
6–8 time			1		1	
7–8 time	1				1	
2–2 time	2				2	
Transcribed in outline	42				42	4
Total	820		167		987	

TABLE 16.—CHANGE OF TIME (MEASURE-LENGTHS)

	Chippewa, Sioux, Ute, Mandan, Hidatsa	Per cent	Papago	Per cent	Total	Per cent
Songs containing no change of time	120	*15*	14	*9*	134	*10*
Songs containing a change of time	658	*85*	153	*91*	811	*84*
Transcribed in outline	42	-----	--------	------	42	*4*
Total	820	------	167	------	987	------

TABLE 17.—RHYTHMIC UNIT

	Chippewa, Sioux, Ute, Mandan, Hidatsa	Per cent	Papago	Per cent	Total	Per cent
Songs containing—						
No rhythmic unit	248	*32*	57	*34*	305	*30*
One rhythmic unit	458	*59*	66	*39*	524	*53*
Two rhythmic units	61	*8*	35	*21*	96	*10*
Three rhythmic units	9	*1*	4	*2*	13	*1*
Four rhythmic units	1	-----	4	*2*	5	------
Five rhythmic units	1	-----	1	------	2	------
Transcribed in outline	42	-----	--------	------	42	*4*
Total	820	------	167	------	987	------

COMPARISON OF PAPAGO SONGS WITH THE COMBINED ANALYSES OF THE CHIPPEWA, SIOUX, UTE, MANDAN, AND HIDATSA SONGS

On comparing the tabulated analyses of Papago songs with 820 songs of other tribes, previously analyzed, we note (Table 1) that the Papago have 47 per cent major and 36 per cent minor in tonality, while the other tribes have 54 per cent major and 44 per cent minor.

Table 2 shows that the percentage of songs beginning on the fifth and keynote is larger than in the songs previously analyzed, while the percentage of those beginning on the octave is much smaller. The percentage beginning on the keynote is 24, compared to 7 per cent in the group of 820 songs. This does not indicate smallness of compass, as many Papago songs lie partly above and partly below the keynote. The percentage beginning on the fifth is 37, compared with 24 in the other songs, while the percentage beginning on the octave is 6, compared with 23 per cent in the larger group. Only 7 per cent begin on tones above the octave, while in the larger group

28 per cent have such initial tones. No Papago songs begin on a tone higher than the tenth above the keynote.

It is interesting to note (Table 3) that the percentage of songs ending on the keynote is much smaller in the Papago than in the combined songs. The percentage of Papago songs with this ending is 41 and in the other songs it is 57 per cent. The songs ending on the fifth constitute 44 per cent of the Papago and only 30 per cent of the combined group. Thus it is shown that the songs of the Chippewa, Sioux, Ute, Mandan, and Hidatsa have a preference for beginning on the fifth or octave and ending on the keynote, while the Papago prefer to begin their songs on the keynote and end them on the fifth.

Only 10 per cent of the Papago songs end on the lowest tone of the octave (Table 4), contrasted with 87 per cent in songs previously analyzed. In 17 per cent of Papago songs the tone lower than the final tone is a fourth, many such songs ending on the keynote approached by an ascending fourth.

A compass of 7, 8, and 9 tones is found in 71 per cent of the Papago songs (Table 5), compared with 39 per cent of the former group, while the percentage of songs with a larger compass is 1 per cent in the Papago and 29 per cent in the combined songs of other tribes.

The principal group in Table 6 consists of songs on the second and fourth five-toned scales ("minor and major pentatonic"), and in these we find that the Papago contains a slightly smaller percentage on the second and a much larger percentage on the fourth five-toned scale.

The percentage of songs containing no accidentals (Table 7) is 88 per cent in the Papago and 85 per cent in the combined group.

A melodic freedom of Papago songs is shown by a percentage of 73 in the Papago (Table 8) and 59 in the larger group, while the percentage of harmonic songs is 6 in the Papago and 21 in the combined songs of other tribes.

Only 33 per cent of the combined songs begin with an upward progression while 63 per cent of the Papago have this beginning (Table 9). There is less difference in the total of ascending and descending progressions (Table 10), the percentage of ascending intervals in the Papago songs being 41 and in the larger group 36 per cent.

In Table 11 it is shown that the percentage of major seconds in Papago songs is 48 per cent, compared with 44 per cent in the larger group, while the proportion of major and minor thirds is considerably less. The relative proportion of ascending and descending intervals is similar in the Papago (Table 12) to that in the songs of other tribes, while the average size of the interval is slightly smaller (Table 13).

The percentage of songs beginning on the unaccented part of the measure is 2 per cent greater in the Papago than in the songs of other tribes, while the percentage of songs beginning on the accented part of the measure is 2 per cent smaller (Table 14).

Papago songs show a larger proportion beginning in double time and a smaller proportion in triple time (Table 15), the difference being 11 per cent in double and 9 per cent in triple time. A change of time occurs in 91 per cent of the Papago songs (Table 16), contrasted with 85 per cent in the larger group.

The use of a rhythmic unit differs only slightly, the Papago having 34 per cent without a rhythmic unit and the larger group having 32 per cent of such songs, but the Papago songs have 25 per cent with two or more rhythmic units (Table 17), while the larger group has only 9 per cent with this rhythmic structure.

In the songs of other tribes it has seldom been difficult to designate one tone as the keynote of the melody but among the Papago we find songs which are so free in melodic form that it is not considered advisable to designate any tone as keynote. These are classified as "irregular in tonality" and comprise 6 per cent of the number of songs. Allied to these are songs in which the third above the apparent keynote is lacking, these constituting 10 per cent of the number; there are also two songs which are classified as "both major and minor" in tonality. The Papago melodies, generally speaking, contain greater variety and are more pleasing to the ear than the songs of the other tribes under observation. Melodic freedom, as found in Papago songs other than those classified as irregular or lacking the third, may be defined as a prominence given to the second and fourth, with a lack of prominence of the triad based on the keynote of the melody.

With this melodic freedom we find two variations from the usual custom of repeating a song over and over without a break in the time. A Papago said, "Some kinds of common songs can be sung from the beginning to the end, over and over, but the very old songs and the medicine songs must be sung twice through, then the last part sung twice through, and then the whole song sung twice and the last part twice, and so on to the end of the performance." In certain songs the first half is sung twice, then the last half is sung twice. The time is usually maintained when parts of a song are repeated, but there is usually a slight break in the time between repetitions of the entire song, as in the common melodies. In addition to this slight break in the time there was frequently a change of one or two notes in beginning a repetition.

Other distinctive peculiarities of Papago songs are a prescribed manner of singing certain classes of songs. A *glissando* was used frequently in the Limo songs and those connected with the ceremony for bringing rain, and three sorts of medicine songs were sung with special degrees of loudness and speed.

A peculiarity of singing heard among the Papago consisted in the sustaining of a tone above the general trend of the melody, this tone being held by two or three women's voices for the space of perhaps three or four measures, after which the voices descended and joined the others in the remainder of the song. This was heard at a dance held in an isolated place a few miles north of Vomari. It was said that only a few women in the tribe could sing this "drone," and it appeared to be regarded as an embellishment to the melody. This peculiarity was not noted among the tribes whose tabulated analyses are here compared with the Papago but was heard once among the Pawnee, during the Morning Star ceremony. There was no opportunity to make a phonograph record of this peculiarity in either tribe. Among the Makah, Quileute, and Clayoquot, studied in 1923 and 1926, it was permissible for a woman to sing in a high monotone if she did not know the melody being sung or if she "could not carry a tune." By this means she could join the other singers. In these tribes the high monotone was known as "metal pitch." It was seldom used and was not held in high esteem.

The various classes of Papago songs appear to have more rhythmic distinction than in other tribes. For example, Owl Woman's songs used in treating the sick are characterized by a steady forcefulness of rhythm.

The words of Papago songs are always continuous throughout the melody, which is in contrast to other tribes under observation. Some songs of other tribes are sung with no words whatever, the tones being separated by means of a peculiar action of the throat, while in many songs the words are used with only part of the melody, the remainder having vocables or vowel syllables, as ho, ah, or ay. In three classes of songs the first word is preceded by a word or syllable which is either meaningless or obsolete. Thus the koöp songs begin with aliwĕrci, the songs connected with expeditions to obtain salt begin with hiciä, and the wakita songs begin with hǫi, hǫi.

No accompaniment was used with the songs concerning Elder Brother, the songs of the tiswin lodge, and the wind dance. A gourd rattle accompanied the songs for treatment of the sick and the wakita songs. Rattle and basket drum were used with the Limo and bat dance songs; and rasping sticks, either with or without a basket resonator, were used with the songs of expeditions to obtain salt.

The manner of shaking the rattle varies more in the Papago than in other tribes. The common rhythm is an accented and an unaccented stroke, corresponding approximately to the first and third counts of a triplex, but a doctor shakes the rattle "in accordance with the instructions received in his dream." Thus some doctors shake the rattle four times sharply before they begin to sing, while Garcia, who recorded more songs than any other Papago, preceded his singing of medicine songs with a "roll" of the rattle for a few seconds.

Among tribes previously studied a considerable number of songs have been recorded with instrumental accompaniment, the rhythm of which is indicated in the transcription of the song. This was impossible among the Papago as they use no percussion instrument with a loud tone. A limited number of songs were recorded with the accompaniment of a gourd rattle but the phonograph record of the instrument is not clear. It was manifestly impossible to record the pounding on an inverted basket, with which certain classes of songs are accompanied. One song (No. 125) was accompanied with rasping sticks, this being indicated in the transcription.

PHONETICS

CONSONANTS

c	is pronounced like *ch* in *church*.
g	as in *get*.
j	is pronounced like *j* in *judge*.
h	is pronounced as in *how*.
ħ	represents a gutteral sound as used in Sioux words.
k	as in *kin*.
ŋ	represents a nasal sound as used in Sioux words.
p	as in *pin*.
s	as in *same*.
ṡ	as in *shall*.
t	as in *tin*.
z	is pronounced as in *azure*.
th	represents a hard sound like *dh*.

VOWELS

a	as in *father*.
e	as in *they*.
ĕ	as in *met*.
i	as in *marine*.
ĭ	as in *knit*.
o	as in *note*.
û	as in *but*.
u	as in *rule*.
ù	as the German ü.
y	as in *yet*.

DIPHTHONGS OR CONNECTED VOWELS

ǫi	pronounced like *oy* in *arroyo*.
ąi	pronounced like *ai* in *aisle*.
ąu	pronounced like *ow* in *now*.

Two dots above a vowel are used only to indicate that that vowel has a sound separate from the vowel which immediately precedes it.

SONGS CONNECTED WITH LEGENDS

The Papago watch the stars and when they see the Pleiades cross the sky in one night they say that the proper time for story telling has arrived. These nights are the longest of the year, and the Pleiades rise in the east at evening, cross the zenith, and set in the west just before sunrise, their setting being considered the end of the night. Comparatively few men are considered competent to tell the old tribal stories, and it is often necessary to send a long distance to secure their services. Two men go together, one telling the stories and the other assisting him. These men tell stories four nights and, in that time, can relate the entire series, beginning with the creation. There are said to be six divisions of the Papago tribe, each speaking a different dialect and having its own version of these stories. The words of the songs differ slightly in the several dialects but it is said that the melodies are always the same. The stories here presented are from the divisions of the tribe living at San Xavier and at Vomari. The more complete stories were related by Sivariano Garcia of San Xavier, who is not one of the regular story tellers but has been an attentive listener, thus learning the stories and their songs.

There are two classes of tribal stories. The first and most important class consists of stories that must be told in a prescribed order, while the stories in the second class may be combined in any desired order to form a night's story telling. To the first class belong the following: (1) The ashes people; (2) the gambler; (3) the old woman who ate the children; and (4) the peacock. To the second class belong the stories of the origin of the flute, also that of corn and tobacco, which is called the "mind clearer." The principal character in these stories is Elder Brother (also called Montezuma and Ithoi), and the more important stories relate his adventures with Earth Magician (Tcivut makai), Coyote, Brown Buzzard, Beater Wind and other personages. In each story there are pauses at about equal intervals, the usual number being three, though some stories contain only two. These pauses always occur at the same places and are introduced at points of special interest. The story teller says, "Now we will smoke," or announces the pause in some similar phrase, and the people are at liberty to lie down, walk about, or go outside the lodge. During the telling of the story they are required to sit up and pay strict attention. There is no feast in connection with the stories, but tobacco is given the story tellers before they begin their work.

It is not the intention of the present work to enter into a detailed consideration of Papago mythology. The only versions of the stories here offered are those that were recorded in connection with the songs. The first and second stories of the principal series are given in extended form; the third and fourth stories may be summarized as follows: There was an old woman who used to go around the villages, picking up the children and calling them her grandchildren. Then she carried them away, crushed them and ate them. At last the people decided they must get rid of her, so Elder Brother went to her house and said, "There is a big dance in the next house.

WIFE AND CHILD OF MATTIAS HENDRICKS

a, Burden basket

b, Basket bowl in which tiswin was served

Why don't you go and join the fun?" The old woman went to the dance and they gave her a cigarette made of a certain plant. She smoked it and fell asleep. Then they carried her across the line into Mexico. They carried her to a little mountain and put her in a tunnel. It was a deep tunnel and they put her in the farther end, piled wood across the entrance, and set fire to it. She was so strong that she rose up and split the top of the mountain but Elder Brother drew it together again. Mattias Hendricks, who recorded numerous songs, said he had seen the split in the mountain and the footprints which are about 12 inches long and 4 inches wide. He said it seemed as though Elder Brother stood astride the split, as his footprints are on both sides of it. The final story of the series is a continuation of this and states that an old woman came to the place where the animals were eating the old woman who was burned in the tunnel. They did not give her any, but she got hold of some charred blood and took it home, and it turned into a peacock.

The following narrative contains portions of the first Papago creation myth, the informants selecting the portions most closely associated with songs.[2] This narrative was obtained at Vomari village, about 7 miles from the Mexican border. Mattias Hendricks (pl. 8, *a*) was chief of this village. His mother (pl. 8, *b*) was among the informants who united with the singers in giving these stories. The other singers at Vomari were Jose Hendricks (pl. 14, *a*), Jose Ascencio (pl. 17, *b*), and Rafael Mendez (pl. 17, *c*). The wife and child of Mattias Hendricks are shown in Plate 9.

Story of the Ashes People

In the old times there was a flood that covered the whole earth. Elder Brother gathered gum from a certain bush (usabugum) and made a big olla. He took every sort of animal with him, and got into the olla. Last of all came Coyote and wanted to get in. Elder Brother told him there was some bamboo growing in the west. He told Coyote to get some of this bamboo. Coyote brought it. Then Elder Brother cut off the end and put Coyote inside, letting his tail hang out. The flood came while Elder Brother was doing this, and soon everything was afloat.

When the water subsided, Elder Brother came out of the olla and Coyote came out of the bamboo. They met four times as they were walking. Coyote was all muddy and could not walk very well because of the mud, but he sang the following song as he was walking toward Elder Brother.

---

[2] For a more complete version of these and other stories see Frank Russell, The Pima Indians, Twenty-sixth Ann. Rept. Bur. Amer. Ethn., 1908.

No. 1. Song of Coyote After the Flood

(Catalogue No. 1000)

Recorded by Jose Manuel

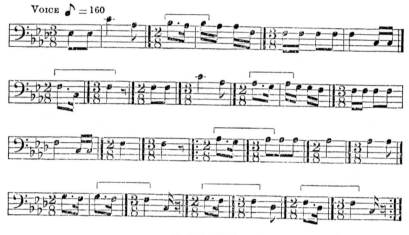

TRANSLATION

I can not walk, I am dragging along,
I cried! Ah, Ah!

Analysis.—This song contains all the tones of the octave and moves freely within its compass of eight tones. The key[3] is F minor but the song opens with the triad on A flat, the relative major. This is followed by the triad on F minor and does not reappear in the song. The tone D is used effectively at the close. It is also interesting to note the absence of the third (A flat) in these measures. The fourth is the most frequent interval except the whole tone which occurs often as a passing tone.

When they met the fourth time Elder Brother said, "Little Brother." Coyote did not like this and said, "I was first."

Elder Brother said, "How much water was there when you came out?" Coyote replied, "About 4 inches on my front leg."

Elder Brother said that when he came out the water was chest-deep on him, and that showed that he came out first.

Then he sang this song about the olla in which he had floated.

---

[3] Throughout these analyses the terms key and scale will be used frequently. It should, however, be understood that their use is for convenience, not with the full significance of the terms as used by musicians.

No. 2. Song of Elder Brother After the Flood

(Catalogue No. 1001)

Recorded by JOSE MANUEL

TRANSLATION

Black refuge where I dwell.
I am going forth with it.
I am there.

Analysis.—The keynote of this song appears to be G, but the third above that tone does not occur. The seventh is also lacking and the tone material is that of the first five-toned scale, according to Helmholtz.[3a] The most prominent interval is the descending minor third. The phrases are clearly defined and usually comprise three measures.

·After the flood, Elder Brother, Earth Magician, and Coyote began their work of creation, each creating things different from the other. Elder Brother created the spirits of men and gave to them the "red evening" which is regarded by the Papago as one of the most beautiful sights in that region. The sunset light is reflected on the mountains with a peculiar radiance.

[3a] See footnote, p. 7.

No. 3. Song of Elder Brother After he had Created the Spirits of Men

(Catalogue No. 996)

Recorded by MATTIAS HENDRICKS

TRANSLATION

I have created you here, I have created you here.
The red evening I bring to you.

Analysis.—In this, as in the song next preceding, the third above the apparent keynote does not occur. Like the preceding song, it begins and ends on the same tone. More than half the progressions are whole tones.

No. 4. Song of Elder Brother After he had Created the Wind and the Clouds

(Catalogue No. 997)

Recorded by MATTIAS HENDRICKS

TRANSLATION

I suffered to the bottom of my heart but at last I created a great deal of wind and at last I created many clouds, so now I am singing for joy.

Analysis.—This song is classified with E as its keynote, although C sharp is a particularly prominent tone. Except for the opening interval the melody progresses entirely by minor thirds and whole tones. Like several other songs of this series it ends with an ascending minor third. The phrases contain five, six, and seven measures, respectively, and each phrase has its individual rhythm.

Earth Magician had a bad temper. The things he made were criticized by the others and he became very angry. Then he began to sink into the earth.   Elder Brother caught at him as he disappeared and became infected with a "cause of sickness." Endeavoring to shake this from his hands he disseminated sickness among men. (See pp. 82, 83.)

No. 5. Song of Earth Magician when Disappearing in the Ground

(Catalogue No. 1035)

Recorded by JOSE HENDRICKS

TRANSLATION [3b]

Here I sink, and I know all sorts of things.

Analysis.—There is a peculiar quality in this melody which may be regarded as wistful.   The ascending fourth is a prominent and also the final progression.   Two rhythmic units occur, each having the same count divisions in the opening measure.   The tone material is that of the first five-toned scale which omits the third and seventh above the keynote.

Elder Brother had a rival named Brown Buzzard, whose power was so great that he could make boiling water bubble out of the ground near his house.   He said that he would kill Elder Brother but that after some years he would come to life and then worse things would happen to the people.   Four times the people tried to kill Elder Brother but he always came to life in four days.   In their third attempt they boiled him in a big olla, but he put up his head and looked out of the boiling water.   If the fire went out he got out of the olla, replenished the fire and got into the olla again.   The fourth attempt to kill Elder Brother seemed to be successful.   He

---

[3b] Compare words of No. 13.

was shot by Brown Buzzard, who went to him, after he was dead, and sang a song. In this song Brown Buzzard said he would not destroy all the things that Elder Brother had created, but would keep the wind and clouds for the benefit of the people.

No. 6. Song of Brown Buzzard After Killing Elder Brother

(Catalogue No. 983)

Recorded by MATTIAS HENDRICKS

TRANSLATION

I have done the worst thing now in killing you, my brother, but I am going to leave your wind and your clouds.

Analysis.—This melody is characterized by a descending trend. The phrases are short and the tone material is that of the fourth five-toned scale.

Elder Brother remained dead so long that children played with his bones and made bridges of his ribs. One day the children ran home and told their parents that Elder Brother was sitting there and fixing a clay canteen. As he worked he sang this song.

No. 7. Song of Elder Brother After Returning to Life

(Catalogue No. 980)

Recorded by MATTIAS HENDRICKS

TRANSLATION

There is an old man sitting down and fixing his vaäko (canteen), fixing his vaäko.

Analysis.—This is a melody of unusual beauty and bears some resemblance to oriental music. It is minor in tonality and contains a similar number of intervals in ascending and descending progressions. These intervals are 1 fourth, 4 minor thirds, 12 whole tones, and 8 half tones. The song is harmonic in structure and begins and ends on the keynote. The ascending fourth at the close is effective, also the frequent progression, D sharp-C sharp-D sharp.

The old people said to the children, "We told you not to disturb those bones or something bad would happen." Every one was afraid. Elder Brother said he had come back as he had promised and that he was going away but would return soon.

Elder Brother tried to walk but he staggered and in this way he started across the sky to find Brown Buzzard who killed him. Elder Brother rose up in the sky. In the middle of the sky was a "talking tree." When he reached the tree he broke off four branches and took them with him. The branches of the talking tree gave him power wherever he went in the world.

No. 8. Song Concerning the Talking Tree

(Catalogue No. 991)

Recorded by MATTIAS HENDRICKS

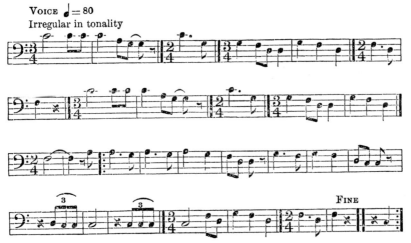

VOICE ♩ = 80
Irregular in tonality

Analysis.—This song is classified as irregular in tonality. Other songs thus classified are Nos. 12, 14, 24, 31, 33, 36, 88, 119, and 145. These are melodies whose tones are not clearly referable to a keynote, and a majority are based upon the interval of a fourth. They are transcribed generally without signature, deviations from pitch being indicated by accidentals. The first half of this song is built upon descending fourths. The latter portion opens with two phrases on descending fifths, followed by a return to the interval of a fourth. The song is characterized by phrases with a descending trend, many having an upward progression at the close.

Elder Brother traveled four days until he reached the sun.   Then
he went across the sky with the sun and saw where he could find a
man to help him kill Brown Buzzard.   He went into Ashes Hill and
found Earth Magician lying on a bed.   When Elder Brother entered
the room, he turned and said, "What sort of a traveler are you?"

Elder Brother answered, "I am here to talk with you."   Earth
Magician said, "I am in bed and have no time to talk."

Elder Brother waited.   After a long time the other man said, "It
is getting dark; you had better go.   I have no time to talk."

Elder Brother stayed until the man had done this four times, then
the man got up and sat by the fire.   He directed Elder Brother to
sit down.   Elder Brother had brought tobacco, and they began to
talk the matter over.

Elder Brother stayed there about 16 days, and they made plans
for their journey to find the man who had killed him.   Earth Magician directed his servants to prepare for the journey, making extra
strong bows and arrows and preparing the food they would need.
The servants went with them, and they started for the place where
they would emerge from Ashes Hill.   When they reached the place
they sang this song.

No. 9. Song Before Emerging from Ashes Hill

(Catalogue No. 981)

Recorded by MATTIAS HENDRICKS

TRANSLATION

Now we are going to look over the world and see what is going on.

Analysis.—The intervals characterizing this song are the ascending
fourth and the minor second, the latter comprising almost half the
entire number of intervals.   The song comprises three periods, each
containing five measures and having an individual rhythm.   The
fourth and seventh degrees of the scale do not occur.   Other songs
with this tone material are Nos. 11, 20, 41, 43, 55, 62, 65, 69, 92, 99,
121, 143, 151, and 165.   These are the scale degrees absent in the
fourth five-toned scale, but the tonality of these songs is minor, the

third and sixth being minor intervals, while the fourth five-toned scale is major in tonality, the corresponding intervals being major. This song was recorded on two occasions, and the records are identical in every respect.

After singing the song they selected four pure young men, who went first into the world, and after they had gone the others followed them. When the people came out of the mountain they saw a beautiful world with green grass and many flowers. Elder Brother looked about and then sang this song.

No. 10. Song After Emerging from Ashes Hill

(Catalogue No. 982)

Recorded by MATTIAS HENDRICKS

VOICE ♩ = 80

TRANSLATION

The world we have come into looks so grassy,
We come out to look over the world.

Analysis.—A downward gliding of the voice and a *nota legato* characterize this interesting melody. The progression C-B flat-C is used effectively; also the whole tone between G flat and A flat. The tempo is slow and the melody tones are those of the first five-toned scale.

The people emerged in the east and traveled toward the north, then to the west, and south, some completing a great circle and returning to the east. On this journey they continually fought the earlier inhabitants of the land. From time to time groups of people left the company and settled down, the Papago remaining in the Sacaton Valley. As they journeyed Elder Brother gave names to the mountains. He would listen to the people as they talked about the beautiful mountains, then he would tell them the name of the mountain in a song.

It was said that the people saw a little cloud on top of a mountain and said, "We thought that we had everything with us. We thought we had all the clouds. What can be the name of that mountain that has a little cloud inside." Elder Brother sang the following song, telling the people that the mountain which they saw was Raven Mountain (Hawantohak). The whole crowd said to themselves, "That is Raven Mountain," and it is called by that name to this day.

No. 11. "It is Raven Mountain"   (Catalogue No. 985)

Recorded by MATTIAS HENDRICKS

TRANSLATION

Here we are on our way and see the distant mountain.
See, the mountain far from us that has the cloud is Raven Mountain.

Analysis.—In this melody we find a peculiar haunting quality suggesting oriental music. This has been noted in other songs of this group. It is minor in tonality and lacks the fourth and seventh tones of the octave. About one-third of the progressions are whole tones. Next in frequency is the major third. As in many of the songs of this series the first and last tones are the same. Attention is directed to the ascending minor third at the close of the song.

A mountain at each of the cardinal points was named from some circumstance of the journey. When they were journeying in the north a man had his lunch in a frogskin and threw it away on a mountain which is called Frog Mountain to this day. When they were in the west they named the mountains "Crooked Mountains."

When they were in the south a man killed a big bird, cut off the head, and left it there. This mountain is still called Head Mountain. A mountain at the east of the present site of Tucson was named Turkeyneck Mountain. One of the men cut the skin from around the neck of a turkey, turned it inside out and put his lunch in it. He finished his lunch when on this mountain and threw away the skin of the turkey neck, from which the mountain was named.

A beautiful picture of the multitude is suggested by the words of the following song. The people were looking for a good camping place.

Some favored one place and others said, "Come, we have found a better place," so they swayed from place to place. Elder Brother looked upon the swaying crowd and in a song he told them what they resembled.

No. 12. " White Feathers Along the Edge of the World "

(Catalogue No. 984)

Recorded by MATTIAS HENDRICKS

VOICE ♪ = 126 (♩ = 63)
Irregular in tonality

TRANSLATION

Downy white feathers are moving beneath the sunset and along the edge of the world.

Analysis.—This song is classified as irregular in tonality. Other songs thus classified are Nos. 8, 14, 24, 31, 33, 36, 88, 119, and 145. It is interesting to note the prominence of the fourth in the framework of these songs. In the present instance it occurs chiefly as C–F, appearing in both ascending and descending progression. About 54 per cent of the intervals are whole tones.

Four incidents of the journey were related and their songs recorded. The first is as follows: In the great throng of people who traveled with Elder Brother, after he emerged from Ashes Hill, there were two brothers who had their old grandmother with them. This little group could not keep up with the crowd when it was moving, and at evening they always camped a distance behind the others. The two brothers had to go in the evening and overtake the party to find what the people would do the next morning. They built a big fire and left their grandmother near it. They kept doing this for a long time and at last they grew tired of it. The older brother said, "I guess we had better kill our grandmother and be able to travel with the rest, so we will know what is going on all the time. Perhaps we might meet some of the people we are going to fight and we would not see them because we are always behind."

The younger brother said, "All right, but we must tell our grand-mother and see what she will say about it."

They told their grandmother and said, "Well, grandmother, we would like to know what you think of this plan that we kill you, because you know that we are always behind and do not know what is going on over there. So we thought we would kill you and keep up with the crowd."

She said, "Well, grandsons, it is all right, because I have been living a long time and have seen many things in this world. I would like you to be with the crowd and see what is going on." She sang the following song, but she felt so badly that she was crying rather than singing. This quality of tone was imitated by the singer when recording the song.

No. 13. "I Have Been in This World a Long Time"

(Catalogue No. 986)

Recorded by MATTIAS HENDRICKS

TRANSLATION

Oh! I have seen many things in this world and I have been in this world a long time.[3c]

[3c] Compare words of No. 5.

Analysis.—Two renditions of this song were recorded and transcribed, the first only being analyzed. A comparison shows a slight difference at the opening and close, and the addition, in the repetition, of a plaintive phrase ending on the second. The song opens with a brave rhythm in a long phrase which has a descending trend of 10 tones. Subsequent phrases are shorter and progression is chiefly by the major second, this interval comprising about 65 per cent of the entire number of progressions.

The old grandmother said, "After I die, find some fine sand and bury me in it. When you come back this way, stop and see what you find."

The boys then sang the following song. They sang it four times and "when they came near the end of the fourth time their grandmother began to die."

No. 14. Song With Which Two Boys Killed Their Grandmother

(Catalogue No. 987)

Recorded by MATTIAS HENDRICKS

Voice ♩ = 69
Irregular in tonality

TRANSLATION

Our grandmother says it will be all right that she dies,
Because she has been alive a long time.
That is why she does not mind dying,
Because we can not keep up with the crowd.

Analysis.—This is the first song recorded among the Indians which is said to have caused the death of an individual. The tones are not clearly referable to a keynote and the song is classified as irregular in tonality. Other songs thus classified are Nos. 8, 12, 24, 31, 33, 36, 88, 119, and 145. The song is peculiar in that the last tone is higher than the first. There is no change of measure lengths. As in the song next preceding, the compass is unusually large. Attention is directed to the brave, clear rhythm of the opening measure and the plaintive phrase at the close.

The boys buried their grandmother in the sand and joined the crowd on its journey. As they were returning they came to the place where they had buried their grandmother and saw a plant growing.

It was tobacco. Ever afterwards they did not smoke because they said the tobacco was the flesh of their grandmother.

The second incident is concerning the rain.

The people were camping near two mountains called Tatka[4] when a storm came and the rain fell steadily for 10 days. Some old medicine men went out together and "killed the rain," so the rain stopped falling. When Elder Brother found that the medicine men had killed the rain he said, "That is not right. The rain does no harm. It is good for us because the people we go to fight will stay at home if it rains and so we will get them." He sang this song to tell the people what would happen to the world if the rain were stopped. It is to correct this action of the medicine men that the "tiswin making" and the rain making ceremonies were devised. (See pp. 137–175.)

No. 15. "The World Would Burn Without the Rain"

(Catalogue No. 983)

Recorded by MATTIAS HENDRICKS

TRANSLATION

Now, now I have found what you did,
The world will burn if you do this,
Now I have found it out.

Analysis.—This song is classified with E as the keynote, although the third above that tone does not appear. In the latter part the keynote is the highest tone, which is an unusual structure. The fifth constitutes 17 per cent of the intervals, which is an unusually large proportion. The two rhythmic units have no resemblance to each other.

---

[4] A railroad now runs between these mountains.

The third incident is concerning the inhabitants of Casa Grande. Elder Brother, traveling with his people, drove out the former inhabitants of the country. He tore down their houses and temples and even went to Casa Grande, where the ruins now stand. A man and his daughter lived in that ruin. The man's name was Sivanimaka.

When Elder Brother came to that place the man stood on top of his house. He stood on one foot with the other foot on his knee. His daughter was beside him and she stood on both feet. Elder Brother and his people tried to kill them, but the man had certain power so he could not be killed if he remained in that position.

Among Elder Brother's people there was an old woman and her two grandchildren. She spoke to them and said, "You had better finish them up." She went to her burden basket and took some feathers from a box. She sang a song, and the children turned into birds called Visuk. (The song is forgotten at the present time.) The birds flew into the air. The first smote down the man and the second smote down the woman and killed them. Ever since that time the Casa Grande ruins have stood as now.

The birds flew back to the old woman who sang this song.

No. 16. Song After the Inhabitants of Casa Grande Were Killed

(Catalogue No. 998)

Recorded by JOSE MANUEL

TRANSLATION

Good luck, my grandmother.
All that you have done will be sounded through the world.

Analysis.—Twenty-six of the thirty-six progressions in this song are whole tones. The song begins and ends on the same tone and is based on the fourth five-toned scale. The change of tempo is unusual. The crisp, sharp rhythmic unit is interesting in connection with the use of the song.

The burden basket (*kiĥo*), which forms the subject of the next song, is a peculiar contrivance by which the women of Piman tribes were enabled to carry loads of mesquite wood and other material weighing, in some instances, about 100 pounds. It consisted of a conical netting stretched on a hoop, with four sticks, two of which were about 3 feet long. A separate long stick, called a "helping stick," formed a tripod, thus making it possible for a woman to load the basket before assuming the burden.[4a]   The position of the basket on the ground probably suggested the idea that it was "walking." The specimen illustrated (pl. 10, *a*) was obtained at Santa Rosa. The headband is missing but a portion of its cord remains.   According to Mason, the "buttonhole or half-hitch stitch" of this netting does not appear in tribes north of the Piman but "occurs in Central America, in Latin South America as far south as Tierra del Fuego, where it will be found to be the only attempt at textiles."[4b]

The people rose up again and went toward the south.   As soon as they went out from the place where they had camped the burden basket walked behind them.   Coyote came and saw the burden basket walking.   He spoke to it and said, "You certainly are walking," and immediately it stopped.

Elder Brother said to the old woman, "Now I am going to give you strength so that you can carry the burden basket and never be tired."   So he sang this song.

No. 17. Song That Gave Woman the Strength to Carry the Burden Basket

(Catalogue No. 999)

Recorded by JOSE MANUEL

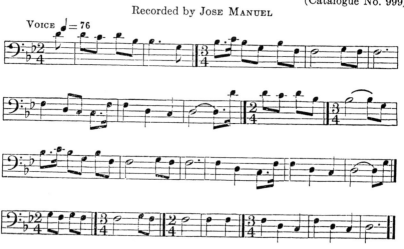

TRANSLATION

Going toward the east where the road goes;
Where the burden basket walked.

[4a] Mason, Otis T., Origins of Invention, London, 1895, p. 251.
[4b] Mason, Otis T., Primitive Travel and Transportation, U. S. Nat. Mus. Rept. for 1894, p. 470, Washington, 1896.

Analysis.—This song is characterized by a compass of nine tones and a freedom of upward and downward movement between the highest and lowest tones of the compass. Like many songs of this series it ends with an ascending progression. It is based on the fourth five-toned scale, and the major second constitutes 55 per cent of the intervals. Next in frequency is the minor third.

The fourth incident was the encounter with Brown Buzzard. When the Papago came to Brown Buzzard's house they caught him and were going to kill him, but he said, "Do not kill me. I will do something so that your evenings will pass pleasantly." He removed his scalp and fastened it at the end of a pole. When evening came he held up the scalp and sang all night. This was the beginning of the custom of taking scalps and of dancing the scalp dance. This also is the reason why the buzzard has no feathers on top of his head.

No. 18. Song of Brown Buzzard After Removing His Scalp

(Catalogue No. 989)

Recorded by Mattias Hendricks

TRANSLATION

You must enjoy yourselves in the evening.
Look at me. See how I look and yet I am happy.

Analysis.—The rhythmic units of this song have the same beginning as the unit of No. 16, which was sung after the inhabitants of Casa Grande had been killed. This song is based on the second five-toned scale, part of the song lying above and part below the keynote, as in many others of this series. The ascending fourth is a prominent interval, but 70 per cent of the intervals are whole tones which occur most frequently in descending progression.

Brown Buzzard also sang the following song to amuse them.

No. 19. "See My Scalp Hanging on a Pole"

Recorded by MATTIAS HENDRICKS

(Catalogue No. 990)

TRANSLATION

Get up and dance.
Look up and see the end of the pole where my scalp is hanging.
I want you to enjoy yourselves.

Analysis.—This song is minor in tonality, with the fourth raised a semitone in every occurrence. In this respect it resembles No. 15, but it differs from that song in having the accidental only on the last count of the measure. This song is peculiar in that the approach to an accented tone is usually by an ascending progression. The compass is seven tones, the highest of which occurs with frequency in the first portion, while the lowest is of frequent occurrence in the latter portion of the song.

After their journey the Papago settled in the Sacaton Valley near Crooked Mountain (*Kakotku*).

The second story of this series was related and its songs recorded by Sivariano Garcia of San Xavier. (Pl. 16, *b*.)

Story of the Gambler

As already stated, the Papago settled in the Sacaton Valley. Among the people there lived an old man and an old woman. They had with them an orphan child who was one of the Ashes people mentioned in the first story. Because he was one of the Ashes people he could not at first understand the language of the Papago. All their ways were strange to him. When the child was old enough to speak and to understand their language, the following incident took place:

It was in the early spring when the wild plants that the people ate were coming up. The old woman told him to get up early and get a plant called "owl feathers" that the people used for food. The little boy got up, took a little basket, and went into the woods. He came upon an owl which he chased and finally caught. He took off the feathers, put them in a basket, and went home. When he showed them to his grandmother, she said, "That is not what I wanted. There is a plant called 'owl feathers.' That is what I wanted." She told the boy to take the feathers into the woods and throw them away. He did this. The next morning she told him to go out and get some "crow's feet" so she could cook them for his dinner. Early in the morning he got up and walked in the woods with his little basket. He came upon some live crows, chased them, broke off their feet, and put them in his basket. When he took them home and showed them to his grandmother, she said: "Why did you do this? There is a plant called 'crow's feet' that grows under the trees and which we eat. I did not want you to get the feet of live crows. You must take these somewhere and throw them away." The next morning she told him to get up early, go out with his little basket, and get "skeleton heads." He went to the burying ground, filled his basket with skulls, took them home, and showed them to his grandmother. She said, "Why did you do this? There is a certain plant called 'skeleton heads' that we eat. You must take these back where they belong."

In those days the people married early and while the boy was doing these things he became old enough to marry. One day his wife put the ollas in a burden basket and went early to get the water. She returned while he was still in bed. The grandmother told him to get up and wrestle (steady the ollas on the frame so the water would not spill, and thus help his wife). He got up and fought with her, breaking the ollas, so his wife went back to her home. When the boy went into the house his grandmother began to talk to him and said: "It seems as though you had no brains. I wanted you to help your wife and you fought with her, broke the ollas, and she has gone back to her home. Now you will go about among the people and you will have no wife."

By that time he was old enough to go out every day with the hunters for meat. It was customary for the hunters to go to a certain place and then divide into two parties that were to meet farther on at a given place. The two parties drove the game toward that place, where it was killed and then taken back to the village. The boy went on his first trip and the hunters as usual stopped and discussed where there was most game. The leaders spoke to the boy and said, "You go in a certain direction and hang. The others will go in another direction and drive the game toward you." The boy always minded well, so he went to that place. He saw a tree that leaned to one side, so he threw down his bow and arrows and hung himself in the tree. When the other hunters came to the place they saw him and said, "Why did you do this?" He replied, "Because I was told to." They said, "It was not that. You were told to stay here and if any game passed this way you were to kill it." That day they got no game. The next day they went out again and the boy was told to go to a certain place. The leader told him that if an old man came along he should kill him. The boy went to the appointed place. Along came his grandfather. The boy shot him with his bow and arrows. When the other hunters came they said: "What have you done? You were told to wait here and kill any old game that came along." All the hunters were there, and the leader and others scolded the boy, but an old man spoke up and said, "It was found long ago that this boy always did as he was told. You should speak plainly to him and say exactly what you mean. Instead of 'an old man' you should say 'an old buck.' " After all the hunters were assembled they picked up the boy and took him to the camp. They boy stayed there a while and then followed them toward home. As he came near the village he began to feel as though something would happen to him when he got home, so he started to go straight toward the west.

He traveled a long time, always going toward the west. The reason of this was as follows: His strange actions had been caused by an evil medicine man named Beater Wind, who lived in the west and compelled the boy to come toward him. Beater Wind had foreseen that the boy would do something like the killing of his grandfather, so he made a new house for the boy near his own and was living in it when the boy arrived. All the time that the boy was going toward the west Beater Wind lay in the new house with his back toward the door. Some one came in the door and sat down. Beater Wind could feel it and turned over and said, "I did not build this house for you to enter first. The person for whom I built it is coming." The man who entered was Brown Buzzard. The house was full of "medicine," which was said to be something like the heat vibrations that rise from the desert in the summer.

Beater Wind had put this medicine in the house for the boy, but Brown Buzzard was so angry at Beater Wind's words that he spread his wings against the house and took out every bit of medicine of every sort. He sang this song.

No. 20. "Am I an Eagle?"   (Catalogue No. 954)

Recorded by SIVARIANO GARCIA

TRANSLATION

Am I an eagle?
My feathers are filled with mysterious power.

Analysis.—A careful observation of songs in minor tonality will show that some omit the sixth while others emphasize it in an effective manner. This song belongs to the latter class and the emphasis is obtained by an ascending progression to an accented tone, after a rest. This occurs halfway through the song. The second is repeatedly emphasized in the latter portion of the song. Although the song is minor in tonality the interval of a minor third occurs only once. The major third and whole tone are the most frequent intervals and occur about the same number of times. The song has a range of an octave and a steadily descending trend.

When Beater Wind found that Brown Buzzard was doing this he turned to him and said, "I did not mean any harm. You can enter this house if you want to." Brown Buzzard was already offended, so he walked out of the door and flew over the highest and the lowest mountains and dropped into each mountain top some of the medicine that he had taken out of the house. Because of this some of the mountains became full of medicine, as the house had been. Brown Buzzard said that because of this medicine there would be a roaring of wind or noise of thunder and a shaking inside of these mountains before a storm and this would be a warning to the people.

The boy approached the house after Brown Buzzard had flown away. He went inside the house and sat down by the door. Beater Wind turned over, saw the boy, and said, "Have you come?" The boy replied, "Yes." Beater Wind took him in front of the house where he had cleared a big circle. He put the boy in the middle of the circle and went over to one side. Then he went back to the boy, took him up, and threw him toward the east. He went again to the boy, took him up, and threw him toward the north. Then he threw the boy toward the west and toward the south. He thought that the boy must be dead and yet he knew that he had not fully killed him. Beater Wind went home and lay down a while. Then he thought he would go back and see if the boy was getting up yet. The boy was "coming to," but lay there, his long hair tangled and filled with sticks or whatever was on the ground. Beater Wind picked him up and carried him to a place where they sat down together.[5]

While they sat there Beater Wind fixed the boy's hair as it was when he arrived. He cut several sticks 4 or 5 inches long and pointed at the end and told the boy to use these instead of his hands in scratching his head or body. Beater Wind put these sticks in the boy's hair and told him that henceforth it would be the custom that if a man killed an enemy he must use one of these sticks until he had gone through a certain manner of purification. (The following acts of Beater Wind were the beginning of a custom which was later called the *Limo* and used throughout the tribe.) Beater Wind took the boy quite a distance from the house and fixed a place where he was to stay four days without food or water. At the end of four days the boy was as though he had been sick for years. On the fifth day Beater Wind came to him with a little food and about one swallow of water. From that day on, for four days, he got about the same amount; then for four days he got about double that quantity of food. This was followed by one more period of four days during which the food was double that in the third period. After each period Beater Wind had the boy bathe and come nearer the house. Beater Wind was doing all this to "straighten out" the boy. While the boy was fasting Beater Wind was thinking all the time, keeping watch of the boy, and seeing that his mind was clearing. At the end of 16 days (four periods of four days each) Beater Wind saw that the boy was going to be all right, so on the seventeenth day he allowed him to enter the house and gave him a full meal.[6]

The boy stayed in Beater Wind's house quite a while and then he decided to go home. Beater Wind said, "All right. I have done what I wanted to do. I have straightened out what I wanted to straighten out in you. It is all right now for you to return and live

---

[5] Garcia said that a speech should be inserted at the point where Beater Wind picks up the boy. He said he had heard the story many times but the speech was always omitted because there was no one present who could give it correctly.

[6] It was said that "ever since this incident it has been the rule that no medicine is strong except that obtained by a severe test of the man himself. If a man gets his medicine around here it will not last long. If he will have a strong medicine he must get it from the ocean or the mountains."

like other people." The boy came out of the house and started toward his own home. As he went along he entered every mountain and learned songs. The four kinds of songs which he learned are called *komatan* and *koöp* (used in treating the sick), *kohemorle* (used in the rain ceremony), and *hicuhcolita* (songs that come from the ocean). He learned these and he knew then that all these songs would in the future be used for curing the sick and performing other remarkable acts beneficial to the people. These were very powerful medicine songs.

After entering these great mountains the boy reached the village, went into his own house, and lived as Beater Wind had taught him, staying at home all the time and not mingling with the people. There was much gambling in the village. There was one young man who constantly stole, gambled, and lost, then he would go to another village, steal, gamble, and lose again. This had gone on for a long time. The fellow was very rough in all that he did, he gambled all the time and was called "Wanta," meaning "gambler."

FIRST PAUSE

It was the custom in the village for each boy to have an intimate boy friend or chum, but the gambler was always alone. He went about by himself, for no one liked to go with him. In some way it occurred to him that the boy had been away and returned yet stayed at home all the time. He thought that he would go to the boy's house and hear what he had to say. So that evening he went to the boy's house, entered, and sat at one side. The boy never turned toward him at all. He stayed until late and then went home. The next morning the grandmother said, "A young man was here last evening hoping to be spoken to, but you did not speak to him. I do not know how long he stayed." The gambler came again the next evening, entered, and sat in the same place as before. He sat a long time but the boy did not say a word. He stayed until late and then went home. The next morning the grandmother spoke as before, adding, "That is not right. He may want to talk of something important or ask you some important question." The third night the gambler came as before but still the boy would not speak to him. The next morning the grandmother spoke as before. On the fourth night the gambler came again and sat as before. The boy turned without rising and said, "I wanted to speak to you before. I suppose you have wanted to ask me something, but I did not speak." The gambler said, "I did not bring my tobacco, hoping you had some, but to-morrow I will bring my tobacco, because I want to ask something from you."

The gambler went home and next day he went around and stole some tobacco, which was the way he had been getting everything.

In the evening he went to the boy's house and made a thin corn husk cigarette. He took the first puff and offered it three times to the boy, who refused it each time. The fourth time the boy rose from his bed, took the cigarette and smoked, talking as he smoked, and said he knew just how this young man lived and that was the reason why he was not welcome in that house, but that he felt sorry for him after he had been there so many times. The gambler said, "That is the way I have lived. Everywhere I go each boy has a chum but I have been among these people year after year and have no friends, so I thought I would see you and ask if we could not go together as friends." After the gambler had finished, the boy said, "I will tell you right now you must stop these things you are doing and then you will get on better with the people. You can come here and stay all you like but I can not go about with you." The gambler said, "All right, that is good. I will stop what you tell me to stop." So he did. He went out by day and wandered about, but evenings he stayed at the boy's house.

One evening, quite a long time afterwards, the gambler told the boy exactly how he had lived before the boy became his friend, how he gambled and always lost but he would play the next day and lose again. The boy said, "If you want to win in gambling you must let me make you some game sticks (*ginskut*), then you can win the game. You can not win if you make the sticks yourself nor if any one makes them excepting me." The gambler said, "All right, make me some, for I want to win back what I have lost." The boy said, "To-morrow you must go and look for the inside of some dry cactus; bring it to me and I will make you some game sticks, then you will play a better game." The young man went out the next day, got the material, and placed it before the boy. Then he went away. The sticks previously used by the gambler were made of the same material and had the same marks as those made by the boy, but the marks were made with charcoal. When the boy had finished the sticks he blackened the marks with the darkness of the night, taking the black out of the air. The boy cut the sticks all the same length. The first one that he made he called *gins* and on the surface he cut and marked stripes like the women used to paint on their chins. The next one he called *sikoh* and on that he made marks representing the rays of the sun. The next one he called *cawooh* and this he marked to represent a bird in flight. The last one he called *giihk* and he made two marks on each side of it to represent the entire set of four sticks. When he had finished the sticks he put them under his pillow and waited for the gambler. On the second night the gambler came and said that a man had wanted to play with him but he told the man that he could not play until he had made some sticks. When the gambler said this he told a lie for he knew that the sticks were already made. The boy said, "You can not take these sticks to-night. Go out to-morrow and if a man asks you to play you must not tell a lie but you must say that you will get your sticks." The gambler said, "All right." The next morning he found a man who wanted to play and said what the boy had told him to say. Then he went to the boy and said, "I want the sticks now." The boy took out the sticks and laid them before him and said, "I made these sticks for you. Take them, and if the first throw shows the first stick you will know that you are to win the game, but if the last stick shows up you will lose. According to this showing will be your good or bad luck right along. For the first four games that you win you must bring me half your gains. You must take care of these sticks and put them under your pillow every night." So the gambler went off with the sticks.

The gambler and his opponent played from morning until sunset. It was as the boy had said. He turned the first stick on the first throw and won every game. He took half his winnings to the boy to pay him for the sticks and took good care of the sticks as he had been told to do. He played every day afterwards and 10 or 15 men came each day to play with him, but he won every game. Then the men came from other villages to play because they had heard that he could not be beaten. The people wondered what had happened to him. He used to be easy to beat, but now it seemed impossible to beat him. In time the most distant villages came to gamble. The people in his home village bet on him every time and always won from the other villages. After a while all the villages had played and he had not been beaten.

Over toward Phoenix there was a mountain called *Mohatĭk*. Elder Brother had a house in this mountain. Elder Brother had houses in four mountains, one at each of the cardinal points. The houses were all alike and one was in Baboquivari Mountain. It was about Elder Brother's turn to try to play with the young man. He said to himself, "I do not see how this boy can be so powerful. I am the creator of these trees, animals, and mountains, and I do not see how anyone can have stronger (medicine) power than mine. The other games they play are the games that I taught them." When Elder Brother had finished talking he left his house and as he was going along he talked with everything he had made, such as the birds and animals, hoping that these things would help him take away the power from the gambler so that he could win. While he was traveling he was trying to find out whether he could do this but he reached the gambler's place without knowing whether he had received this power.

SECOND PAUSE

Elder Brother reached the village, stopped at the first house he came to and asked if the gambler were anywhere around, saying he had heard of his power and wanted to see for himself what kind of a man he was and what his power might be. They told him where the gambler lived and said he was then at home.

Elder Brother reached the house and the gambler came out. Elder Brother said that he had come to play to see which would win. Of course he had brought things to wager and he threw them on the ground for the gambler to see, and to say what he would bet against him. Elder Brother told the gambler to go in the house, get the sticks with which he had won all the games and begin to play. So they began the game. For a while Elder Brother lost and the people began to make fun of him. At first the gambler had been afraid of him but he grew more confident. Elder Brother bet three times and lost. The fourth time it was getting toward evening and he lost again. Amid the jeering and ridiculing after the fourth game he got up and walked toward his home, and as he walked it came to his mind that something bad was going to happen to all the people and that it would be worse for them than the jeering was for him. He said to himself, "If any man is as powerful as I am he can upset all my doings, and then things will not happen to the people as I say they are going to happen."

When he got home he could not forget the jeering and that night he kept thinking. The next morning he told his neighbors that something disagreeable had happened to him and that he was going to get rid of some of the people who caused it. He also said to the people, "You know where the largest birds sleep. Go out and get all the feathers you can find. With these feathers I will do what I want to do." When the feathers were brought he parched some corn and in another dish he heated some feathers so they curled up. Then he ground the corn and the feathers together. This was on the third day of his preparations. He told the people that by the end of the fourth day he would have made a beautiful maiden and that on the fifth morning he would be ready to gamble again. On the fourth day he made the beautiful maiden and told her that on the following day he would start from his house and at the same time she would start in the sky traveling with the sun. He told her that she must watch where he went and come down to the village where he stopped. The next morning he left his house and she came out with the sun as arranged. He reached the village about noon and the girl came down to a place where there was a pond. There were children playing around the pond and they saw this girl coming, dressed in green. They ran to the village and came to the place where the gambling was to take place and where all the people were assembled. They said there was a strange maiden dressed in green near the pond. Elder Brother said, "I don't see where she came from." All the people wanted to know but nobody started to go and find out. Then the gambler said he guessed that he would go. When he said this Elder Brother said, "You had better not go. The game is just about to begin. Let someone else go and tell us about it." Then the gambler said, "It will only take a few minutes; I guess I will go." Of course Elder Brother knew who the maiden was and he also saw that his power was gaining ascendancy over that of the gambler. At last Elder Brother said, "All right. Go over and see her, but hurry back or we can not have enough games."

When the gambler reached the pond he saw the girl on the other side. She was mixing meal. He went near her, watched a little and turned back. The girl said, "Don't go; you had better have some of this *pinole* before you go." When the girl called him he went over and sat on his haunches. She handed him the *pinole* and he drank a little. She said, "Drink some more." He drank twice and she told him to shake himself. Then his flesh began to feel queer. He drank a third time and then she began to sing, and as soon as she began to sing he knew there was mischief going on. Feathers began to come out on his body. The following is the maiden's song.

No. 21. "Feather Meal Give Me to Drink" [6a]

(Catalogue No. 955)

Recorded by SIVARIANO GARCIA

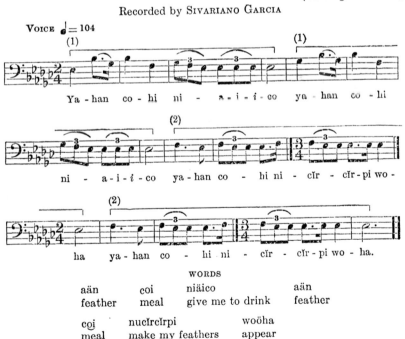

WORDS

aän	coi	niäico	aän
feather	meal	give me to drink	feather
coi	nucïrcïrpi	woöha	
meal	make my feathers	appear	

Analysis.—In contrast to the preceding songs this has a compass of five tones and contains only the minor triad and second. Attention

---

[6a] In the orthography of this and other Papago songs the writer gratefully acknowledges the assistance of Fr. Schwarz, O. F. M., who is connected with St. Catherine's Mission, Topawa, Ariz.

is directed to the different rhythms of the first and second parts of the song. The keynote is the first and last, as well as the lowest tone. It is interesting to note the accented tones. G is most frequently accented in the first portion of the song, and F accented in all except two measures of the latter portion.

As he drank the fourth time he was sure something was going to happen and thought he had better sing while he could. So he sang the following song to counteract the magic which the girl was working.

No. 22. "My Feathers Are Growing Longer"

(Catalogue No. 956)

Recorded by SIVARIANO GARCIA

WORDS

Wanitho	ci	makaj	coĭ
I will become	like	a medicine	man

niäthanur	vavazaza
my feathers	are growing longer

Analysis.—This song comprises three rhythmic periods, all ending with the same phrase. The descending fourth C to G forms the framework of the first phrase and the fourth G to D is the framework of the last phrase. The principal interval is the minor third. This song is based on the second five-toned scale and ends on the third above the keynote. Nos. 1 and 8 also begin on the seventh and are minor in tonality.

The song was of no avail, as the girl had finished singing her song. The feathers on the gambler's body grew longer and he became an eagle. Then the girl began to disappear and faded away.

Elder Brother was waiting and he began to talk, saying, "What has become of the man? We want to begin a game." But Elder Brother knew that by that time he was changed into a bird. A child went running toward the pond, got half way there, and came back saying, "I saw a great black bird with an awkward beak, but no one was there." After hearing this report Elder Brother said, "All right, people, something bad is going to happen. I am going home. You had better get your bows and arrows and kill that bird." His opponent having disappeared, it was the same as a victory for Elder Brother, so he took all the wagered articles and started home. On the way he stopped and sang the following song for the eagle, so that the people could not hurt him.

No. 23. "The Eagle Will Destroy Us All"

(Catalogue No. 957)

Recorded by SIVARIANO GARCIA

WORDS

Húmo	kúpahakú	natho	húmo
now	the eagle	is made	now

tokiyo
it will destroy us all

Analysis.—This song is analyzed with F as its keynote, although the third occurs only once, on an unaccented beat. Like the song next preceding, it ends with a short tone, approached by an ascending progression. A similar ending appears in No. 40. The general character of this melody is especially interesting in connection with its title. The principal interval is the minor third.

Meanwhile the people had rushed to the pond. The eagle flew upward but the people could not hit him. He alighted on a tree and the branches broke; then he came down on a hill and almost fell over. He was very large and did not know how to alight. Then he flew higher and higher so that the people could scarcely see him. From there he saw the mountain where he thought he would like to stay, so he came down and lit there. He lived up there and began to kill small game for his food, going farther and farther away until he had killed all of the animals that were good for his food. This went on for many years.

After he had cleared the country of game he thought he would begin on the people and start with the children. After he had been killing the children for many years and had killed about all of the small ones he killed the older people. The villages near him were gradually cleaned out and he got nearer to the village where he used to live when he was a gambler. The people where he used to live were getting excited. They held meetings to talk it over and remembered how they laughed at Elder Brother and that on his second visit he had said something bad would happen. Perhaps it was this, and they said they must do something before the eagle got to their village. At their meetings they tried to find a man who had power enough to kill the bird. They inquired in all the villages that remained but could find no one strong enough to do it. While they were holding another meeting and trying to find a man to kill the eagle there was a man in the crowd who did not say a word until the last minute. Then he spoke, saying, "At every meeting you have talked and talked but no one has mentioned a man who left here not long ago. This is his work. We will have to see him, for he is the only person who can kill the eagle." Then they all spoke up and said, "We will see Elder Brother and find out whether he is willing to save us or wants us all to be killed."

They sent a man over to Elder Brother's house. When the man got there he told Elder Brother what the people wanted and that he was sent to ask whether Elder Brother would be willing to save them, as the eagle was killing people every day. Elder Brother said he would do it, and he told the man to go back and say that in four days he would be at the village and would begin his preparations to kill the eagle. When the man returned to the village he told the people that Elder Brother would do it and would be there in four days. The people waited four days. Night came and he had not arrived. He did not come all that night. Then the people did not know what to do. The men said, "It is only a little way; he ought to be here. Probably he will say again that it will be four days." So they sent the man again the next day. When he reached Elder Brother's house he said, "What is the matter? This is the day you promised to be at the village." Elder Brother said, "Yes, I said that I would be there at the end of four days and I will be there at the end of four days. Go back and tell the people again that I will be there at the end of four days." The man returned to the village and said, "Elder Brother said he would be here at the end of four days." Four days passed and again he did not come. The people held another meeting and again sent a messenger to Elder Brother's house, who returned with the same report. When this had occurred four times the man who had suggested sending for Elder Brother spoke again and said, "You know very well that Elder Brother talks backward sometimes; perhaps he is doing that now and means that he will come in four years." The people began to see that was what he meant and that he was going to give the eagle four more years in which to destroy them. So they waited four long years for Elder Brother.

At the end of four years he came to the village, and when he arrived he said he should need a number of things and did not tell what they were. It was necessary for the people to guess one thing after another until they suggested what was in his mind, thus exerting themselves toward the securing of a benefit for the tribe. (This custom is frequently noted in connection with events depending on dreams.) Following this custom the people brought many things to Elder Brother, but he always said they were not right. The people had about given up, for they could not find even the first thing that he wanted. They held a meeting and the man who spoke at the other meeting said, "You have tried everything around here. Over in the west is *wahok*, a stone like clear glass; you had better try that." They went west and got the stone and showed it to Elder Brother. He said it was what he wanted. After they got that stone he asked for another thing to take with him, but did not describe it fully. He said he wanted *wasiuh* (very hard wood). They looked everywhere and brought the hardest sticks they could find but he said they were not right. Then the same man said, "Look in the west where you found the stone." They went and got the sticks at that place and Elder Brother said they were what he wanted. Then Elder Brother said, "There is one more thing; I must have a stick to use for a torch." He gave the right name but they had a different word for it and could not understand him. They sent people out to look and tried many. They went to the same man, who said, "There are some right near here; go and get them." So they got a bundle of those sticks and Elder Brother said they were what he wanted. These sticks were about 6 feet long and he tied them in four bundles. He put the clear stone in the fire and melted it so that it would spread out thin on the ground and he could sharpen the edge of it for a knife. Taking the first sticks that were brought him he selected and sharpened four of them, these sticks being 6 or 8 inches long. After he was ready he waited until four years from the time at which he began his preparations. When he was ready he said, "I am going, but there is one thing I want to do before I start. I will travel during the day until I get to the place at which the eagle is destroying the villages; after that I will travel at night."

He traveled four days and got to the place where the eagle was killing people. From there he traveled at night, using a torch each night, and when daylight came he hid so that he would not be seen by the eagle. On the second night he started out with his second torch. On the third night he was again on his way and the next day he hid from the eagle. His last torch he lit for his last night's travel, and that night he reached the foot of the mountain. He looked up in the night and it looked as though it had no end. He looked up for a while, then went over, and sat down.

THIRD PAUSE

Along toward morning it was so cold that he had to make a fire, so he made a fire in a little can and sat close to it. About daybreak he could hear a roaring inside the mountain. Just before the sun rose the eagle came out and was circling around his house so Elder Brother had to cover up the fire. Four times the eagle circled over the house, then he flew straight east to the place where he had been killing the people. In the morning Elder Brother looked at the rocks and saw there was no projection by which he could climb. He took the four sticks that he had sharpened and stuck them into the rocks for handholds and for his feet to step on. Then he sang this song:

No. 24. "He Walked Up the Slippery Rocks"

(Catalogue No. 958)

Recorded by SIVARIANO GARCIA

VOICE ♩ = 104
Irregular in tonality

Ka-ni-ŋa *na*   va-va-hi   nah - pi-o-ni   ka-ni-ŋa *na*

va - va   wah-po-la   ka-ni-ŋa *na*   va - va   nah -

pi - o - ni   ka-ni-ŋa *na*   va - va   wah-po-la

ta - ca-i   ko - i - tha   cai - *cai* - i - i - mù - na.

WORDS

Kaniŋa	vavahi	nahpiöni	wahpola
It was	rocks	slippery	arrow shafts
tacaï	kojtha	caiïmùna	
stick in	on this	walked up	

Analysis.—This song is classified as irregular in tonality and is transcribed without a signature. Other songs classified as irregular are Nos. 8, 12, 14, 31, 33, 36, 88, 119, and 145. The song consists of two periods having the same rhythm and containing A sharp, and two closing periods in a different rhythm containing A natural. Ascending and descending intervals are about equal in number, and the progressions, with only four exceptions, are major thirds and whole tones.

When he got up about halfway and looked down he began to tremble, he was up so high and the rock was so straight below him, so he sang a song to overcome his fear.

No. 25. Song to Overcome Fear　　　　(Catalogue No. 959)

Recorded by SIVARIANO GARCIA

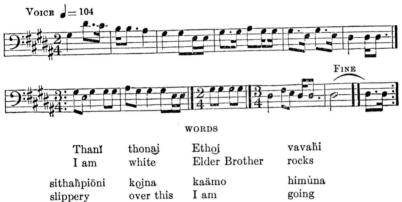

WORDS

Thanĭ	thonaj	Ethoj	vavahĭ
I am	white	Elder Brother	rocks
sithahpiöni	kojna	kaämo	himŭna
slippery	over this	I am	going

Analysis.—It is interesting to study this song in connection with its title. We note the beginning on the accented count of the measure and the ascending fifth as the first progression. The song has a compass of an octave and moves from the highest to the lowest tone of the compass in the first six measures. The change to triple time is effective. The keynote is emphasized in the next three measures but does not appear at the close of the song. The principal interval is a major third, although the song is minor in tonality.

Elder Brother was getting almost to the top. A woman that the eagle had taken up alive was up there. She heard sounds and wondered how a man could have gotten there and where he came from. She thought someone was coming, and then thought that perhaps the sound came from the dead people lying at one side.

When Elder Brother reached the top and saw the woman sitting there he walked toward her and began to tell why he came to the top of the big rock. He said that he did not expect to see any living person, and she said that she never thought she would see a living person up there and did not see how he got up. He had already told her what he came for and he inquired the usual time for the eagle's return. She said, "When the people were near he came back early,

but now he has to go farther, so he does not get back until noon."
The woman had a baby (eagle) sitting at her side. He asked if the
baby could talk and she said, "No." The woman said, "When the
eagle comes home he looks everywhere and kills anything he finds."
Elder Brother said he would do his best to keep out of sight. Then
he turned into a little brown snake, crawled into a crack between the
rocks and said, "Can you see me?" "Yes; I can see you easily,"
cried the woman. Then he turned into a green fly and said he would
fly over the dead and maybe the eagle would not bother him. She
said, "It is not safe; there is not even a fly alive up here." Then he
turned into a very small brown fly and hid among the dead. She
said, "No; he turns over every dead body there. He is so afraid
that something will happen to him." Then he changed into a very
small fly and he flew around four times, each time wrapping a different color of mist around him—green, black, white, and yellow. Then
he crawled into one of the oldest corpses; he crawled far into it, and
she thought he might be safe there.

As for the things he had brought, the knife and the four sticks,
the woman hid them under her trash pile in a corner. He stayed
there and about noon he heard something like a windstorm coming
and as the eagle came nearer he could hear the people groaning.
The eagle laid them down. The eagle walked back and forth and
turned over the dead. He asked his wife if anyone had been there
and she said, "No." He sat down beside the pile of dead and began
to turn them over and throw them to one side. When he got to the
last one, in which the fly was hidden, he said, "Too old; better throw
it away." His wife said, "No; the food may give out. The baby
is getting old enough to eat, and we may have to cook that one for
him." He and his wife walked toward the house and he said, "My
heart feels queer. Didn't some one come here?" She said, "No;
who would dare to come up to this place?" They got into the house
and she began to give him his dinner. After sitting a while he grew
sleepy, so he laid down and went to sleep. She began to sing and he
said, "What is the matter? You never sang like that before." She
answered that she was glad they had so much food. He said, "All
right," closed his eyes, and went to sleep. She had been singing
softly, then she sang louder, and as the eagle did not move his eyelids
she knew that he was sound asleep. The following is her song:

No. 26. Song to Put the Eagle to Sleep

(Catalogue No. 960)

Recorded by SIVARIANO GARCIA

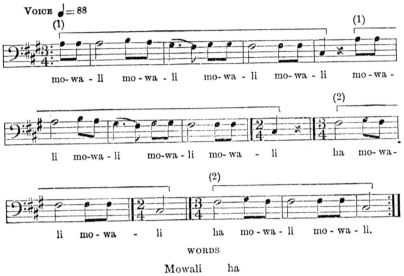

WORDS

Mowali	ha
Fly	ho

Analysis.—This song resembles No. 24 in that it comprises two long phrases followed by two short phrases in a different rhythm. The structure is peculiar in that, with three exceptions, the intervals are fourths and whole tones. A further peculiarity is that the third occurs only as the lowest tone at the end of a phrase. The melody has a soothing quality, perhaps due to the long tone at the beginning of each measure.

Then Elder Brother sang the following song (recorded by Garcia), the tune being the same as in the preceding:

WORDS

niäkahai	mohoko	nahputho	sikosimoko
(no meaning)	dead	are you	sleep-head

TRANSLATION

Are you dead with sleep?

After she had told the fly he came out and changed back to human form. She got Elder Brother's things from under the trash pile and gave them to him. Then he said he was going to do what he had come to do and told her to hold tight against the rock for the rock would shake as soon as he killed the eagle. After he had cut off the head of the eagle and of the baby he ran and stood against the rock beside the woman, and as the eagle rolled and jumped about, after his head was cut off, the rock shook like an earthquake. This kept up until the eagle was dead.

Before Elder Brother left the old woman's house he strung a string across her room, saying, "If this breaks you will know I am dead, but so long as it is not broken you will know I am alive." The shock of this earthquake broke the string and Elder Brother's people began to fear that he had failed.

At last the eagle was still. Elder Brother went over to him, pulled off his long feathers and downy white tufts of feathers, also those from the baby eagle. The tufts from the baby he threw toward the east and those from the father to the north, west, and south. He did this so that from the east white clouds would rise, and from the north and west black clouds would come, and from the south pinkish clouds would come. Then Elder Brother told the woman to heat some water. He sprinkled this hot water on the dead people and told them to wake up because the rain was near. They began to wake up, one at a time. Then he took his big knife and struck it against the face of the rock and a crack appeared. This was for the people to climb down. When all were down he questioned them as to where they came from. The first lot spoke and told where they lived and he sent them there. Then he sent back four groups of people that lived in different villages. The fifth lot had been dead so long that they could not talk the language of the people who were alive. He questioned them again but they would not talk, for they spoke a different language. Elder Brother said, "I don't want you to be among my people. I will send you away and you can find your way back to the other side." He also sent the Yaqui along the shore of the ocean because they also spoke a different language. He cut one of the largest eagle feathers and gave it to the Spanish people, saying they would find it something easy to write with, so they could talk to each other at a distance. He sent them across, saying they would find that was the best place for them to live. Afterwards he sent away the woman and he was left alone. He decorated his hat with large feathers and also with eagle tufts; then he started home.

Back at the house where his string was broken, the old woman had medicine power and she knew Elder Brother was alive and had killed the eagle. So she sang and danced.

Before Elder Brother went away he told the people to watch a certain chain of mountains. He told them to watch a low place in it and said that if he had killed the eagle there would be white clouds over that place. So the people watched the old woman dancing and singing, and they also looked for the clouds in the low place. At last something appeared that looked like clouds but it was Elder Brother's hat decorated with tufts of eagle down. Then they remembered his words and said to each other, "It must be that the old lady knows more than we know and Elder Brother has killed the eagle."

After Elder Brother came down from the high place where his hat showed he did not come home at once but went to a quiet place and lay down for several days. The old woman was out walking and came upon him, asleep from exhaustion. After she found him she went home and began to make an olla to cook gruel for him, and a little olla for him to drink from, and a plate, and a little spoon for the gruel. When she had finished making the dishes and had made the gruel, she got some water, took it over, and set it beside him. This is her song.

No. 27. Song of the Old Woman Who Attended Elder Brother

(Catalogue No. 961)

Recorded by SIVARIANO GARCIA

FREE TRANSLATION

You have done it right, you little bit of an Elder Brother.
Henceforth the villages will be safe and I am on the ground,
I will get along better.

Analysis.—In the first part of this melody we seem to catch the fussiness of the old woman, and in the latter part her joy at the safe return of Elder Brother. The song begins and ends on the fifth above the keynote and progresses chiefly by whole tones, though the minor third occurs with frequency.

After giving him the food she cared for him 16 days. She had also made ollas to carry water for his cold bath and she cared for him in every way, as Beater Wind had cared for the boy at the beginning of this story. At the end of the fourth day she moved him nearer the house and did the same after the next period of four days. At the end of the third period of four days she took him inside the house and continued her care until the end of the fourth period of four days, when he took a bath and was entirely free.

Then he lay around the place for a while. He knew everything was settled and that everything would go on the same as before the gambler was made into an eagle.

STORY OF THE ORIGIN OF THE FLUTE [65]

In one part of the big village in Sacaton Valley Elder Brother had a sister named Acorn Eater, who lived alone. In the village was a man named Lion. (This man's name was said to refer to a large animal, not a "bobcat.") He decided to marry this girl and on that day he went hunting, killed game, took some of the meat over to the girl and told her his plans. He put the meat at one side and told the girl. Then she went out, took what he had brought and threw it away. She told him to go, and said she was getting along better without a husband. Soon afterwards a man named Tiger did the same thing and she told him what she had told the first man. After these two had failed there was a man named Blue Hawk who thought he would try his luck at winning the girl. He went out and killed some game but she did the same to him as to the others. There was a fourth man who tried. His name was Eagle and they were the four meanest people in the village. She turned Eagle away also.

Elder Brother heard that some men in the village were trying to marry his sister so he thought he would go over and tell her whom she should marry. He told her that he did not see why she refused those four young men, all of whom killed game and brought it to her. Then he told her that he wanted her to marry Gopher. Of course his sister turned her back on him and said she did not want to marry anything that looked like Gopher. Elder Brother went away when he saw that she would not mind him.

The place where they got water was quite a long distance away and they had to cross four ranges of hills. Gopher lived under ground and he heard what the girl said when her brother wanted her to marry him. His magic power was great and the next day he made her go to the place where they got the water, and by his power she became pregnant. She had great difficulty in making the return journey to her home and by the time she reached the last of the four ranges of hills she was obliged to crawl. She sang the following song facing the west, then the south, east, and north. When she had sung the song four times her two babies had been born. Both were boys.

---

[65] Cf. "Origin of the Flageolet." Bull. 80, Bur. Amer. Ethn., pp. 80–84.

No. 28. "The Rocks are Making a Noise"

(Catalogue No. 962)

Recorded by SIVARIANO GARCIA

VOICE ♩ = 76

WORDS

Vavaȟi [7]	kohona	hononi	wûma	iäšoäkima
Towering rocks	sounding	evening	with them	I am crying

Analysis.—The interval of a fifth forms the framework of the opening measures of this song and the whole tone is the principal interval in the latter portion. The keynote occurs only on unaccented counts in two measures, midway the length of the song.

The next morning she felt better and went home. About noon the people in the village were playing *ginskut*. They saw her coming and wondered. One man said he believed that what she carried in her arms were babies. Quite a while afterwards Lion found out about it and thought he would go over and see the babies. He took some game as before and she sent him away again, saying the father was someone whom she did not know. All those men who had tried to marry her did as before and she again sent them away. Coyote found out and he said to the people, "I am going over to see my babies. They belong to me." Coyote did as the others had done but in getting game he killed only animals that crawled, such as snakes and lizards. She threw them away and told him to go. For many months, as the children began to learn to eat, old Gopher came and brought them roots, which are the food of the gophers. The girl knew he was the father of the children and she took the roots inside for the babies to eat. The people did not know yet who was the husband of this young girl.

In the spring, when edible plants are coming up, she used to go after them and leave the two boys at home. While she was gone old Grasshopper and Cricket began to jump about and bother the children, who began to cry. She heard the babies crying, came running to the house and saw Grasshopper and Cricket jumping about. Cricket crawled into a crack and Grasshopper hid in the grass. She went into the house, took hot ashes from the fire and filled the crack, and she set fire to the grass, but Cricket and Grasshopper were gone before she got there. She kept on gathering plants every day and

[7] This is the same as the first syllable of Vavakivari. See p. 3.

left the babies in a hammock for more safety. The babies were now able to talk together. One day they were left in the hammock and lots of seeds were scattered below the hammock. A flock of quails came and made a noise under the hammock. One boy said, "Do something so they will not keep us awake." The boy threw something among the quails and they lay down as if they had been shot. Then the children went to sleep. When their mother came she found the quails lying there. She put away what she had brought, threw out the quails and came back. The babies waked up and cried. She did not know what to do with them and finally decided they were crying for the quails. She got them and the babies stopped crying at once. Then she found that one of the little fellows had killed the quails. She made a fire and began to roast them.

Several men in the village said the children were theirs. After the boys were old enough to talk and understand she told the people to gather at one place. She said she would turn the children loose, and if their father were there the children would crawl toward him. So she got the people together, turned the children loose, and they crawled around the circle. Coyote was about the last one. They were crawling along and not looking around. When they came near to Coyote, he tried to call them, but they went right by and went to their mother. She said, "Now, you see that the father of these children is not present, and you must keep still. I do not know what you have been saying."

Afterwards she told them who was the father of the children. All the people went home except Coyote, who stayed and called himself their grandfather. As they grew older they went around the village like other children. When they were old enough to go far away, their mother said, "You have been here among the people, not knowing what I have in store for you. About this season certain things will be there all the time." Then the boys began to ask her to tell them exactly where these things were, for they wanted to see them. She said, "They are very high; it is hard to get up there." They decided to go, but their mother said, "You had better not; you do not know the ground and besides if you reach the place you can not climb so high." They kept wanting to go and she tried to dissuade them, but finally she let them go. They asked her the number of days it would take to get there. She said, "About four days." She made a lunch for them to take. They left home, went quite a distance, and camped; they went on the second day, camped again, and so on for four days. On the fifth day they were at the place where these things were. They got to a great rock, and, coming closer, the younger boy saw them first. The boys looked up quite a while, and then both saw them. The younger said, "See if you can get our pets (young eagles) so that we can take them home." The boy turned himself into a little snake that can climb a rock, went up about halfway, slipped, and fell to the ground dead. The younger boy went to work and brought him to life. Before the older boy rose up the younger boy stood beside him singing this song.

No. 29. Song When Restoring a Boy to Life

(Catalogue No. 963)

Recorded by SIVARIANO GARCIA

VOICE ♩ = 76

FREE TRANSLATION

He lies face downward.

Analysis.—The framework of this melody consists of the descending tones C sharp, A, F sharp, and C sharp, the only additional tone being G sharp. Six of the twenty-one intervals are fourths and nine are major seconds.

After the older boy came to life he told his younger brother that it was his turn to try to get them down. He turned into a tuft of feathers, which the wind carried to the top of the rock. He got two eagles and came down with them. When he had brought them down, he fainted and his brother revived him, singing the same song that had been used for himself. As soon as the younger boy got up he walked over to where he had put the eagles and took the larger one. His brother said, "Take the smaller one; you are the youngest." He said, "No; I will take the larger. I went up there and brought them down." He went on, and finally the older one took the smaller bird and they started home. The first night they camped and all night the wind blew as hard as it could, and they had to sit up all night. It stopped the next evening, but rain began to fall and they had to sit up all night again. The third night the ground was damp and it turned cold, so they had to sit up all night. The fourth night it snowed all night and the eagles were killed. The boys burned the eagles and everything that they had, and on the morning of the fifth day they were crying over the death of their pets and singing this song.

No. 30. Lamenting the Dead Eagles

(Catalogue No. 964)

Recorded by SIVARIANO GARCIA

WORDS

Hayah	niroika
Oh	my pet

Analysis.—In this song we note the prolonged tone on the first count of the measure which characterized No. 26, which was sung to put the old eagle to sleep. Both songs are minor in tonality, the present song containing only the minor triad and second. This song contains six sorts of ascending intervals but progresses chiefly by whole tones. The tempo is more rapid than in a majority of these songs.

All that day they cried on the way home and they cried as they entered the house where their mother was cooking for them. They had no eagles. She said, "I do not see why you did not get them. They are always there at this season.". But she knew the eagles were dead. She tried to make them eat but they would not. Then she told them to stay there and she would go to another place where there were little eagles and she would get some that would look just like those that had died. She went to the place where they had burned the birds and dug down in the place where they had their fire, got out the young eagles and took them home. She put them outside the house and told the boys to go outside and see their pets. They stopped crying at once. The older boy told the younger to peep through the door, saying, "They may not look the same as the others." The younger boy said nothing but went outside and got the larger bird which he had claimed before. Then they began to quarrel about which should have the larger bird. The mother went out and said that the younger child should take the younger bird as it would grow up to be just like the older bird.

Coyote was living there with them and he killed lizards and other small animals for the eagles to eat. He also made a house for the eagles to live in. After the eagles got older their feathers grew very long. The boy's mother said, "The feathers are too long. I will pull them but others will grow."

No. 31. "I Will Pull Out Their Feathers"

(Catalogue No. 965)

Recorded by SIVARIANO GARCIA

FREE TRANSLATION

I will take any young birds and raise them.
When their feathers grow long I will pull them out.

Analysis.—This song is classified as irregular in tonality. Other songs thus classified are Nos. 8, 12, 14, 24, 33, 36, 88, 119, and 145. As in several other songs with this classification, the melody is based on the interval of a fourth. Examination of this song shows the descending intervals C to G and G to D as the framework of the melody. The rhythm is simple, consisting chiefly of eighth notes.

The boys pulled out the feathers of the eagles and turned them loose. Afterwards their mother told Coyote to go and get a kind of tree that she was going to use in making bows. Far in the east there was a mountain and at the foot of the mountain was a tree that made good bows and arrows. Coyote said, "All right, those mountains are right next my feet, I can get that tree." He went toward the east, cut two saplings for the children and one for himself and brought them home. He threw down the two for the children and their mother pulled off the bark, curved them by the heat of the fire, and put strings on them, doing this at once.

Coyote cleaned the wood of his tree nicely and bent his bow by leaning the tree against another tree so that when dry it would be in the proper form. The mother had used the whole tree except the rough outer bark but Coyote scraped off part of the wood on each side of his bow. He told the woman she was doing something that no one ever did and that his way was right. Then she sent Coyote to another range of mountains where there was wood that was good for making arrows. He went again and returned in a short time.

When Coyote brought the sticks the woman made arrows by just stripping off the bark. Coyote put water in a dish and put his sticks to soak, intending to take off the bark and polish them with an arrow polisher. He made his arrows as smooth as possible but the woman had better arrows and they were finished long before Coyote finished his. When they were making the bows Coyote had sinew for his bowstring but the old woman used her spittle. He told her she was doing something that no one had ever done and that people would take his way. After finishing the bows and arrows the old woman sang the following song.

No. 32. Song After Making the Bows and Arrows

(Catalogue No. 966)

Recorded by SIVARIANO GARCIA

VOICE ♩ = 69

TRANSLATION

Bows now are made,
Arrows now are made.
Toward the west we will try them.
You can watch them fly, my boys.

Analysis.—No rhythmic unit occurs in this song but the rhythm of the song as a whole is suggestive of firmness and confidence. A compass of nine tones is accomplished in the first two measures, and a compass of an octave within two measures occurs twice in the later portion of the song. Five sorts of descending intervals occur, which is an unusually large variety. About one-third of the intervals are fourths, an interval frequently associated with motion and vigor. Each of the four rhythmic periods ends with an ascending fourth.

Coyote and the two boys went toward the west and stood together to try their bows and arrows. The old woman sang her song over and over as they pointed their arrows toward the points of the compass, changing one word according to the direction in which they were shooting—west, south, east, and the last time toward the north. The first time she sang the song through once and at the last word the boys acted as though they were going to shoot toward the west but they did not shoot their arrows. Coyote shot his. The same was done toward the south and east, Coyote letting go an arrow every time. Then they turned toward the north and this time, at the last word of the song, all three let their arrows go. Coyote's arrow went only about a third of the way, whirling around, then falling. The boys went to get their arrows but Coyote did not go. He said that people never went to get their arrows when they were in war; they let their arrows go.

FIRST PAUSE

.In the evening their mother told the boys that there was game near by. She said that she had seen jack rabbits and if they wanted to get some game they could go and shoot one. Afterwards they brought home jack rabbits and other game every day. Once she went out to gather "Elder Brother's beans." When she came home she told the boys that she had seen a deer that was not afraid of her and she would like to have the boys go and see if they could get it. Next morning the old woman got up early and went on ahead. The boys stayed in bed until almost sunrise, then they followed her, after eating their breakfast. They reached the place where their mother had seen the deer and the younger boy stood by a tree. An old buck walked off into the woods. They tracked the old buck and while they were following the tracks their mother came walking. She asked them what they were looking for and they said they had lost the tracks. Then the younger boy said, "That was no buck, that was our mother; she was showing us how a deer looks. We will find game like that before long."

Coyote stayed at home and fixed up the meat while the boys got the game. After they had grown older their mother told them something else. She said, "I have a plant. It stands in the water, but I do not think you will ever get to it because it is in such a dangerous place." They wanted to see what they could do so they left home the next day. After traveling four days they reached a place where tall cane stands in the water. On that day it looked as though there would be rain and lightning, but they walked on until they came to an oblong lake and saw cane (commonly called bamboo) standing at one corner of the lake. One boy said, "Our mother said the plant was in a dangerous place but it is near the shore." They went toward it but the bamboo moved to the next corner; when they came near it the bamboo moved to another corner, until it had been in all the corners, and then it moved to the middle of the lake. They stopped and began to talk, saying it did look dangerous. A red snake was coiled around the bamboo, reaching almost to the top. This snake was what they had thought was lightning. The elder brother changed himself into a water snake and said he was going to enter the lake, and if he met anything he would probably be killed. Their mother had told them that they had a grandfather in the water—it was a beaver. The boy came to a beaver, lying right in his way, and he said to the beaver, "Get out of my way; I want to get to my bamboo." He went to an alligator and told him to get out of the way and then he came to a large animal which the old people say once lived in the water and did not come out at all. Before this animal could move out of his way the boy ran back to the shore, tired out. He was so tired that he fainted and his brother revived him. Then he told the younger brother to see what he could do. The younger brother turned himself into a fish, met the beaver, the alligator, and the large animal that lived in the water, and he finally reached the rattlesnake coiled around the bamboo. He said, "Grandfather, get out of my way and let me get my bamboo." The snake said, "You had better let me cut it for you." The snake cut it and it fell toward the older boy who was on the shore. He could almost reach it, and he got into the water and seized the large end of it. The younger boy was in such a hurry to get out that he climbed over his grandfather. He got so tired that he fainted on the shore, but the elder brother did not take care of him; instead they quarreled about which should have the larger end of the bamboo. The younger boy said that he ought to have it because he went into the water to get it. So they took the whole bamboo to their mother, who was the one to decide it. When they got it home their mother cut two lengths of two joints each and made them each a flute. After the flutes were finished she put ornamental designs on them. She gave the flutes to the children, who blew right into them, but could not play tunes. She paid no attention to them, knowing that some day they would be able to play tunes on the flutes. She kept hearing them blow as hard as they could. One day she asked for one and said, "Now listen and you shall hear how it should be played." She took it and began to play, and after she handed it to the boy and told him to play he was able to play just as she had done. Then she did the same with the other boy. This is the melody which she played on the instrument. It was said that the following words were sung, if no flute was available when the story was told.

No. 33. "Four Fires on the Ground"

(Catalogue No. 967)

Recorded by SIVARIANO GARCIA

FREE TRANSLATION

One in the corner, in the square on the ground,
A fire in each corner, four fires on the ground.

Analysis.—The peculiar sequence of tones in this song suggests D as a keynote, though that tone occurs only in the first measure. This song contains no change of time, which is unusual, and about two-thirds of the intervals are whole tones. (cf. flute melodies, pp. 217, 218.)

After the mother had played on the flute she let the boys go and of course they both played the same tune. They played that tune early in the morning and it could be heard quite a long distance. One morning the old woman said she was going north to the edge of the world to see if there she could hear the sound of the flutes. She went north and stood at the very edge of the world and there she could hear the sound of the flutes so clearly that she began to dance. When she got home she said, "That sounds fine. It seems as though it sounds better when I am at the edge of the world than it does when I am near by."

Every morning the boys went hunting and in the afternoon they came home, raced with their wooden balls (cf. pp. 200, 201), and then they played on their flutes. One morning they were up at daybreak and went around the house playing as usual. At that time the earth was young and it used to rain every other day. The earth was damp and the flute could be heard a long distance.

Over in the east lived Brown Buzzard. He had two daughters. The older one got up very early and she heard this music in the west. She stopped and listened, thinking it was some sort of bird, but still she knew it was not a bird. She went in the house and called her sister to come and listen. The sister did not come, but said, "It is some sort of bird whistling and singing." The elder sister said, "It is not a bird; it is something different and it is coming nearer." Finally the other sister went out to hear. The elder girl said they must try to find out what this was. The younger girl refused to go at first but the elder sister kept coaxing and after a while she consented. They dressed in their best. In those days they had beads and other ornaments and they put tufts of eagle feathers on top of their heads. At evening they came to a house and the man who lived there asked where they were going. They said they had been hearing something wonderful the last few nights and wanted to find where it was. The man said they would not hear that sound anywhere except at his house, so they had better stay there that night. The girls said they would do so. The man went up in a high tree and began to make a noise like a bird. The younger sister asked the elder, "Is that the way it sounds?" The elder one said, "No." They would not sleep there when they found it out, so they ran away. The man tried to call them but they kept running and he fell out of the tree. They went on and came to another place. Everything happened as before. A man went to the top of a tree and tried to sing but the girls ran away. This man was an owl. The next evening the same thing happened again. This time it was a little screech owl. The girls refused to listen and ran away. They went on and after a time they came to a little hawk's house and everything happened exactly as before. When the little hawk told them that the bird sang early in the morning the girls said, "Show us a little so we can hear if it is right." He went to the top of a tree and made a sound that really was a little like that of a flute. The elder one said, "That sounds right; let us stay." The younger one said, "No." The elder one believed the younger one and they went on. They began to run toward the west. On the fifth day they felt that they were getting nearer the place so they stopped and sang a song.

No. 34. "Who is Going to Marry Me?"

(Catalogue No. 968)

Recorded by SIVARIANO GARCIA

VOICE ♩ = 76

FREE TRANSLATION

Who are you, nice boys?
Who is going to marry me?

Analysis.—A question and answer seem to be suggested in this melody, the first two phrases ending with an upward progression, and the last two phrases containing only a downward progression. The compass of the song is only three tones and it is minor in tonality.

Of course the boys could feel that the girls were approaching, so they played the following tune on the flute. As in the previous instance, the words are sung if a flute is not available.

No. 35. "The Girls are Approaching"

(Catalogue No. 969)

Recorded by SIVARIANO GARCIA

FREE TRANSLATION

From the east the girls are approaching.
They came to the place of the singing,
They are here.

Analysis.—The rhythm of this song is an interesting contrast to the rhythm of the song next preceding. The melody is said to have been played on a flute but the tones are not those of the flute played for the writer. The melody tones are those of the first five-toned scale in which the third and the seventh above the keynote are omitted.

They played the tune once and then stopped, for they knew the girls would arrive during the day. While the boys were racing with their balls that afternoon the girls arrived. The girls were at a distance from the house when the boys got home. The boys knew they were the ones who had been coming toward them. The two boys went into the house, got their flutes and went on top of the house. They noticed that the girls were brightly adorned and made this song about them.

No. 36. "A Fillet of White Eagle Down"

(Catalogue No. 970)

Recorded by SIVARIANO GARCIA

FREE TRANSLATION

I am showy, I am showy, with glittering belt and a fillet of white eagle down.

Analysis.—Only three tones occur in this song, which is classified as irregular in tonality. Other songs thus classified are Nos. 8, 12, 14, 24, 31, 33, 88, 119, and 145. The interval of a fourth constitutes half the progressions. This interval is prominent in other songs classified as irregular in tonality, also in No. 26 (concerning the eagle), and has been noted frequently in songs concerning birds.

The girls came and sat beside the house. The mother was inside the house cooking and Coyote was outside fixing the meat that the boys had brought. Screech Owl came over and sat down at one side. Coyote had a long stick, and each liver that he took from the game he put on this stick. He had quite a number on the stick, and he called, "Screech Owl, take these and roast them for your supper." Screech Owl did not like to have his name spoken before the girls, so he said, "You mean yourself; you cook them for your supper." He was ashamed about the speaking of his name, but anyway he went over and got the livers and started for home. There were certain plants they used for making gruel. The gruel was greenish in color. The mother had some in a big olla and was cooking it. After it was cooled she put a generous amount in dishes for her sons, but for the girls she put only a very little in each dish. When she put it before them the elder girl said, "That is not a meal; I am hungry." After the mother had placed the gruel before them she went off and sat with her back to them. They began to eat the gruel, and as they ate it there was just as much as at first. They ate until they were filled, but there was just as much in the dish as at first. The old woman asked why they did not eat it all and said, "It is easy to eat that all up." She put in her hand and scooped it up and ate it all at once. The mother made up the bed for the boys and they went to bed, but she let the girls sit outside. Finally they came in and the old woman said, "Where do you come from to disturb my children like this?" She kept awake. Finally the younger son got up and took his flute and struck it against the big post in the middle of the house and broke it to pieces. After that his brother never played his flute because he did not want to play it alone. He left it in the house and it was destroyed with the house later. The girls stayed there some time, and at last they decided to go back and see their father. They told their husbands, who said that was all right. They got home at last and told their father how they had come. Their father knew that the younger girl would have a child and he said, "If it is a girl, we will take care of it; if it is a boy, I am going to roast and eat him." The old man was getting blind, and when the child was born they told him it was a girl. He said they must take good care of her so she would grow up to be like her mother. But the child was a boy. They took good care of the little boy and dressed him like a girl until he was old enough to run around.

When the old man found that the child was a boy he decided to harm him, so he told his daughter that he was going after wood and wanted the child to follow him. He went on ahead. When the little boy overtook the old man there was a big log on the ground. The man pretended he wanted to have it put on his shoulder and told the boy to help lift it, but instead of putting it on his shoulder he let it fall on the boy. He thought that he had killed him and went home, but when he got there he saw the child sitting beside his mother. He said, "What does this mean?" This went on day after day. The old man tried four times to kill the boy and every time the boy was sitting at home when he got back. Finally the old man saw that he could not harm the boy.

The husbands of the girls had no luck after their wives went away. They killed game once in a while but not so often and they kept thinking of their wives over in the east. So one day when they were out hunting the younger questioned his brother as to what he thought of going to see their wives. The elder one said, "No; we had better not go." The younger kept wanting to go, and finally the elder said, "Well, we had better find out from our mother whether she wants us to go." When they got home that evening they asked their mother, saying that the younger boy wanted to go and see how his wife was getting along. The elder boy said he did not care but that the younger one wanted to go. Their mother said she did not like to have them go, for if they went she would worry all the time; besides, she knew that the father of these two girls was a man who would not spare their lives if they entered the house. The younger brother wanted to go very much, so he said they would go—he did not care if it was dangerous. Finally the elder brother decided he wanted to go in order to protect his younger brother. The old woman finally said they could go and that they would see for themselves whether they would have any trouble in getting there. The next day when they were ready to go, the old woman said, "If anything dangerous happens or if anything speaks to you at your first camp you had better turn back and come home." They left the next day and went quite a distance. Their mother "jumped right into their tracks" and that brought them back home. They did this four times. When their mother saw they were determined to go a fifth time, she said, "All right; if you see anything dangerous this time you had better fight your way through and go on."

Then they went, and at evening as they were walking, the elder one, who was going ahead, dropped suddenly face downward on the ground. The elder brother knew that something bad was going to happen. The younger brother was braver than the elder. He made

a little fire and fixed the camp right there. After lying for quite a
while the elder boy got up and came to the fire. The younger said,
"This shows that our mother was right; we had better turn back."
The elder said, "No; things our mother says do not always happen;
sometimes she is trying to fool us." So they camped. The younger
one went ahead the next day and when he got to the place for camp
at night he dropped down. The elder one made a fire and sat down
by the fire and when the fire got bright he put on more wood so he
could see a long way by the flame. A headless wild cat came and sat
across the fire from him. He touched his brother and said, "Get
up and see, I guess this is what our mother meant." After the younger
boy got up the headless wild cat disappeared. The younger boy said,
"It is nothing; we will go right on." The next day they went on
again, the elder boy leading, and at night he fell down. The younger
boy made a fire and sat down beside it, and along came a big owl,
talking and trying to tell them something. He wakened his elder
brother and said, "You had better wake up and listen. Perhaps we
are already dead." Then his brother got up and said, "I tell you
again, things our mother says do not always come true; perhaps she
is trying to fool us." Next day the younger brother made a fire, and
a screech owl sat on the opposite side of the fire; he sat there and went
away. The boy wakened his brother and said, "I want to tell you
something that has happened. We have been traveling four days
and nights, and every day and night something has happened, but
we have gone on, hoping each time that nothing more would happen
to us. We will go on again and I think we will get there to-day,
but I do not know whether we will be safe there or not." They went
on to Head Mountains and sat down. They got up on the top of
these mountains and decided to make a song about their trip.

No. 37. Song on the Mountain Top   (Catalogue No. 971)

Recorded by SIVARIANO GARCIA

Analysis.—This song is in a rapid tempo and has a simple rhythm
without a recurrent rhythmic phrase. The keynote is the first and

also the highest tone in the song, which is unusual. One-half of the intervals are minor thirds.

Then they went on to another range of mountains called Frog Mountains. They went on the top and from there they saw their wives' houses, so they knew they were near the place. After they got on Frog Mountains they sang another song which had the same tune as the preceding but mentioned Frog Mountains instead of Head Mountains.

After singing this song the elder boy began to encourage his brother, saying they would get there soon and they would together find out what would happen. He told his brother not to be afraid as it had been their plan to go there in spite of danger. They flew from there to the house and they put something on their claws that shone like stars. One came down on the head of one of the girls, the other on the lap of the other girl. Their father heard the girls laughing and sent the little boy to find out, as he had never heard them laugh like that. The little boy said, "Give me some roasted pumpkin seeds to eat as I go along." The old man gave him four or five which the boy ate and then ran back. The old man asked, "What are they doing?" The boy said, "I do not know. I ate the pumpkin seeds and so I came back." He sent the boy again and the boy said, "You better give me some roasted corn to eat as I go." The boy came back as before. The old man sent the boy again and he said, "Give me some popped corn." And the fourth time the boy said, "Give me some hard corn." With this he went clear over to the place and peeped in the door, then he cried out and ran back to the old man.

SECOND PAUSE

When he came crying to his grandfather the old man asked what was the matter there to make him cry. He said, "One was with my mother and the other with her sister." Then the old man said, "All right, the time has come for me to do something. I have never spared anything that has come into my house and I will not do so now." The old man got up and went into the next house where he got his club and his shield, then he went to where they were, peeped in the door, and said, "Oh, these are my sons-in-law." The boys said, "Yes." The old man went back and put his club and shield where he kept them. He had intended to do almost anything, but now that he had seen his sons-in-law it seemed as though he could not do it. He knew that these boys had great medicine power and he no longer wondered why his girls went so far to find them when there were people living all around them. Then he thought of his neighbors, who were the meanest people in the world and who had wanted to marry the mother of these boys. He thought of Lion, Tiger, and the two others.   He talked with them and they all said the boys' medicine was stronger than theirs.   They came and looked at the boys.   Then he went to Blue Hawk (the fifth animal who wanted to marry the girl).   Blue Hawk said that if the old man wanted to get rid of the boys he would not go to look at them but would stay in his house and get ready.   He sang the following song.

No. 38. "Terrible in Its Power to Destroy"

(Catalogue No. 972)

Recorded by SIVARIANO GARCIA

FREE TRANSLATION

Hanging motionless in the sky yet terrible in its power to destroy.

Analysis.—It is interesting to study this melody in connection with its title.   It contains four phrases, each with a fourth descending to D. The tones E flat and F occurring at the close of certain measures give a peculiar melodic effect.   The song contains all the tones of the octave and has no change of measure lengths.

Afterwards Blue Hawk flew to the east and then back and swooped down on the house and knocked out the west side of it, singing the above song.   He rose up, came back, knocked out the east side of the house and sang again.   Then he flew toward the north and knocked out the south side of the house.   Then he flew toward the south and knocked out the north side.   After knocking each side he sang the song.   While coming back after knocking down the last side he flew low over the boys and tried to destroy their medicine power. Then he flew west, came down and knocked down both boys.   Then he flew up high and went home.

After the boys were killed the old man dragged them to his house and made a place in which to keep them.   While the old man ate them he saved everything so he could crush the bones and get all the grease.   The little boy sat near.   Some grease splashed in his mouth and he liked the taste.   He ran to his mother saying, "What is that grease that my grandfather has?"   His mother said, "Do not go near that place.   All that remains of your father is there.   Do not go near the old man, go somewhere else."   The little fellow wandered off, but soon got back to the old man.   He had the bones all crushed in a big dish and was sucking off the grease.   The old man handed a bone to the boy, but then drew it back and put it in his own mouth. The boy ran to his mother and told her what the old man had done. She said, "I told you not to go around the old man.   He is making fun of you."   The old man ate up everything.   They lived there quite a while afterwards.

The old woman knew that the boys had been killed and she played on the flute; then she began to cry.   One of the tunes she played was recorded as a flute melody (p. 217) and also as a song which was not transcribed.   The song corresponding to the second flute melody (p. 218) was not obtained.

When the little boy was old enough to go far away his mother said, "I think you are old enough to go, and if you want to see your grandmother she lives straight west."   Of course the mother of the two boys knew that they had been killed and was almost crazy thinking about it.   One day the little fellow said he would like to see his grandmother and would go wherever she lived.   His mother said, "All right.   It is quite a distance but there are people living all along."   The little boy started next day and went as far as the last camp of his father and uncle.   He found ashes and wondered if any one wandering like himself had camped there.   The ashes looked fresh and he stirred them and found fire.   He sat there and near by was the place where his father had fallen; opposite was where his uncle had sat.   Both men appeared slowly.   The boy went and tried to set them up but they acted as if they were drunk and could not sit up.   Then they began to disappear again.   Then the little fellow knew that his father and uncle were traveling right with him. The next night he came to their third camp.   They appeared again and he tried to set them up again but they could not remain in position, and they finally disappeared.   The fourth night he came to their first camp and there he got them set up.   He acted affectionately as a child would act toward his father and then saw that his uncle was disappearing.   He hastened to him and tried to keep him from disappearing.   Then he ran to his father because he, in turn, was disappearing, so he went back and forth again and again.   His uncle said, "My poor child, you can not keep us from disappearing; we are different now that we are dead.   You must let us go.   You know that your old grandfather chopped us up.   If we had any bones we might be able to sit up for a while and tell you what we would like to tell you."   Of course because they had been chopped up they could not give any power to the boy.   He had some magic power of his own, or he would not have been able to see them.

The boy arrived at his grandmother's on the fifth day and stayed there.   She went away to get food every day and told him to stay inside the house, saying, "There is something near here that swallows children and it will get you." He thought one day that he would go and find what the thing was. He went to that place and before he got there he saw many flint stones and he picked up some sharp ones and went toward the place where the thing lived. (It was a large animal said to have lived in the water.) Before he knew it the animal came out and said, "Where does this little thing come from? The children around here are afraid of me. I will swallow this little thing." He swallowed the little boy, but before the little boy died he looked around and saw a thin place. He struck at this thin place with his flint, cut it, and got out. He started back home but stopped to see what the animal would do and he saw it fall over.

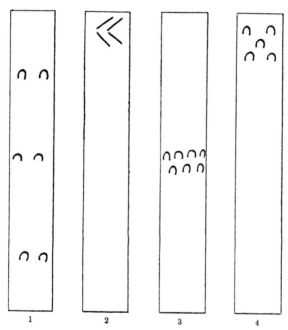

FIG. 1.—Implements used in bamboo game

He went home. When the old woman got back he said, "I went to that place where you told me not to go and I was swallowed by the animal but I killed him and have come home." The old woman could not believe it, so the boy took her over and showed her the animal. The old woman thought at once that the little fellow would follow in the footsteps of his father and uncle. The next day he was going out again and she told him not to go as something in another part of the village was ugly and killed children all the time. After she had gone the boy went over that way to see what strange sort of thing it might be and stood next to a tree. A big snake was lying down. He looked over and saw the boy by the tree. The snake fairly flew over and hit the tree with his head. He was going so fast that this killed him. The boy went home as before, took the old woman over and showed her the dead snake.

He lived with his grandmother several years. When he was old enough to understand it thoroughly the old woman related the life of his father and uncle and finally came to the manner of their death. While she told him this story the little boy cried. When he stopped

crying he said that he did not know that was the way they were
killed, but now he understood. He said that he was going back
home to get even with his grandfather. Then the old woman said,
"My grandson, I don't believe you can do it; the man is old, you are
young and you have not so much magic power as he. I do not think
you can do it." The boy said, "I will see my grandfather and find
out whether·he has as much power as I, for I want to get even with
him." She asked the boy to tell what he intended to use in killing
his grandfather. The boy said he would take some bamboo. They
had only one piece originally and four joints had been cut off for
making the flutes, so the old woman cut off four pieces, each one
joint in length. After she had done this the little fellow said he
would take those pieces but he did not know just which one of them
he would use. So he took the four bamboos. No. 1 is called "Old
woman," and he took this first. With his medicine power he made
it fly. It went just a little distance and fell down. No. 2 was
called "Old man." This went a little higher, but it also fell down.
No. 3 was called "Black in the middle," and that went up still
higher but not high enough. No. 4 bamboo was called "Head."
(These designs, sketched from a set in actual use, are shown in fig. 1.)
He made the fourth bamboo fly up and it went up to the sky and
descended to the ground. The old woman had been watching.
The boy said, "This is the one; I think I can do it with this one alone."
Just as he was getting ready to leave the old woman called him to
her. He stood before her, and she put her hands on his shoulders
and said she would do something to him so he could not be seen and
would reach his destination safely. She sang the following song for
him:

No. 39. Song to Make the Boy Invisible

(Catalogue No. 973)

Recorded by SIVARIANO GARCIA

FREE TRANSLATION

My poor grandchild, my poor grandchild,
It is the head gaming stick that always wins,
Throw it forward.

Analysis.—Attention is directed to a comparison of the rhythmic units in this song. An hypnotic effect is produced by repetitions of rhythm that are almost but not quite alike, so these units are interesting in connection with the use of the song. It is also interesting to note the rhythmic completeness of the song as a whole.

When she had finished singing she said, "This is all I will do for you. You may go, but I will know if anything serious happens to you." He went on and after a time he began to feel queer. He thought that it was the old man's power and said, "The old man knows I am coming and is making his medicine." Then he sang the song that the old woman had sung to make him invisible but changed the words slightly. There were four camping places, as there had been when he came, and he camped again where his father and uncle had camped, but they did not appear.

When he reached home he saw the old man sitting and he said, "All right, grandfather, we will gamble." The old man said, "I do not gamble with young people. I play with old people and win. I do not see how a boy like you could beat me." The boy kept teasing him to gamble and the old man kept on refusing. The boy had already sent his "head bamboo" up to the sky, and before it got back the old man had consented. The boy heard it coming down with a sound like a windstorm. The boy said, "It sounds as if we would have a windstorm." Then the bamboo came down on the old man's head and went right down to the ground. After the boy had killed his grandfather he took off the scalp and put it on a pole. He did not go near his mother. Then he started back and camped in the same places as before. He got to the old woman's house on the fifth day. When he arrived he did not know what to do. He put the scalp, fastened on a pole, beside the door; then he went in and sat down by the fire. The old woman turned over and saw the boy's clothing splashed with blood, so she knew that he had killed his grandfather. She went outside, took up the scalp pole and danced with it, singing the following song.

This is the first *Limo* song that was ever composed. The first line refers to the successful warrior who must undergo an ordeal of purification, while the second line refers to the people who rejoice in his victory. The word *Limo* is here used with reference to the entire procedure that followed the return of the warriors. In definite use it indicated only the action that took place after they had completed their purification. (Cf. pp. 193–197.)

No. 40. "The Man Who Has No Joy"

(Catalogue No. 974)

Recorded by SIVARIANO GARCIA

FREE TRANSLATION

Who is the man who killed an enemy and has no joy?
I am having all the joy alone.

Analysis.—There is an effect of tragedy in the repeated semitones of the first six measures of this song. The keynote does not appear until the seventh measure, but is persistent until the close. Whole tones and half tones comprise all except three of the intervals.

The people heard her and came over and sang with her. Soon the whole village was there. After that big dance they were tired out. She took the little fellow to a quiet place and cared for him four days. During every night of this time the *Limo* songs kept coming to him. One of the old *Limo* songs refers to two girls who could not decide which songs they liked best and so wandered from one dancing circle to another. During the *Limo* several dances were often in progress at the same time. (See p. 197.)

No. 41. "From One Dance Circle to Another"

(Catalogue No. 975)

Recorded by SIVARIANO GARCIA

FREE TRANSLATION

Twin girls, they go from one dancing circle to another,
Returning to the place from which they started.

Analysis.—It is interesting to compare this song with its title and to trace in it an element of humor, the wandering quarter-note succession being twice broken by short rhythmic phrases. The varied measure lengths are unusual, but were indicated by the accents. No secondary accent occurred in the fourth measure. It will be noted that quadruple time rarely occurs in these transcriptions.

After his final bath the boy told the old woman that he was going back to see how his mother was. He said, "Do what you like, but if you stay here I will come back to you." The old woman said, "I am going across the ocean into another land, but after you have seen your mother you are to come to me." After the little boy was gone she tore down her house, put the longest beam on her shoulder, and started for the ocean. She carried it a while, then she threw it down and went off, saying, "Each year when the leaves come out, if there are leaves on this beam the people will know they are going to have a good crop." The beam was a mesquite log. Then the old woman crossed to the other side of the ocean.

When the boy had been at his mother's house a few days he told her that he was going to follow his grandmother's trail and see if he could find her. He went to his grandmother's house, found it torn down, and thought she must have started about the same time that he did. After the boy had left his mother's place the mother and her sister decided to follow and live with him where he lived. The boy got to the ocean and walked and walked but found no way to get across, so he decided to cross by magic. He put his bow on the shore and it stretched into a rainbow bridge to the other side of the ocean. He had started across it when his mother and sister arrived. They begged to go, too, and said, "You have gotten even with our father, now we want to go and live with you." They sang this song.

No. 42. Song of the Women by the Sea

(Catalogue No. 976)

Recorded by SIVARIANO GARCIA

Voice ♩ = 80 (♪ = 160)

FREE TRANSLATION

Where am I running from, that I come here?
Am I a crazy woman with a painted face?

Analysis.—This song consisted of three phrases, each followed by a closing period of three measures. The plaintive query expressed by the tones G sharp, F sharp, G sharp appears at the close of the three long phrases, and the same sequence persists in the last phrase, until the song ends on F sharp. The song contains only the minor triad and second, and is melodic in structure.

When the boy had crossed the bridge he told his mother and her sister to follow. When they were halfway across he twisted his bow and they fell into the water. He stood on the other side and told them that he did not want them to follow because of their father's bad acts. He said they would always travel along the shore of the ocean and never be with him. They turned into two kinds of birds that run along the sand at the edge of the ocean.

The boy followed his grandmother and lived with her.

The making of the first bamboo (cane) flute was described on page 62, and the singing of these flute melodies with words was mentioned on page 71. Songs 33 and 35 were also used either as flute melodies or songs with words, being sung only if a flute was not available when the story was told.

FLUTE MELODY NO. 1 (P. 217)

Recorded by SIVARIANO GARCIA

Analysis.—This melody was recorded on two cylinders and the records are identical. The melody is played twice through and the latter portion is then played twice, this procedure being the same as in the singing of the old songs. Garcia played this slowly, apart from the phonographic recording, and the melody was noted by ear, with the position of the fingers when each tone was produced. The first finger of the left hand was held steadily above the upper sound hole and the various tones were produced by changes in the positions of the first three fingers of the right hand. (Pl. 1.) The melody contains the tone B-C sharp-D sharp, and G sharp below B. These tones were produced in the following manner:

B_____All fingers raised.

C sharp_____First finger closing the upper sound hole.

D sharp_____First and second fingers closing the two upper sound holes.

G sharp_____First, second, and third fingers closing all the sound holes.

G sharp was less clearly given than the other tones.

106041°—29——7

FLUTE MELODY NO. 2 (P. 218)

Recorded by SIVARIANO GARCIA

Analysis.—This melody contains one tone less than the preceding and is less definite in form. The tones are the simpler tones of the instrument and the rhythm is simple, diversified by rests. The tempo was steadily maintained. The effect produced by this record is that of a performance rather than the playing of a definite melody. It is as though the performer had at his command certain melodic and rhythmic material and produced it according to his fancy. The first three measures form a pleasing phrase which is once repeated. This is followed by a repetition of the original phrase. The measures not transcribed did not differ from the earlier portion of the song and the tones are indistinct. These are followed by a new phrase, after which the player returned to the opening phrase of the song. The record is about one and a half minutes in length and the phrase which follows the untranscribed measures is of frequent occurrence on the remainder of the cylinder.

The foregoing story mentioned the "bamboo game" (*waputa*) which is a favorite game of the Papago at the present time. It is described as a "hidden ball game" by Stewart Culin.[8]

In the bamboo game there are two opposing players, each having an assistant. Any number of spectators may be seated around them. The game implements consist of two pairs of short bamboo reeds (see p. 73), two small red beans, 100 grains of corn for keeping count of the points won, and five short sticks for keeping count of the games played. The reeds are filled with sand and a red bean is concealed in one of each pair. Each player in turn hides the bean, his opponent guessing which reed contains it. After the guess has been made the player's assistant empties the sand from the two reeds, showing which contained the bean.

The player seated at the right in Plate 11, *a*, is holding his pair of reeds while the player at the left is preparing to guess which reed holds the red bean. The player's assistant is emptying the reed in Plate 11, *b*. The grouping shown in Plate 11, *c*, would occur only when two or three grains of corn remain, these not being enough to register the usual score for a successful guess. In such a case the players put the remaining corn in a pile and each side takes a pair of reeds and conceals a bean. Thus both sides are hiding and both sides are guessing. Whichever side guesses correctly receives the corn. The pictures accompanying this and the description of the "stick game" were posed at San Xavier by Indians who habitually play these games.

---

[8] Games of the North American Indians. Twenty-fourth Ann. Rept. Bur. Amer. Ethn., 1907, p. 354ff.

a, Preparing to play

b, Conclusion of play

c, Preparing to settle a close score

a, Preparing to play

b, Watching sticks in the air

c, Counting the score

STICK GAME AT SAN XAVIER

The foregoing story of the origin of the flute was recorded at San Xavier in March, 1920. The following autumn it was read to Papago at Sells, who said the inclusion of the bamboo game was a Pima version, and that in the true Papago version of the story the boy killed his grandfather after playing the "stick game" with him. They said the wonder boy challenged his grandfather to the game and, as the two sat facing each other preparatory to playing, he sang the following song, recorded by a man living at San Xavier.   (Pl. 13, *b.*)

No. 43. "I Will Toss Up the Sticks "

(Catalogue No. 1066)

Recorded by LEONARDO RIOS

TRANSLATION

Now I toss up the sticks.
I will throw the sticks for the corner.
(The highest score was made by this throw.)

Analysis.—This song is peculiar in that the first and last tones, as well as the larger part of the melody, are on the upper part of the compass.   The fourth constitutes about 20 per cent and the major third about 40 per cent of the intervals.

As the boy sang he threw the sticks near his own feet, then nearer and nearer to his grandfather, until at the fourth throw the sticks were at his grandfather's feet and the game was won.   He sang this song after he had won the game and in it he calls upon his grandfather to pay his stake.   In games or contests between mythical characters the stake is a life.   It was said, "The boy was half crying as he sang the song because he felt so sorry to kill his grandfather, but he felt he must do it in order to avenge the death of his father at the hand of the old man."   After singing the song he killed his grandfather with a club.

No. 44. "It Is Time to Pay Your Wager"

Recorded by LEONARDO RIOS   (Catalogue No. 977)

VOICE ♩ = 76

TRANSLATION

The time is come to pay your wager;
The time is come.

Analysis.—This is an interesting example of a minor melody in which the tone below the keynote is used effectively. It is also an example of a melody with four rhythmic periods in which the rhythm of the third period is different from that of the others. Twenty of the twenty-seven progressions are whole tones.

The "stick game" (*ginskut*) is played every afternoon at San Xavier, a set of sticks being concealed under a cactus ready for use. This is a dice game, the sticks being dice.[9] Songs Nos. 43 and 44 are commonly sung to bring success in the game. The four gaming sticks are made of the rib of the saguaro cactus, which is smooth and hard. The decorations are shown in Figure 2. The lines on No. 1 indicate the four days' fasting of a warrior on his return from a victory, on No. 2 they represent bird's claws, on No. 3 they represent the rays of the sun, and on No. 4 they represent the lines of paint on the face of a warrior.[10] The ground is marked with dots arranged as in Figure 3. The loop at the corner is called a "house." The dice sticks are thrown upward by one player after another, and the score counted by the position of the sticks when they fall on the ground. Each player has a different article that he moves along the dotted lines in accordance with the score that he makes. One player, for instance, may use a bone and another the bowl of an old spoon in counting his score. In the description of the game given the writer it appears that all the players start from one "house." In the play described by Culin it appears that only two are playing and they start from opposite corners. The object in each case is to progress around the square to the point of starting

---

[9] Stewart Culin, op. cit., p. 149. Cf. also Russell, op. cit., pp. 175–177.
[10] Cf. a somewhat different marking on p. 40.

and to "reenter the house." If one player overtakes another at a counting hole, he sends that player back to the "house," or starting point. The manner of play as described at San Xavier is as follows: A player takes the four dice sticks in his hands and rests them on a stone so the ends are exactly together; then he lifts them up and strikes them sharply with the stone (pl. 12, *a*), thus projecting them into the air. When they fall, the score is counted and the player's article (bone, or bowl of spoon) advanced the proper number of dots on the ground. In Plate 12, *b*, the

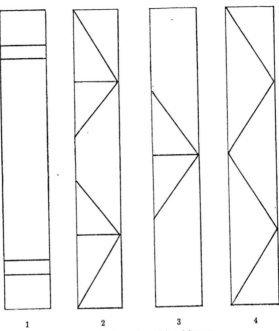

Fig. 2.—Implements used in stick game

sticks are in the air and may be discerned as white lines against the foliage of the background. In Plate 12, *c*, the sticks have fallen, the score has been computed, and the player in the center of the foreground is moving forward the article with which he keeps his score. The score used at San Xavier differs somewhat from that described by Culin. It was said that if all the sticks fell with the decorated side uppermost the score was 5, if only three fell thus the score was 3. If all fell with the plain side uppermost the score was 10. If only one stick fell with the decorated side uppermost the score depended upon the decoration of that stick. If No. 1 were the only

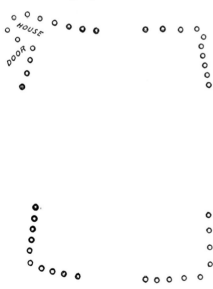

Fig. 3.—Diagram of ground on which stick game is played. (From a native drawing.)

pended upon the decoration of that stick. If No. 1 were the only one thus exposed the score was 4; No. 2 gave a score of 6; No. 3 counted 14, and No. 4 counted 15, the other three sticks, of course, falling with the plain or undecorated side uppermost.

Both of these games are usually witnessed by a number of spectators, and there is considerable betting on the result.

TREATMENT OF THE SICK

It is the belief of the Papago that only a portion of human illnesses and ailments are due to material causes. The portion thus attributed consists of bruises, cuts, and minor bodily discomforts, but what we term "major illnesses" are explained in a different manner. The causes for these are believed to be psychic in character. Certain illnesses were attributed to sorcery and the treatment of such illnesses was in reality a contest between the psychic ("medicine" or "magic") power of the doctor and that of the person believed to be working the evil on the patient. Part of the doctor's skill consisted in his ability to determine who was working the evil, after which he matched his power against that of his adversary. If his power were the stronger his patient would recover; if his were the weaker the man would die. Other illnesses were attributed to spirit birds and animals, to the spirits of the dead, and to other causes of like nature, but in every instance the cause of the disease imparted the secret of its cure to some medicine man, or "doctor." Singing formed a part of the treatment of the sick and the songs were imparted together with instructions for the treatment. Herbs and other material remedies were sometimes administered, but the knowledge of their use was supposed to be obtained in "dreams."

The term "doctor" will generally be used in this chapter to designate a man who treats the sick. The term "medicine man" is more general in its application and may be applied to anyone who achieves results by "magic." The power of a medicine man was psychic in its character and, continuing this terminology, a medicine man may be regarded as a "developed psychic." He might use his power in treating the sick, or he might be a clairvoyant, or he might use his power to evil ends, thus developing his power in the way he desired.

The Papago have a tradition that sickness was scattered abroad when Earth Magician disappeared into the ground. (See p. 21.) Comparison with the beliefs of certain other tribes makes it clear that the "sickness" thus spread abroad was not a definite ailment but a general disposition toward illness which became present in the air. A parallel in our own thought is the statement that "the air is full of malaria," or "there is miasma in the air" of a certain locality.   As Earth Magician sank out of sight Elder Brother seized the feathers on top of his head.   The down came off these feathers and Elder Brother, feeling that he had "bad medicine" (a substance filled with potential harm) on his hands, tried to throw it away.   He scattered the down to the winds, which carried it everywhere, and sickness became prevalent among the people.

The ills of the Papago may be grouped under four headings: (1) Sickness attributed to the action of "bad medicine men," or those who use their psychic power to evil ends.   The nature of these "sicknesses" was not determined.   The cure consisted in the overpowering of the "bad medicine" by a "good medicine" that was stronger, the treatment being essentially a conflict between the psychic power put forth by one man with evil intent and that put forth by another man with good intent.   (2) Diseases attributed to spirit animals or birds.   These were believed to cause functional troubles, such as cough, soreness of the eyes, and digestive derangement. The treatment consisted in the singing of songs imparted to the doctor by the animal or bird that had caused the trouble, the singing usually being attended with some physical treatment, such as stroking with feathers or some other object, which had also been directed by the animal or birds causing the disease.   (3) Accidents and injuries.   For some injuries a cure was provided by a spirit animal of the sort that produced the injury.   Thus the present paper contains songs given by a horse to cure an injury caused by a vicious horse.   (Nos. 58–61.)   These songs were used by doctors in a manner similar to those given by animals or birds for the cure of organic or functional disorders.   (4) Diseases attributed to spirits of the dead. These were nervous disorders and were treated in a manner similar to diseases attributed to birds or animals.   The spirits supposed to cause these disorders were spirits of dead Papago as well as those of Apache slain in war.   Material remedies were not administered unless the means above described had failed to produce results.

To these ills may be added a "love bewitchment" believed to be produced by the singing of certain songs.   This was treated by a medicine man who sang the proper songs.   The victim of this "bewitchment" was said to be "crazy" and the treatment was akin to that of a nervous disorder.

In explanation of the first class of ills, enumerated above, it was said that in former times there were "bad medicine men" who spread diseases of various sorts.   Hugh Norris, the writer's interpreter at Sells, said that long ago he saw two of these evil men whom everyone feared.   Many deaths in a single day were often attributed to their

deeds. None of the people would speak to them. When accused,
this sort of medicine man frequently placed the blame on innocent
persons and allowed them to be killed.

The work of these evil men was done either by putting poison on
the persons of those to be affected or by diffusing it in the air, causing
sickness and death throughout the village. For the latter purpose
the medicine man used a contrivance resembling a bomb with a time
fuse. The man had been told in his "dream" how to mix a poison
that would become volatile after a short period of time. The mixture
was said to be red and to have the blood of the medicine man as one
of its ingredients. He put this mixture in a piece of jointed straw
about 1½ inches long. The joint of the straw closed the little recep-
tacle at one end and a plug was inserted in the other end. The medicine man knew how many days would elapse before the mixture would
"begin to work" and push out the plug, liberating the poison. If
one of these poison tubes was found before the plug was expelled it
was burned and the evil reacted on the medicine man. Since the
poison was mixed with his blood, the burning of the poison was said
to affect the blood in his body. His skin turned black and sometimes
the skin on his face cracked open. The moment the heat of the
flame touched the poison tube he began to cough, then he could neither
sleep nor eat, and if the tube were consumed by the fire he died in
two or three months. Sometimes the fire was not hot enough to
entirely destroy the substance in the tube and then he might live a
year or so. An instance of this was said to have occurred only a few
years before the present inquiry was made.

The presence of a poison tube might be detected by a medicine
man but not by other persons. A medicine man, suspecting this
danger, might go to the chief and say he feared that "poison had been
set for them." The chief would select three medicine men to help
the one who suspected the danger and they would set a night for the
search. They would have a fire and the singers would begin to
sing. The medicine men would sit together during one or two songs,
then go to the top of a hill, smoke, and act as they would if trying
to locate an enemy. One man might say he felt that the poison tube
was in a certain house or corral and they would go there and look for
it. If it was not there the men would return to the top of the hill and
try again. Sometimes the location of the poison tube was shown by a
light which, at a distance, looked like a candle and flickered like a
candle in the wind. As a man approached the light it grew smaller
until it looked like a small live coal, and if he came too close it disappeared entirely. After finding the tube and destroying it the men

would use their power to locate the medicine man who placed it, and would report their suspicions to the chief, who would act as he thought best in dealing with the man.

The destruction of a poison tube was attended with considerable danger. It was said that a poison tube was once found in an old house near San Xavier. An old medicine man located it, seized it with his hands and fell unconscious. He fell on some cholla cactus but was so deeply unconscious that he did not feel pain, nor know when his friends pulled the cactus spines from his flesh. He remained unconscious for about 10 minutes. Other men took the tube from him, carried it away, and burned it. Few medicine men had sufficient power to take hold of a tube alone and a group of men usually kept together so that if one took hold of the poison tube he could be saved by his associates. The men wrapped the tube in a cloth and ran with it to a fire, throwing it into the flames. Then came a slight explosive noise like a cork popping out and they saw the coals fly upward a little. The medicine men held out their arms and did not make a sound until the slight explosion took place, then they dropped their arms and began to moan like a person in pain.

These poison tubes were sometimes seen by persons who dared not touch them. Several years ago Mr. Encinas, the interpreter, saw one that had not opened. It was destroyed by a medicine man just as the sickness was beginning. This man was in his home about 10 miles from San Xavier when he saw a light over the village. He came to the village to treat a sick man and told the people he had seen the light and that it indicated the presence of a poison tube. Taking several medicine men with him, he found the tube and burned it. He said it was so powerful that if all the poison had been liberated it would have killed the whole village, beginning with the old people.

Among the Papago there were men called "sun medicine men" who claimed to get their power from the sun. It is said they were able to "take the light of the sun and throw it into the night." The strange brightness was said to be stronger than daylight and by it the medicine man could see objects many miles away. The song next following is the song of such a medicine man and is addressed to those who are searching near him for a poison tube. He does not offer to help them for he knows the tube is far away.

The next song was recorded by the writer's interpreter at San Xavier. (Pl. 13, a.)

No. 45. "A White Wind from the West"

(Catalogue No. 1072)

Recorded by HARRY ENCINAS

TRANSLATION

From the west a white wind is coming out.
Stand there and look, it is not near,
It is beside the ocean, there you will see it.
By the reflected light of the sun you will see it.

Analysis.—The larger part of this song contains no interval larger than a minor third. In the latter portion the fourth occurs frequently. The song is minor in tonality, contains the tones of the minor triad and second, and has its beginning and ending on the same tone.

Before proceeding to a consideration of various diseases and their cure we will note certain persons whose peculiar duty was the making of the diagnosis. Such a person was called a *siätikum* and his position was one of great responsibility. He studied the case, decided what ailed the patient, and directed who should be summoned to give the treatment.

The next song is that of such a man named Jose Maria who was living when this material was collected (1920). It is a song which he might sing at any time. Jose Maria did not want others to learn his songs and had a peculiar manner of singing them. He sang the first

b, Leonardo Rios

a, Harry Encinas

a, Jose Hendricks

b, Jose Panco

part without words, humming the melody with lips closed.   Then he sang the words softly, and it was his custom to clear his throat at the end of the first verse.   These mannerisms were imitated by Jose Hendricks (pl. 14, a), who recorded the song.

No. 46. "The Morning Shines on Manasi Mountain'

(Catalogue No. 1033)

Recorded by JOSE HENDRICKS

TRANSLATION

The bright morning begins to shine.
Get up, three of you, and see Manasi Mountain.
On top of it there is yellow water.
I went there, drank the water, and staggered in running.

Analysis.—This song is classified as both major and minor in tonality.   Only one other song (No. 85) is thus classified.   Five rhythmic units occur, a dotted eighth appearing on a different count in each of the first four units, while the last two units contain a triplet of eighth notes.   Few Papago songs show such a clear thematic form.

About two-thirds of the progressions are major seconds and minor thirds.

Similar to the preceding was a song of an old medicine man named Antonio. He sang the song (not transcribed) when "trying to decide what was the matter with the sick person." The words were, "A little black turtle sat cross-legged and the black feathers were like lightning. Red sparks came falling and sprinkling down. The turtle was afraid and moved back, waving his paws round and round."

As already stated, it was the belief of the Papago that certain diseases were induced either by animals and birds or by spirits of the dead. The *siätikum* (or diagnostician) was familiar with the ailments that were prevalent in the tribe and knew what animal, bird, or class of spirits was supposed to cause each ailment. In every such instance there was a doctor to whom the cause of the ailment had revealed the means of its cure. Songs were so closely identified with the treatment that a *siätikum* might say to a person with sore eyes, "Your trouble is caused by the quail. You had better send for So-and-so who knows the quail songs." If the ailment were not serious it might be cured by the singing of the songs, usually accompanied by a simple procedure such as the stroking of the patient's body with some small object, but if the person were very ill, requiring expert treatment for an entire night, the songs were sung by an assistant of the person who gave the treatment. It was said that the songs could be used without the physical treatment, or the treatment could be used without the songs, but they were commonly used together. These songs were the property of certain men and were the means by which they put forth their psychic power for the healing of the sick. Persons of serious mind might join in the songs when a sick person was being treated. By this means they added their quota of power to that of the doctor. For this service they were rewarded by a share of the feast. Thus there were many persons in the tribe who knew the songs that were sung by the medicine men but they would not sing these songs except when led by the medicine men. If the singers or spectators were disrespectful or inattentive they were stricken with the disease for which the patient was being treated.

As indicated, the chief responsibility rested with the diagnostician, who decided what caused the sickness, and who prescribed the sort of treatment to be given. Thus he might say, "The man is suffering from an Apache spirit; you must send for someone who knows the Koöp songs." If a long period of singing was not successful the singer told the patient the *siätikum* had been mistaken in the cause of his illness. The *siätikum* was therefore recalled, and after considering the case again, he suggested some other cause and another singer was summoned.

If several sorts of this treatment had been tried without effect the second method of treatment was used as a last resort. This was by internal medicine. Those who treated by material remedies usually worked in pairs, either two men or a man and his wife. Together they made a decoction of certain herbs, according to instructions received in a dream. The dosage and manner of administering were also directed by a dream. When giving the treatment two such persons were accustomed to seat the patient so that he faced the west. They placed a bowl of medicine in front of him, telling him to look fixedly into the bowl and not move his eyes. Then they took their seats behind him and sang the following song, no rattle being used. The singing was in a tone that resembled humming, and was so low that only the sick man could hear it. They sang the song four times, then went around from opposite sides, took up the bowl of medicine and gave it to the sick man to drink.

No. 47. Song when Administering Herb Medicine

(Catalogue No. 1041)

Recorded by JOSE PANCO

TRANSLATION

Are you going to make a doctor out of me?
You have brought me in here and I see.

Analysis.—The most prominent tone in this song is F but the song is analyzed with C as its keynote. There is an interesting completeness in the rhythm of the song as a whole. The first two periods each contain seven measures and bear a general resemblance to each other but the final period begins with a quarter note and a more positive rhythm, returning to the rhythmic unit in the measure before the close. Only five intervals are larger than a minor third and all these occur in ascending progressions.

Mr. Encinas, the writer's interpreter, said that he once took an herb treatment and that his health was improved for a period of eight years. The medicine was a powerful purgative, yellowish in color and consisting of only one herb. It had no definite taste, and he was required to drink almost a quart of it morning and evening for two consecutive days. There were no songs connected with this treatment. The medicine man died a few years after Mr. Encinas received the treatment, and as he left no son the identity of his medicinal herb has been lost. It was customary to "talk to the plant or tree" when gathering a medicinal substance and also when administering it.

The following list shows animals and birds said to cause disease, with the symptoms of the ailments.[11] Songs used in treating the first five ailments were recorded.

Deer	Weakness and cough.
Badger	Swelling of the throat.
Horned toad	"If a person steps on a horned toad and kills it he will have a large sore on the part of his body corresponding to the injured part of the toad."
Rattlesnake	Pain around the heart.
Lizard (brown)	Severe internal fever.
Bear	Swellings and soreness.
Dog	Mouth affected, no appetite.
Gopher	Pains around the heart.
Jack rabbit	Boils, especially on the neck.
Rat	Soreness of mouth, affects only infants.
Turtle	Severe lameness.
Blue hawk, eagle, woodpecker	Symptoms not given but were said to be the same in diseases caused by these birds.
Butterfly	Dysentery.
Quail	Sore eyes.
Owl	Sleepiness.
Woodpecker	Boils and sores on the head.

SICKNESS CAUSED BY SPIRIT ANIMALS OR BIRDS

Jose Panco (pl. 14, *b*), who recorded the next five songs, is using them at the present time (1920) in treating persons suffering from the "deer sickness." He received the songs from his grandfather, who told him of their origin. Not many miles from San Xavier is a mountain called "Kawit" and below this is a village. Panco's grandfather said there once lived in this village a man who went out to hunt every day. On his last hunt he had gone quite a distance when he saw a deer running toward him. The deer came toward him, then turned and ran away from him, going toward the west.

---

[11] For a longer list see Frank Russell, op. cit., pp. 260–268.

The hunter could not get near enough to shoot the deer. Suddenly
it turned into a human being and led the hunter into the ocean.
The man was gone a month. One day he returned but he was shy
like a deer. Outside the village was an empty house and he went
there at night, when everything was quiet. He went there and sang
all night. The people asked themselves who could be doing that
singing. One night they surrounded the house and a man went in.
He saw a deer sitting in one corner and singing. The deer tried to
run past him and escape but he said, "Don't try to run away. I do
not want to hurt you. I only came to see you." They caught him
and took him home. He was very thin, as he had eaten nothing but
cactus fruit and other deer food for a whole month. They fed him,
and after he got well he told the people that if they wanted to learn
his songs they might come to the fireplace (chief's
house). Night after night he sat there but no one
came.

Soon afterwards there was a general "gift dance" to
get food at a neighboring village and all who took
part in the dance were taken ill with coughing, which
is now known to be a symptom of the deer sickness.
A *siätikum* attended one of the dancers and sent for
this man who had lived on the food of the deer and
returned with the strange new songs. He came and
sang his songs, and the singers learned the songs and
sang with him, but the sick man did not get any
better. The *siätikum* was summoned again to see if
there were some other cause for the illness. He said
that a deer must be killed, skinned, and cut in quarters
by an old man known to be expert in the work. He
said they must also appoint four expert women to cut

FIG. 4.—Gourd rattle

up and cook the deer. They must be responsible for every portion of
it, even to the smallest particle of blood. Not a bone could be broken,
it being required that the carcass be disjointed. If a bone were
accidentally broken they must kill another deer. The meat was to
be eaten by the singers who were to sing the songs for the treating of
the sick. The tail of the deer was taken for use in the treatment,
and all the scraps of meat were wrapped and hidden so securely that
no dog, coyote, or other animal could ever find them. When this was
finished all the sick people were gathered at one place, and a great
crowd of spectators and the singers were there. The man who had
received the songs led the singing of them and treated the sick people,
stroking them with the tail of the deer. They recovered, and ever
since that time the songs have been used in treating this sickness.
Jose Panco is shown in Plate 15, *a*, treating a patient. In his left hand
is the deer tail (pl. 15, *b*) and in his right the gourd rattle (fig. 4) with

which he accompanies his songs. The rattle was obtained by the writer but Panco did not wish to part with the deer tail. On the wooden handle of the rattle are 12 marks, 6 cut in the wood on each side. One mark has been added each year since he began to use the rattle, the last mark being freshly cut and the first ones being dark, as might be expected from 12 years of use. The following group represents only a part of Panco's songs. They were in pairs, each song of the pair having the same melody but the words being different. For convenience they are designated as parts 1 and 2 of the same number. The village mentioned in the first song is that in which the hunter lived and in which the songs originated. The native term "ye'ogam" is literally translated "sandy loam fields."

No. 48. "Sandy Loam Fields"

Recorded by JOSE PANCO

(Catalogue No. 1036)

TRANSLATION

Part 1

Sandy Loam Fields, on top of these lands Elder Brother stands and sings.
Over our heads the clouds are seen, downy white feathers gathered in a bunch.

Part 2

After hearing these songs the women gather on Sandy Loam Fields,
Their heads decorated with clouds of feathers.

Analysis.—This is a gentle, pleasing melody which would be acceptable to a sick person. It contains a measure in 5–8 time, which occurs in many similar songs. This is the first of six healing songs recorded by Panco, all of which are on the major and minor pentatonic scales (fourth and second five-toned scales).

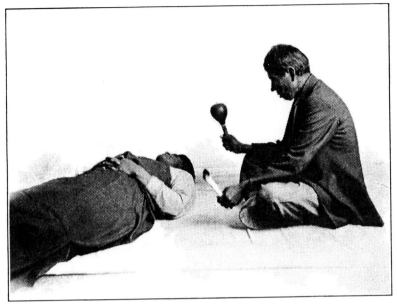

a, Jose Panco treating sick man

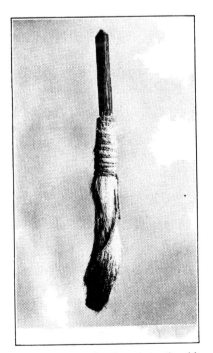

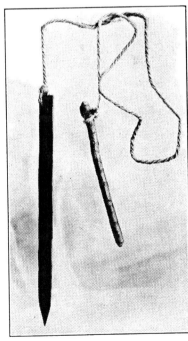

b, Deer tail used by Jose Panco in treating sick man

c, "Bull-roarer" used in Viikita ceremony

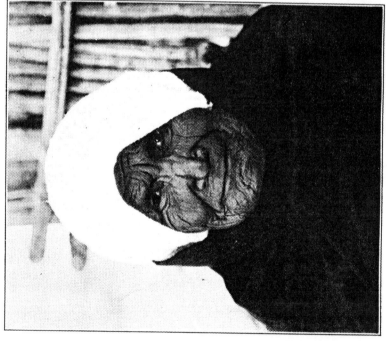

b, Sivariano Garcia

a, Owl Woman

No. 49. "I Will Sit and Sing"

Recorded by JOSE PANCO

(Catalogue No. 1037)

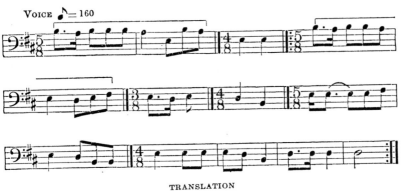

TRANSLATION

Part 1

I am going to sit here and sing, I am going to sit here and sing.
On top of our ground you will see green scum drying up.
(This refers to land on which water has recently been standing.)

Part 2

I am going to stand here and sing, I am going to stand here and sing.
On top of our ground you will see foam drying up.

Analysis.—This song comprises three periods containing, respectively, three, four, and six measures. Each period begins with the 5–8 measure which occurs often in songs for the sick. The rhythmic peculiarities of the melody are such as would hold the attention of a listener. About two-thirds of the progressions are whole tones.

No. 50. "Out of the Mountains"

Recorded by JOSE PANCO

(Catalogue No. 1038)

TRANSLATION

Part 1

That bird comes out back of Frog Mountains.
It stretches its arms trying to reach Cokwigan Mountains (in Mexico).

Part 2

A measuring worm comes out of Long Mountains (Santa Rita).
It stretches itself, trying to reach Iöhlikûm (Queen Mountains, part of Baboquivari range).

Analysis.—In considering a group of songs like these of Panco't
it should be borne in mind that they were sung in sequence, and thas
the patient was expected to show improvement while the songs were
being sung.   In the present melody we find a firmness and vigor
instead of the gentleness of the two preceding songs.   An ascending
seventh occurs twice and the rhythm of the song is lively and varied.

No. 51. "Singing to the Leaves and Flowers"

Recorded by Jose Panco   (Catalogue No. 1039)

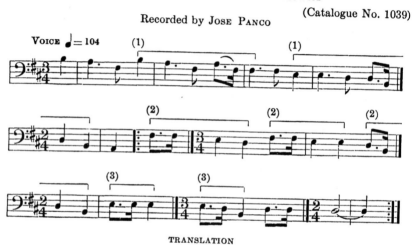

TRANSLATION

Part 1

Crazy woman, crazy woman, trying to sing to mescal leaves,
How can she sing to them and make the wind come?

Part 2

Young children trying to sing to *baȟwi* flowers,
How can they sing to *baȟwi* flowers and bring rain?

Analysis.—Almost one-half of the progressions in this song are
minor thirds, in contrast to the preceding songs by Panco which
progress chiefly by whole tones.   It is a graceful melody with two
rhythmic units that begin in the last count of the measure and a third
which resembles the second but is accented differently.   Attention
is directed to the effect of firmness produced by the accented quarters
and dotted quarters, while the melody becomes more lively with the
entrance of the third rhythmic unit which has the shorter note on the
accented count.

No. 52. "Toward the Mountains" (Catalogue No. 1040)

Recorded by JOSE PANCO

TRANSLATION

Part 1

Hanamikan Mountain calls itself doctor and stands by itself.
Toward it I am walking.

Part 2

Thatkam calls itself brave, standing toward Hanapkam Mountain.

Analysis.—This is the most vigorous of the healing songs recorded by Panco. It has a compass of nine tones, while the preceding songs had a compass of an octave. A dotted eighth note followed by a sixteenth occurred once in the rhythmic units of preceding songs and occurs twice in the first unit of this song, adding to the briskness of the rhythm. The interval of a fourth is used effectively at the close and constitutes 27 per cent of the progressions. The tone material is that of the fourth five-toned scale.

The badger is said to cause an affection of the throat accompanied by swelling. The following is one of the songs given by the badger for the treatment of this trouble. The singer (pl. 16, c) resides at Vomari.

No. 53. Song of the Badger Medicine (Catalogue No. 1024)

Recorded by RAFAEL MENDEZ

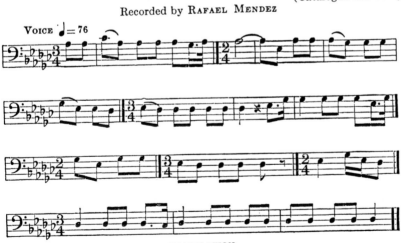

TRANSLATION

I know everything in the bottom of my heart.
From Coyote I learn all this.
I get it and keep it within me, and hold it there.

Analysis.—This song is classified with G flat as its keynote, although the third above that tone does not occur. It is an example of an Indian song consisting of pure melody without tonality. The song progresses by minor thirds and major seconds except for two intervals of a fourth.

It is the belief of the Papago that the horned toad is a "medicine animal." It is said that he "once got up a sickness," so the medicine men gathered the sunshine and covered him up, to put an end to him, but he escaped and went directly to the man who did it and sang the following song to him.

No. 54. "They Covered Me with Sunshine"

(Catalogue No. 1021)

Recorded by RAFAEL MENDEZ

TRANSLATION

Gray horned toad, the sun shines on you.
The sunshine they gathered.
With that they covered me but I got out from it.

Analysis.—This song is peculiar in that the fifth above the keynote does not occur while the sixth occurs with frequency and prominence. The song is not particularly rhythmic and the principal interval is the minor third. Other songs of this group with a similar tone material are Nos. 69 and 92. There was an exact degree of force used in singing horned toad songs, both being sung in a low tone and somewhat drawled. This manner was followed by the singer when recording the songs.

It is said that the Papago formerly mixed a certain dried, pulverized flower with "something from the rocks," and put a little of this mixture in a cup of water. The man who drank it became crazy for four days. A similar effect was obtained by combining the powder with an equal quantity of tobacco, making it into a cigarette which the man was asked to smoke. After a medicine man had prepared the remedy for this condition he sang a song with the following words:

"Gray horned toad, earth flower they mixed. They gave it to me to drink intending to make me crazy." This song was not transcribed.

The next two songs are "rattlesnake medicine songs," and were sung with the same degree of loudness as the Koöp songs, while the horned-toad medicine songs were sung in a lower tone.

No. 55. "A Painted Snake Comes Out"

(Catalogue No. 1022)

Recorded by RAFAEL MENDEZ

TRANSLATION

Here we begin to talk.
We call a name toward the east and a snake comes out, nicely painted.

Analysis.—This song contains only four intervals larger than a whole tone, which is interesting in connection with the words. A similar song is No. 68. A certain correspondence has been noted between the structure of songs concerning animals and the motion of the animals.[12] The fourth has been found to characterize songs concerning birds, and particularly large intervals are found in the songs said to have been received from a horse (Nos. 58–61). The tonality of this song is minor and special emphasis is placed upon the tone above the keynote.

In the country of the Papago there lives a wasp that makes a small, straight hole in the sand. It digs its hole 4 or 5 inches downward, then the hole is turned at an angle. In the words of the following song a snake speaks to a wasp that is digging its hole in front of him and throwing the dust in his eyes.

---

[12] Cf. Bull. 75, Bur. Amer. Ethn., p. 200.

No. 56. Song to a Little Yellow Wasp

(Catalogue No. 1023)

Recorded by RAFAEL MENDEZ

TRANSLATION

Little yellow wasp, you throw the dirt in my eyes.
I do not know what to do with you.
All I can do is to make a long-drawn breath, hoping you will die in four days.

Analysis.—The measure divisions and intervals of this song are appropriate to its title. It contains no rhythmic unit and frequent changes of time. The tones are those of the second five-toned scale and two-thirds of the intervals are whole tones.

The following was said to be a "general medicine man's song," probably used to cure a disease caused by a brown lizard.

No. 57. "Brown Lizard"

(Catalogue No. 1042)

Recorded by JOSE PANCO

VOICE ♩ = 76

TRANSLATION

He hangs it on both sides of himself and rolls around, then he gets up and dances with these on either side.

Analysis.—This is one of the most pleasing melodies recorded by the Papago. It begins and ends on the same tone and contains no rhythmic unit. Five sorts of ascending intervals occur, giving variety to the progressions.

The Papago had songs for the curing of injuries as well as diseases. The four songs next following were sung to cure an injury caused by a fractious horse. As in other healing songs the remedy was provided by the cause of the difficulty. These songs are attributed to a black horse, which was heard singing them. They are called "devil songs" by the English-speaking Papago, from *javolt*, meaning "devil cactus." The singer (pl. 16, *a*) lives at Sells. He was with the United States cavalry when Geronimo was captured.

No. 58. Song to Cure an Injury by a Horse

(Catalogue No. 1014)

Recorded by Jose Manuel

TRANSLATION

The devil's power shines over us now.
We can see it shine on the tail of a black horse and we can also see the shining on the top of every mountain.
We know it will cure you.

Analysis.—An interesting resemblance is noted in these songs, which are the only ones attributed to the horse. They contain an unusually large proportion of quarter notes, with few half or eighth notes and only one sixteenth note. This gives a particularly steady rhythm. All the songs have rhythmic units and contain large ascending progressions which usually comprise one measure. Three of the songs are on the second and fourth five-toned scales. The present song contains more movement than the others and its rhythm is not unlike the galloping of a horse.

No. 59. "I Came from the East"   (Catalogue No. 1016)

Recorded by Jose Manuel

TRANSLATION

From the east I came half dead with hunger and thirst.
I came to a little water hole but it was dried up.
I knew no other.
I decided to find some other horses or a person who could take me to water.
This boy took me to water but afterwards he treated me badly.

Analysis.—The opening phrase of this song is rather plaintive.
This is followed by a descending phrase 17 measures in length. A
short, appealing phrase is then sung twice, followed by a descending
phrase and a close which suggests a query. This is particularly
interesting in connection with the title.

The following song continues the story:

No. 60. "You Tied Me with a Black Hair Rope"

(Catalogue No. 1015)

Recorded by Jose Manuel

TRANSLATION

Black hair rope is what you used in roping me.
You treated me badly.
You even threw me down and tied me.
Not satisfied with that, you tied a knot in the end of my tail.
That made me disgusted.

Analysis.—The general character of this song is plaintive. The phrases contain four measures, except one phrase which is prolonged to a fifth measure. A majority of the notes are quarter notes. The fourth constitutes one-third of the intervals. The ending is similar to others of this group and suggests a question.

Like the preceding songs, this was sung by a horse, heard by a man in a dream, and used in treating persons injured by horses.

No. 61. Song of a Black Horse   (Catalogue No. 1017)

Recorded by JOSE MANUEL

TRANSLATION

I could go and get some of this yellow poppy flower and a sore would come where it touched your hand, but I have some pity for you though you had none for me when I was in your hands.

Analysis.—This song seems to sum up the rhythm of the three preceding songs, yet it has an individual rhythm. Comparison with the preceding songs will show the resemblance of rhythm. About 26 per cent of the intervals are fourths and fifths. The song is based on the fourth five-toned scale but the sixth tone is particularly prominent, giving an effect of minor tonality.

ILLNESSES ATTRIBUTED TO SPIRITS OF THE DEAD

It was the belief of the Papago that illnesses might be caused by the spirits of Apache killed in war, or by the spirits of dead Papago. Songs were given by the spirits for the treatment of these illnesses, which appear to have been nervous in character.

The spirits of dead Apache were believed to cause three sorts of illness: (1) Koöp, which might affect persons of any age, at any time; (2) Komotan, which affected warriors and unborn children; and (3) Hivicolita, which affected children. The first and second were induced by failure to show respect toward the spirit of the dead Apache and the third frequently attacked the children of warriors who had not undergone the ordeal of purification after killing Apache. Food was taken to the warriors and they were expected to bury any fragments that remained. If one of their children came to the place at a later time, found scraps of food and ate them, the children would develop the Hivicolita sickness. Children who disturbed a "spirit basket" or treated it with disrespect were similarly afflicted. (See pp. 188 and 195.)

The owl is the bird associated with the dead, and owl feathers sometimes taught the songs used in treating this class of diseases, but a majority of the songs, as stated, were received from spirits of the dead. A doctor could give his songs to another if he so desired, or he could transmit the power to treat these diseases and the man could get his songs from some other source. The songs are in groups of four, such a group being called a "rest." The song is sung through twice, then the latter portion is sung twice, while a gourd rattle is shaken. The manner of shaking the rattle depends on the instructions received by the doctor in his dream. For example, some doctors are instructed to "roll" the rattle four times before beginning a song, while others shake the rattle sharply four times before they begin to sing. Garcia, who recorded a majority of the songs in this section, preceded his songs by a continuous "roll" of the rattle. The rhythmic form of these songs is different from that of similar songs among tribes already studied. The words are poetic and do not contain the affirmation which characterized the healing songs of the Chippewa.

The songs of one locality differ from those of another and the place where a song "belongs" or originated is always kept in mind. The first two Koöp songs here presented (Nos. 62 and 63) and the two Komotan songs are "used back in the country," while the other five Koöp songs are used in the vicinity of San Xavier. If these songs were sung apart from their proper use they might produce the diseases they were intended to cure. In such a case it was necessary that the man be treated by one who was skillful in the use of songs.

One of the informants related his own experience, saying he knew many of the songs used in treating these classes of diseases and once became so interested in them that he sang them continually. He said that "his head was full of these songs." His father warned him that trouble would result but he continued singing them. After a time he developed the symptoms of the illnesses which were caused by Apache spirits and he suffered greatly until a medicine man came and sang all night, using the treatments peculiar to his own dream. This relieved the young man and he had no return of the trouble.

Before proceeding further it is important to note the manner of keeping an Apache scalp, and the beliefs concerning it. The scalp of a slain Apache was placed in a basket resembling a small packet. The ceremony connected with this placing of the scalp is described in the chapter on war customs. This "scalp basket" or "spirit basket" was kept with great care and offerings of food were given it. So long as this was done the spirit of the dead Apache was said to be satisfied, but if it were not "properly treated and fed" it escaped from the basket and "put poison in the food," causing disease. If the basket was carelessly treated by its owner he would fall ill, and if one of his children disturbed it the child would be seized with illness at a later time.

When a person was "troubled by an Apache spirit" it was customary to use, in the treatment, certain songs given by Apache spirits for that purpose. The same songs were sung in the *Limo*, which followed the return of victorious warriors. Kiyatan, who recorded Komotan songs (pp. 113, 114), said that in a case of Komotan illness a diagnostician would be summoned and usually directed the sick man to send for a doctor who knew the Komotan songs. The singing of these songs would usually cure the man and he would be up in a day or two. If these were not effective the diagnostician was recalled. He would "look inside," say the sickness was still there, and tell the family they must send for a *siäkum*—i. e., a man who had killed and scalped an Apache. This man would bring his "spirit basket" which contained the Apache scalp fastened to a wooden effigy (see p. 195). He would take out the effigy and press it against the man's body, saying, "Cure this man." He also took white clay from the spirit basket, moistened a little of it and applied it to the chest and forehead of the sick person. The diagnostician did not sing, neither did the *siäkum* who "made passes over the sick man's body, stroking it to get the sickness out." If this did not cure it was said the man either had two diseases or a different disease than the Komotan. The diagnostician would then consider the case again and summon another singer. Eagle feathers were commonly used in treatment of this disease, the doctor stroking the sick man's body with them.

As already indicated, the two diseases attributed to Apache spirits were known as Koöp and Komotan. Both were attributed to careless or disrespectful treatment of a "scalp basket" and the second was the more severe. The Apache spirits were regarded as small, like pygmies. As indicated in a previous paragraph, they stayed in the "scalp basket" if they were properly treated; if not, they came out of the basket and made trouble. In the Koöp they attacked men during dreams and dragged them by a finger or toe. They also "put their little hands on a man's heart and tickle him. This is not so much at first, but if it keeps up a long time it almost drives the man crazy."

The following group of Koöp songs (except No. 70) were recorded by Sivariano Garcia of San Xavier. He is one of the men who are summoned if a man is believed to be suffering from this disease, and these are some of the songs he uses regularly in treating such cases. He also recorded songs now used in treating sickness caused by spirits of dead Papago. (Nos. 72–94.) The present series comprises two "rests" or groups of four songs each and concerns the journey of a Papago in a dream or vision. He is escorted by the spirit of a dead Apache and is obliged to undergo severe experiences in the course of which he receives the songs he is to use in treating diseases caused by the Apache spirits.

No. 62. "Many Spirits Leading Westward"

(Catalogue No. 910)

Recorded by SIVARIANO GARCIA

WORDS

Momoi [13]	kokopa	honūnewewa	nuäna
Many	spirits	westward	leading
ciämowa ŋakiä [14]	nyĕ	moinak	waŋgihona
hanging	my	heart	strengthening

Analysis.—This is the first of a group of seven songs which are minor in tonality and, with one exception, end on the keynote. A peculiarity of the present song is the emphasis placed on the sub-mediant, D flat. This has been noted in other songs of minor tonality and gives an effect of seriousness. A further peculiarity of this song is the prominence of the major third, which constitutes

---

[13] The form of this word used in conversation is *mui.*
[14] The idea is that of an object which pauses or remains suspended in flight, as a bird.

almost half the progressions. The framework of the first five measures is the descending fifth C-F, and that of the next five measures
is the descending fifth A flat-D flat, while the remainder of the song
consists chiefly of the major third D flat-F.

The Apache spirit led the Papago to the house of a medicine man.
He entered and walked to the middle of the room. Before he knew
it there were owl feathers circling around him and singing the
following song:

No. 63. "In the Medicine Man's House"

(Catalogue No. 911)

Recorded by SIVARIANO GARCIA

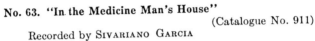

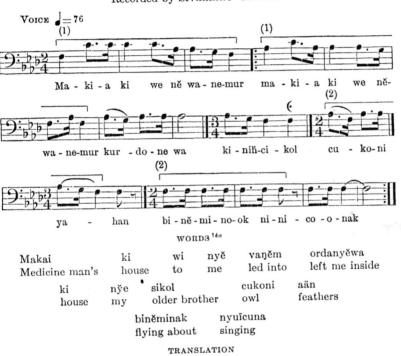

WORDS [14a]

Makai	ki	wi	nyĕ	vaŋĕm	ordanyĕwa
Medicine man's	house	to	me	led into	left me inside
	ki	nyĕ sikol		cukoni	aän
	house	my older brother		owl	feathers
		binĕminak	nyuĭcuna		
		flying about	singing		

TRANSLATION

To the medicine man's house they have led me,
To the medicine man's house they have led me,
Inside the house they have brought me,
Elder Brother is there and owl feathers fly about,
The owl feathers sing in the air.

Analysis.—This song begins and ends on the keynote, which is
also the lowest tone. It has two rhythmic units which have the
same closing phrase. More than a third of the progressions are
minor thirds, and the song is harmonic in structure.

[14a] The words of this song offer an example of mispronunciation by the singer. This frequently occurs
in Indian songs.

The singing owl feathers told the Papago many things that happened on his journey. One of their songs was concerning white bees that appeared when he was almost tired out. When he reached the place where the bees were circling he saw they were over a medicine man's house. Then he knew they were trying to tell him that he had not much farther to travel.

No. 64. Song Concerning the White Bees

(Catalogue No. 912)

Recorded by Sivariano Garcia

Tho-tha mo-mo-vĕld e   tho - tha   mo-mo-vĕld e can no-va-nyĕ

ŋĕ - yo-pa   ni ho-do-nĕ-ko mi-a-wa   ka-mo-va ho-do-nĕ-ko

vo-wi mù-ko mù-ko sma-sma-ma-sĭm tho-tham tho-tham a ya-huś-nu-hu-wa

WORDS

Thotha	momovĕld [15]	can	novanyĕ [16]	ŋĕyopa
White	bees	over there	they will	come out
hodonĕko	miäwa	kamova	hodonĕko	vowi
in the west	they drop	yonder	in the west	toward
mùko	smamsĭm [17]	thotham	• yahuśnuhuwa	
distance	plainly	shimmering white	fluttering	

Analysis.—The count divisions and rhythm of this song are appropriate to the title. The song has a compass of nine tones and has its beginning and ending on the keynote, which is about midway the compass. Although it has so wide a range it contains only the tones of the minor triad and second. Almost half the intervals are fourths and the final progression is an ascending fourth preceded by a descending fourth.

The owl feathers sang another song in which they said that, weary with his journey, he saw a shining white mountain. It looked as though it were far away and he said to himself, "If the end of my

---

[15] The *d* at the end of this word was scarcely perceptible.
[16] The *e* at the end of this word was very softly given.
[17] There is sometimes an apparent vowel between two consonants, as between *s* and *m* in this word, yet no vowel seems intended.

journey is as far as that mountain I can not hold out to reach it."
But as he looked at the mountain he saw arches of white light, like
shining colorless rainbows, that sprang from the mountain and bent
down to the earth between him and its base. By this sign he knew
that the end of his journey lay on this side of the mountain.

No. 65. Song Concerning the White Mountain

(Catalogue No. 913)

Recorded by SIVARIANO GARCIA

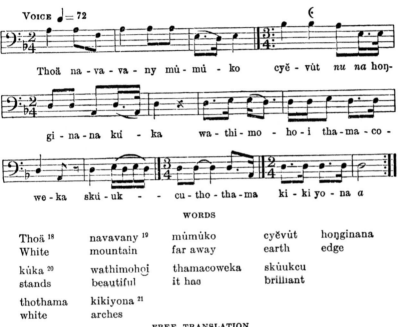

WORDS

Thoä [18]	navavany [19]	mùmùko	cyĕvùt	honginana
White	mountain	far away	earth	edge
kùka [20]	wathimohoi	thamacoweka	skùukcu	
stands	beautiful	it has	brilliant	
thothama	kikiyona [21]			
white	arches			

FREE TRANSLATION

A white mountain is far at the west,
It stands beautiful,
It has brilliant white arches of light bending down toward the earth.

Analysis.—The tempo of this song was not maintained with as
much regularity as in a majority of the songs under analysis. It
contains no rhythmic unit. The melodic formation is unusual, 40
per cent of the intervals being fourths and 47 per cent being whole
tones. As in many songs of this series, part of the melody is above
and part below the keynote.

[18] This form is used with a singular noun, *Thotha* with a plural.
[19] Final *y* very soft.
[20] The word for a bluff is *kuk*, the final *a* denotes position.
[21] This word is used in referring to the arched frame of the old round dwelling.

SECOND GROUP OF FOUR SONGS

One of the dead Apache lingered near the medicine man's house and came in. He was the Apache whom the Papago dreamer had killed and he wanted the Papago to know how he felt after death. He rolled a cigarette and motioned the Papago to sit beside him and smoke it. The Apache spirit sang this song.

No. 66. "We Smoke Together"   (Catalogue No. 914)

Recorded by SIVARIANO GARCIA

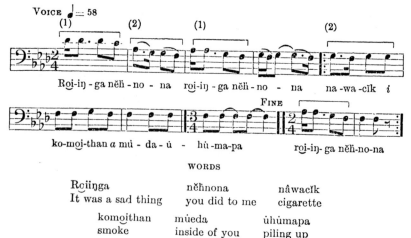

Voice ♩ = 58

Roi-iŋ - ga nĕḣ - no - na   roi-iŋ - ga nĕḣ - no - na   na -wa -cĭk i

ko-moi-than a mŭ - da - ŭ - hŭ -ma-pa   roi-iŋ- ga nĕḣ-no-na

WORDS

Roiiŋga	nĕḣnona	nâwacĭk
It was a sad thing	you did to me	cigarette
komoithan	mŭeda	ŭhŭmapa
smoke	inside of you	piling up

FREE TRANSLATION

It was a sad thing you did,
It was a sad thing you did,
But now we smoke together,
The smoke will pile up inside us.

Analysis.—As this song is so short it was possible to record an unusual number of renditions on one phonograph cylinder. Two sets of words were recorded, the entire performance comprising four renditions of the entire song and eight of the repeated portion. This is interesting, as the melodic relation of the first and second measures is unusual. Attention is directed to a comparison of the rhythmic units.

After the Papago had been dismissed by the medicine man he wandered so far that it seemed he had reached the end of the earth. There he met Elder Brother. This surprised him greatly as he had not expected to see anyone in that remote and desolate place. Just after meeting Elder Brother he sang this song.

No. 67. The Meeting with Elder Brother

(Catalogue No. 915)

Recorded by SIVARIANO GARCIA

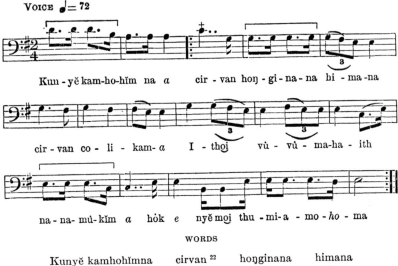

VOICE ♩= 72

Kun-yĕ kam-ho-hĭm na *a*   cir-van hoŋ-gi-na-na hi-ma-na

cir-van co-li-kam-*a*   I-thoị   vù-vù-ma-ha-ith

na-na-mù-kĭm *a* hòk *e* nyĕ moị thu-mi-a-mo-*ho*-ma

WORDS

Kunyĕ kamhohĭmna	cirvan [22]	hoŋginana	himana
I was going there	earth	end	going
cirvan	colikam	Ithoị [23]	avùvùmahaïth
earth	corner	Elder Brother	from two directions
nanamùkĭm	hok	nyĕ	moị [24]	thmiämoma
we meet	the	my	heart	calling for help

FREE TRANSLATION

Going alone to the earth end,
Going alone to the earth corner,
Elder Brother comes from the opposite direction
We meet and my heart is bounding within me.

Analysis.—A compass of 10 tones characterizes this song, which is melodic in structure and contains no change of measure lengths. The first two measures are framed by the descending fourth D–A and the next two measures by C–G. Near the close of the song we find the fourth B–E. The song is melodic in structure and contains all the tones of the octave.

While the Papago was walking on the edge of the world he saw a snake erect on its tail and heard it singing. It came to a mountain and coiled itself around the mountain. He did not learn the snake's song but made up this song about it.

---

[22] This is an old form, the present term being *cyĕvùt*.
[23] This is the formal title of Elder Brother. In songs Nos. 10 and 63 he is called *sikol*, which is the term used in referring to an older brother in a family.
[24] This word is used only in songs. It occurs also in No. 9.

No. 68. Song Concerning the Black Snake

(Catalogue No. 916)

Recorded by SIVARIANO GARCIA

VOICE ♩ = 80

A - li-wĕr-ci scu -uk o waḣ-pa - ma -na ho-du-ŋe -{ko vaḣ-wi

sủ - sủ -lĭn-hĭm-na a cĭ - na- wi-kĭm-tha   ho-du - ŋe vaḣ - wi

sủ - sủ-lĭn - hĭm-na a ci - no - waŋg mi -ḣi - vi   ho- du-ŋe

WORDS

Aliwĕrci [25]	scuk [26]	waḣpamana	hoduŋeko	vaḣwi
(No meaning)	black	snake	west	toward
sủsủlĭnhĭmna	cĭnawikĭmtha		cinowaŋg	miḣivi
going erect	talking while moving		mountain	coiling around

TRANSLATION

A black snake goes toward the west,
It travels erect on its tail,
It sings as it goes toward the west, and coils
around a mountain.

Analysis.—We note with interest the difference between this and No. 55, which is also concerning a snake. In this song the snake is described as traveling and the melody is particularly lively in its rhythm. The progressions, however, resemble the preceding song concerning a snake in that all except three intervals are minor thirds and whole tones.

At length the Papago came to a place where the dead Apache wanted to put him to a severe test. The rocks began to shake as he walked on them. This almost broke his courage but he made up this song.

[25] This occurs at the beginning of many Papago songs. In others the word "*hicia*" is similarly used. *Aliwĕrci* was said to signify "In the beginning."

[26] This is the new language. Cf. No. 71, part 2, which contains the old form *cuçukur.*

No. 69. "The Rocks are Shaking"   (Catalogue No. 917)

Recorded by SIVARIANO GARCIA

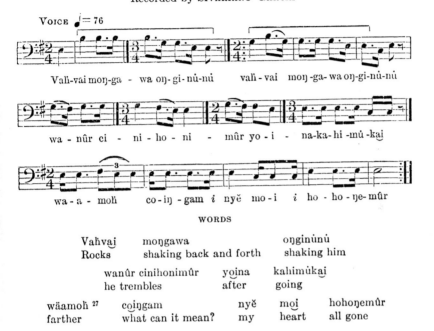

Vaĭ-vai moŋ-ga - wa oŋ-gi-nú-nú   vaĭ-vai moŋ-ga-wa oŋ-gi-nú-nú

wa - nûr ci - ni - ho - ni - mûr yo - i - na-ka-hi -mú -kaĭ

wa - a - moĭ   co-iŋ -gam i nyĕ mo-i   i ho - ho - ŋe-mûr

WORDS

Vahvai	moŋgawa	oŋginúnú
Rocks	shaking back and forth	shaking him
	wanûr cinihonimûr	yoina	kahimúkai
	he trembles	after	going
wäamoĭ [27]	coiŋgam	nyĕ	moi	hohoŋemûr
farther	what can it mean?	my	heart	all gone

Analysis.—This song opens with a phrase on a minor triad, followed by a phrase outlined by the unusual descending progression B, A, E, C. After this we find a quaking phrase in small intervals, and a recurrence of C, especially prominent at the close of the song, but occurring always on the unaccented count. This remarkable formation of melody is interesting with reference to the title of the song. The major third constitutes 9 of the 23 intervals, although the song is minor in tonality.

The following song is a Koöp song recorded at Vomari, the preceding songs having been obtained at San Xavier.

---

[27] This and the next word are used only in songs.

No. 70. Song of the Dawn   (Catalogue No. 1027)

Recorded by RAFAEL MENDEZ

TRANSLATION

It has been a long time since the light began to show, my brother.
Just look, my brother.
Toward us the bows are brightening (referring to shafts of light bent above their
heads like long bows).

Analysis.—This song was recorded by four singers in order to show
the manner in which several men sang together. The opening tones
were sung by Mendez alone, the other voices joining his at *X* and
continuing together until the close of the four renditions. The
slower tempo occurred at the close of each rendition. The song is
harmonic in structure, which is unusual in the present series. The
melody tones are those of the fourth five-toned scale. An ascending
fourth occurs four times and is an interesting peculiarity of the song.
Fifteen of the twenty-five progressions are whole tones. Mendez
recorded the song alone, as well as with the other singers, the transcription being from his own rendition.

The Komotan affected warriors and unborn children. It was a
requirement among the Papago that the father of an unborn child
should provide his own food when on the warpath and avoid the
food of those who had killed Apache. He must also avoid giving
offense in any manner to the spirits of dead Apache. If he failed in
these requirements his child, when born, would be troubled by an
Apache spirit. If he killed an Apache his wife must not drink much
water nor eat any salt until after the birth of the child.

Two songs used in treating the Komotan sickness were recorded
by Kiyatan, whose father was a medicine man of high standing.

No. 71. "The Sunrise"   (Catalogue No. 1075)

Recorded by KIYATAN

WORDS

First rendition

| Tharai | woceracima | hokithab | kakatho |
| Sun | rising | at the side | bows |

| yahaiwa | wùwùcima | hokithab | pûr |
| at the side | lying | at the side | the |

| mawithûr | mamata | vùpùkumi | thiamo |
| lion | babies | pink | that is all |

Second rendition

| Maratha | yutuna | hokithab | pûr | vapakù [28] |
| Moon | setting | at the side | the | canes |

| yahaiwa | wùwùcima | hokithab | kiruhu |
| at the side | lying | at the side | wild cat |

| mamatu | yahaiwara | cùcùwoi | kaiima |
| babies | moving around | uncertainly | that is all |

FREE TRANSLATION

The sun is rising,
At either side a bow is lying,
Beside the bows are lion-babies,
The sky is pink,
   That is all.

The moon is setting,
At either side are bamboos for arrow-making,
Beside the bamboos are wild-cat babies,
They walk uncertainly,
   That is all.

Analysis.—This song has a compass of 10 tones, beginning on the highest tone of the compass and having the lowest tone near the close of the song. The major third is the only interval occurring

---

[28] This refers to pieces of cane used for the shafts of arrows.

more than once in the song. The form of the melody is not of so high an order as the poetry contained in the words.

The following is the "companion song," and was sung to the same melody.

WORDS

Tharai	pi	yoëwa	himùna	waha	pi
Sun	is	slowly	going	and	is

yoïvi	ki	hononye	cucukûr	nakamûrli
slower	in	setting	black	bats

nuïnakûr	maïno	kuma	kokopa	yaäli
will be	swooping	that is all	spirit	children

inowayiv̂urcov	yahaiwara	iyaälhimûr
beneath	moving around	rolling

inowani	wûrwûrmikûr	viviki
around	among	tufts of eagle down

cucuökima
stuck up at intervals

FREE TRANSLATION

The sun is slowly departing,
It is slower in its setting,
Black bats will be swooping when the sun is gone,
That is all.

The spirit children are beneath,
They are moving back and forth,
They roll in play among tufts of white eagle down,
That is all.

Songs were also used in treating sickness caused by Papago spirits. Such songs belonged to Owl Woman (pl. 17, a), who is commonly known by the Spanish name Juana Manwell. The name Owl Woman is a translation of her Papago name. She lives at San Xavier, near the house and well shown in Plate 2, b, c. When she treats the sick her songs are sung by Sivariano Garcia. (Pl. 17, b.)

Owl Woman said that the disturbing spirits were those of Papago who followed the old customs, not those of "Roman Catholic Indians," who, according to Owl Woman, "remain near the villages all the time and loaf around the houses." She said the spirits of old-time Papago usually stay near their graves during the day but at night they go to the spirit land. Owl Woman holds familiar converse with these spirits and uses songs they have given her for the treatment of the sick. She said the road to the spirit land is not far away but only the spirits know its location. The road forks at a distance from the village, one branch leading to the spirit land and the other "going off into space." The spirits travel this road after nightfall as they can see better in the dark than in the daytime.

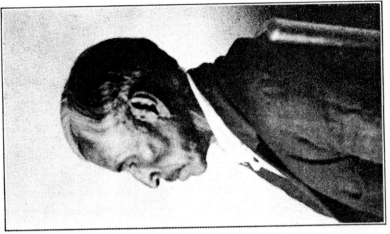

c, Rafael Mendez

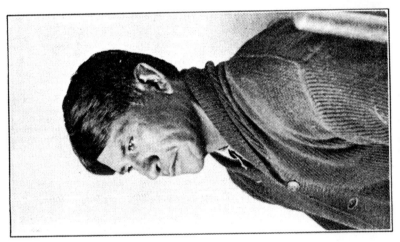

b, Jose Ascencio

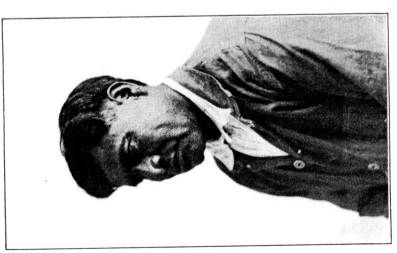

a, Jose Manuel

a, Site of spring in which children were buried

b, Site at which offerings are made

The spirits first revealed themselves to Owl Woman when she was in extreme grief over the death of her husband and other relatives. This was 30 or 40 years prior to the recording of her songs in 1920. The spirits took her to the spirit land in the evening and brought her back in the early dawn, escorting her along a road. They took her to a high place from which she could see the abode of the spirits, and her dead relatives came one at a time to talk with her. If too many had come at once they would have taken her back with them. In these meetings she found her relatives happy and looking neither younger nor older than in life. The spirit land, into which she looked, was thickly populated, the people living "on the ground," as in the old times, and not in houses. She saw blackish waters, beside which the children played. The spirits danced during the night, enjoying the same pleasures as when they were on earth.

When the spirits had taken her many times to their abode and had shown her many things they decided that she should be taught certain songs for the cure of sickness caused by the spirits. It was not necessary that she should go to the spirit land to learn the songs. It was decided that a person, at his death, should go where the other spirits are and "get acquainted a little," after which he would return and teach her some songs.

The time elapsing between a death and the return of the spirit varies from a few days to two or three years. She has seldom received more than two songs from a spirit. When giving her the songs they do not come close to her but stand 30 or 40 feet away. She recognizes them as clearly as she would a living person. In recent years she has gone less frequently to the spirit land, as the spirits have come to her so freely. They tell her many things. For instance, a young woman died who had been married only two months. She came to Owl Woman long afterwards and told of her sadness, saying, "I dropped my tears all the way." Often the sick whom she has treated unsuccessfully return to say they were sorry she could not help them. They say it was the fault of the diagnostician, who did not recognize their disease.

The decision of the spirits was made known to her by the spirit of a man who was killed near the present site of Tucson. He came to her house one night and told her not to be sad any more about her dead relatives, and said that if any of the people were sick she would have songs with which to cure them. The night after this appearance he gave her a song, and later he gave her another (Nos. 72 and 73). It was many years before she used these in treating the sick. Then her grandson was so sick that it seemed certain that he would die and she decided to try her singing. She sang and treated him with the owl feathers and he recovered. She has now received hundreds of these songs, so many that she can not remember them all. It is possible for her to treat the sick without singing, but she prefers to have the songs. The custom is that four songs be sung, then she treats the sick man with a bunch of owl feathers on which she sprinkles ashes from his fire. She strokes his body with them to "get out the sickness" in the manner noted in the description of the deer medicine. There is no singing during the treatment.

Owl Woman taught her songs to her son-in-law, but as he lives in the country she taught them also to Garcia, who lives in the village and whose services are available at almost any time. They usually spend an entire night with a sick person and by morning he is perceptibly better or else she knows that she can not help him. She uses certain songs for the beginning of the treatment, others are sung shortly before midnight, others after midnight, and still others as the day is breaking. If possible they have 15 or 20 other singers, each with a gourd rattle.

The phonographic recording of Owl Woman's songs occupied an entire day. She did not wish to sing into the phonograph and insisted that Garcia record the songs. She sang each song softly in order to recall it to his mind, and toward the latter part of the day she sang with him, but not loud enough for her voice to be recorded. At the beginning of the day, when telling of her visits to the spirit world, she had the appearance of a sibyl, with a strange, far-seeing look in her eyes. The day was chilly and in addition to the white head covering worn by the Papago women she wore her black shawl wrapped tightly around her, as shown in her portrait. In the first two hours Garcia's interest did not falter and he sang one song after another at her dictation. But there came a time when he left out two or three words. There was much talking in Papago. The old woman was suddenly full of animation and fire. The interpreter said, "She is telling him that he must not be discouraged because he forgot those few words. She says he must go on as if nothing had happened." Garcia rallied to his task and the work continued, but the old woman gave closer attention to her singer. Even to one who did not understand the language it was evident that she was encouraging him and holding his interest. She was bright, active, with an occasional witticism at which they laughed heartily. At the close of the afternoon Garcia was singing steadily with little sign of weariness but her face was drawn and tired, as of one who had been under a long strain. How many long nights she had held her singers at their task by the force of her personality, while she watched the flickering life of a sick man!

Each of the four parts of the night has its own songs, which are in groups of four and are sung in sequence. The next two songs are those which were given to Owl Woman by the man who was killed near Tucson and are the songs with which she always begins a treatment.

No. 72. "Brown Owls"　　　(Catalogue No. 931)

Recorded by SIVARIANO GARCIA

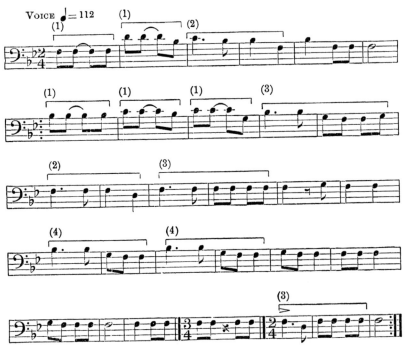

TRANSLATION

Brown owls come here in the blue evening,
They are hooting about,
They are shaking their wings and hooting.

Analysis.—This is the first of a group of 23 songs belonging to a singer of strong individuality and containing many points of unusual interest. A general characteristic is the ascending progression of the first and last intervals. Each song was sung twice through, then twice from the seventh measure, and then once from the beginning, this being his custom. There was a slight break in the time after each partial or complete rendition. The present song contains syncopations (*nota legato*) which are unusual in Papago songs. Attention is directed to the measure following the rest, occurring midway through the song. The absence of a rest at the close of this measure carries forward the interest in an effective manner. The final phrase is effective, with its change of time and strongly accented tone.

No. 73. "In the Blue Night"   (Catalogue No. 932)

Recorded by SIVARIANO GARCIA

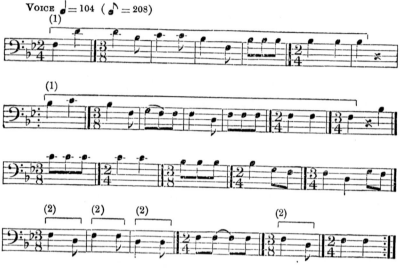

FREE TRANSLATION

How shall I begin my song
In the blue night that is settling?
I will sit here and begin my song.

Analysis.—This song opens with two phrases of seven measures each. The measure division occurring most frequently in these phrases appears several times near the close of the song and is indicated as a second rhythmic unit. Equal numbers of minor thirds and major seconds occur in ascending and descending progression. The melody tones are those of the fourth five-toned scale.

This and the song next following were given to Owl Woman by a man whom she had treated and who died. He returned to tell her what his thoughts were, while he waited for her arrival.

No. 74. "The Owl Feather"   (Catalogue No. 933)

Recorded by SIVARIANO GARCIA

TRANSLATION

The owl feather is rolling in this direction and beginning to sing.
The people listen and come to hear the owl feather
Rolling in this direction and beginning to sing.

Analysis.—A rather mechanical unit occurs throughout this song, though the rhythm is not monotonous. The repeated portion begins with the same rhythm as the song itself, in the fourth measure, and we find that the phrase which occurred on an unaccented count is introduced on the accented count with a change of time. This is an example of the subtle rhythms that occur in the healing songs of the Indians.

No. 75. "They Come Hooting"   (Catalogue No. 934)

Recorded by SIVARIANO GARCIA

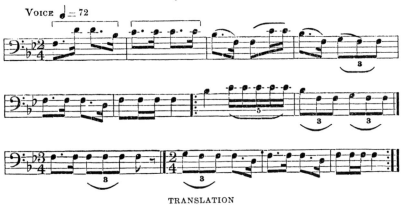

TRANSLATION

Early in the evening they come hooting about,
Some have small voices and some have large voices,
Some have voices of medium strength, hooting about.

Analysis.—A peculiarity of this song is the sliding of the voice in the third and fourth measures. It is a *swaying* melody, first in a higher, then in a lower register. In contrast to the glissando in certain measures the rhythmic unit was sung with clear-cut precision. The melody progresses chiefly by minor thirds and major seconds, which comprise 17 (71 per cent) of the entire number of intervals and are about equal in ascending and descending progressions.

The next song was given to Owl Woman by Nonka Simapere, grandfather of Harry Encinas, who died suddenly, at an advanced age.

No. 76. "In the Dark I Enter"   (Catalogue No. 935)

Recorded by Sivariano Garcia

TRANSLATION

I can not make out what I see.
In the dark I enter.
I can not make out what I see.

Analysis.—The rhythmic unit of this song is similar to that in Nos. 46, 68, and 74. The song is analyzed with G as its keynote, although the third above that tone occurs only once. There is a groping and lack of decision in the melody which is interesting in connection with its title.

The next song was given Owl Woman by her deceased brother and is concerning an old man named Marciano. She had been caring for this old man every night, but he was failing. She was on her way, at evening, to see how he was, and as she went toward the house she felt some one pass her. It was the spirit of her brother. He told her the man would die and gave her this song. The man died before she reached the house.

No. 77. " His Heart is Almost Covered with Night "

(Catalogue No. 936)

Recorded by SIVARIANO GARCIA

TRANSLATION

Poor old sister, you have cared for this man and you want to see him again, but now his heart is almost covered with night. There is just a little left.

Analysis.—The rhythmic effect of this song is largely due to its tempo and to the accented tones in the latter portion. These accents are unusual and very effective. The accent in the connective phrase is also interesting as it occurs on a sixteenth instead of an eighth note. The rhythmic unit is long and does not occur in the opening measures. It comprises two periods of five measures each, the first in double and the second in triple time.

About eight years ago a young man named Jose Louis was sick and Owl Woman went to see him because he was to be taken to the country. It was very late when she went home and on her way she met a young man. She noticed this was one of Jose's friends who had died. Jose was taken to a ranch and died soon afterwards. He came to her a few days later and gave her the two following songs.

No. 78. "I See Spirit-Tufts of White Feathers"

(Catalogue No. 937)

Recorded by SIVARIANO GARCIA

TRANSLATION

Ahead of me some owl feathers are lying,
I hear something running toward me,
They pass by me, and farther ahead
I see spirit-tufts of downy white feathers.

Analysis.—The fourth is a prominent though not a frequent interval in the first part of this song, while the minor third is almost the only interval occurring in the latter portion. The song is longer than the majority of Papago songs and has a sustained rhythm with a long swing from the beginning to the end. More than half the intervals are whole tones and only four are larger than a minor third.

No. 79. " Yonder Lies the Spirit Land "

(Catalogue No. 938)

Recorded by SIVARIANO GARCIA

VOICE ♩ = 112

TRANSLATION

Yonder lies the spirit land.
Yonder the spirit land I see.
Farther ahead, in front of me,
I see a spirit stand.

Analysis.—This song contains two rhythmic units, that in the first part of the song being the longer. It is interesting to note the steadiness of the rhythm in the latter portion. The keynote is next to the highest tone in the compass, which is very unusual in Indian songs. The tone material is the fourth five-toned scale.

An omitted song and No. 80 were said to have been received from Ciko, whose death was tragic in its circumstances. He was killed in a drunken fight and his body was carried around in a buggy and laid on the railroad track so it would appear that he had been killed by a train. This took place about the year 1912. Two years later his spirit appeared to Owl Woman and sang these two songs. The words of the untranscribed song are translated as follows:

Sadly I was treated, sadly I was treated,
Through the night I was carried around,
Sadly was I treated.

The words of the transcribed song are less clear in their application.

No. 80. Song of a Spirit   (Catalogue No. 939)

Recorded by SIVARIANO GARCIA

TRANSLATION

A railroad running west,
He travels westward.
When he gets a certain distance
He flaps his wings four times and turns back.

Analysis.—This song is analyzed with B as its keynote. In this as in the preceding song the keynote is next to the highest tone in the compass. Both songs are concerning spirits. Attention is directed to the two consecutive fourths occurring about midway through the song, giving an ascent of a seventh. The tone material is the fourth five-toned scale.

One day as Owl Woman was resting by a hill a spirit came to her. It was that of a man who died eight years previously and his sister who died at about the same time was with him. The two were riding on one horse. The man said he had just come back to see the condition of his house. He asked what she was doing and she replied that she was going after wood and had sat down to rest. He taught her the two following songs:

No. 81. "We Will Join Them"   (Catalogue No. 940)

Recorded by SIVARIANO GARCIA

TRANSLATION

Yonder are spirits laughing and talking
as though drunk.
They do the same things that we do.
Now we will join them.

Analysis.—This and the two songs next following have the same
opening interval as well as the same general melodic trend. The
rhythm also is somewhat similar in these songs, the first two of which
were said to be received from one individual and the third from
another. This melody is based on the fourth five-toned scale. The
fourth is a prominent interval but progression is chiefly by minor
thirds and major seconds.

No. 82. "My Feathers"   (Catalogue No. 941)

Recorded by SIVARIANO GARCIA

TRANSLATION

I pity you, my feathers,
I pity you, my feathers, that they make fun of,
They must mean what they say,
Or perhaps they are crazy in their hearts.

106041°—29——10

Analysis.—A general resemblance between this and the preceding song has already been noted. This is, however, the more lively of the two melodies. Attention is directed to the effect of vigor produced by the third count in the second measure and by the rhythm of the third measure. This song contains one scale-degree less than the preceding, being based on the tones of the major triad and sixth.

The next song is the first of three given to Owl Woman by Jose Gomez, who died about two years before the recording of the song. He gave her three songs, which is an unusually large number for her to receive from one spirit. Only the first of the three is transcribed, the others being found lacking in interest. The writer commented on this and Owl Woman said, "Jose was not a lively boy, he was slow and sleepy headed." The first and second songs refer to the rehearsals for a dance.

No. 83. "The Women are Singing" (Catalogue No. 942)

Recorded by SIVARIANO GARCIA

TRANSLATION

On the west side people are singing as though drunk. The women are singing as though they were drunk.

Analysis.—The song begins with the same phrase as the preceding and has the same compass but presents some interesting points of difference. The tone E flat which did not occur in Nos. 81 and 82 is prominent in this melody, though it occurs only twice. The rhythmic unit is similar to that of Nos. 46, 68, 74, and 76. An ascending and descending fourth is used effectively in the fifth measure. The song contains all the tones of the octave except the seventh.

The words of the second song are, "On the west side they are singing, the women hear it." The words of his third song are of unusual poetic beauty and are freely translated as follows:

> In the great night my heart will go out,
> Toward me the darkness comes rattling,
> In the great night my heart will go out.

The next three songs are the final songs in this group, sung just before midnight.

No. 84. "I Am Going to See the Land"

(Catalogue No. 951)

Recorded by SIVARIANO GARCIA

TRANSLATION

I am going far to see the land,
I am running far to see the land,
While back in my house the songs are intermingling.

Analysis.—In this song of a journey to the land of the spirits we note that the keynote is next to the highest tone, as in Nos. 79, 80, 84, 87, 88, and 91. Only three intervals larger than a minor third occur in the song, two being ascending fourths and one an ascending fifth. The accidental in the first measure was clearly given in all the renditions.

No. 85. "I Run Toward Ashes Hill"

(Catalogue No. 952)

Recorded by SIVARIANO GARCIA

TRANSLATION

Ashes Hill Mountain, toward it I am running,
I see the Ashes Hill come out clearer.

Analysis.—This song is classified as both major and minor in tonality. Only one other song (No. 46) is thus classified. The distinction between A natural (in the first portion) and A flat (in the second portion of the song) was clearly given, the keynote being the same in both parts of the song. About one-fourth of the intervals are semitones, an unusually large proportion of this interval.

No. 86. "The Waters of the Spirits"

(Catalogue No. 953)

Recorded by SIVARIANO GARCIA

VOICE ♪= 224 (♩=112)

TRANSLATION

They brought me to the waters of the spirits.
In these waters the songs seem to be stringing out.

Analysis.—This song is plaintive and hesitant in character. A minor tonality is suggested by D flat, with F as the apparent keynote. The third above the keynote does not appear. This song is unusual in that it consists almost entirely of eighth notes and contains frequent short rests. Ascending and descending intervals are about equal in number.

The remaining song of this group contains the words, "The spirit person, the spirit person is going around, around me." This is said to mean that the spirit person was making fun of him, or tantalizing him.

The group of four songs next following are sung by Owl Woman between midnight and early morning. Only the first three of the present group of four songs are transcribed. The first and second were received from Francisco Pablo, an old man who died about 1913.

No. 87. "There I Will See the Dawn"

(Catalogue No. 943)

Recorded by SIVARIANO GARCIA

VOICE ♩ = 72 (♪ = 144)

TRANSLATION

A low range of mountains, toward them I am running.
From the top of these mountains I will see the dawn.

Analysis.—An ascending major sixth is the opening interval of this, as of several other songs in this group. The present song is harmonic in structure and is based on the fourth five-toned scale. Like many other Papago songs it begins and ends on the same tone. The keynote is near the top of the compass, a peculiarity noted in several songs believed to have been received from spirits.

No. 88. "I Run Toward the East" (Catalogue No. 944)

Recorded by SIVARIANO GARCIA

VOICE ♩ = 116
Irregular in tonality

TRANSLATION

I am not sure whether I am running west or east but I run on and on.
I find that I am running east.

Analysis.—This song is irregular in tonality. Other songs thus classified are Nos. 8, 12, 14, 24, 31, 33, 36, 119, and 145. The framework consists of the descending fourths C sharp-G sharp, B-F sharp and F sharp-C sharp. More than half the intervals are fourths, the interval associated with motion, and we note the two consecutive ascending fourths midway through the song. The first period of the song contains seven measures, and the second period contains eight measures, the last four measures of the period being alike. The rhythmic interest of the song centers in the opening phrase of the second period.

The last two songs of this group were said to have been received from the spirit of a man who met his death by falling in a well. The "dawn" mentioned in both songs is the light seen by the spirits and mentioned in other of Owl Woman's songs. Black Butte and *Vihuḱput* are commonly known as Dub's Buttes. The man made his first camp at Black Butte. The next day he went on to *Vihuḱput*, where he met his death. He wanted to get water from a well and, having no rope, he climbed down into the well. A rock loosened and fell on him, and he fell into the well. His body was not found until the next day. The first part of the words of this song appear to be concerning his death and the latter part concerning the journey of his spirit.

No. 89. "I Die Here"   (Catalogue No. 945)

Recorded by SIVARIANO GARCIA

TRANSLATION

I am dead here, I die and lie here,
I am dead here, I die and lie here,
Over on top of *Vihuḱput* I had my dawn.

Analysis.—A frequent occurrence of single measures in 3–8 time characterizes this song. These are interspersed with double or triple measures in a particularly steady rhythm, and give an effect of a slight fluttering. The whole rhythm is interesting in connection with the title. The song is on the fourth five-toned scale with the fourth as a prominent interval.

In the following song he mentions Black Butte, which is one of these landmarks.

No. 90.   "I Could See the Daylight Coming"

(Catalogue No. 946)

Recorded by SIVARIANO GARCIA

TRANSLATION

Black Butte is far.   Below it I had my dawn.
I could see the daylight coming back of me.

Analysis.—This song is minor in tonality with a special prominence given to the sixth. This introduces a major third which constitutes 7 of the 21 intervals. As in many of Owl Woman's songs, the first and last intervals are ascending progressions. The melody tones are those of the minor triad and second.

No. 91. "The Dawn Approaches" (Catalogue No. 947)

Recorded by SIVARIANO GARCIA

TRANSLATION

I am afraid it will be daylight before I reach the place to see.
I feel that the rays of the sun are striking me.

Analysis.—The thematic development of this song is interesting
and for convenience in observing this development four phrases
are designed as rhythmic units. It is interesting to compare these,
noting, for instance, that the count divisions of the first unit are
reversed in the fourth. Attention is directed to the change to double
time occurring in the fifth measure of the repeated portion, which
seems to give force and vigor to the song. The tempo is more rapid
than in a majority of these songs.

No. 92. "The Owl Feather is Looking for the Dawn"

(Catalogue No. 948)

Recorded by SIVARIANO GARCIA

TRANSLATION

The owl feather is likely to find the daylight.
He is looking for it.
He is looking to see the dawn shine red in the east.

Analysis.—There is a lack of decision in this melody which accords with its words. The song consists of two periods each containing five measures. The dotted eighth which is unaccented at the opening of the song appears on the accented count at the beginning of the second period.

No. 93. "The Morning Star"   (Catalogue No. 949)

Recorded by SIVARIANO GARCIA

TRANSLATION

The morning star is up.
I cross the mountains into the light of the sea.

Analysis.—This, like the preceding song, is based on the fourth five-toned scale, but the melodies are different in every respect. This song consists of three periods containing four measures each, followed by seven measures in a monotonous style somewhat resembling a chant. The intervals include ten minor thirds and ten whole tones, four of each being upward and six being downward progressions.

The next song was omitted if the medicine woman saw that the person whom she was treating would recover. If, however, she saw that he would die she talked with his relatives, told them that he would not recover, and sang this song.

No. 94. Song of a Medicine Woman on Seeing that a Sick Person will Die

(Catalogue No. 950)

Recorded by SIVARIANO GARCIA

TRANSLATION

I think I have found out.
I think I have found out.
With the owl songs I have found out and I will return home.

Analysis.—This song is transcribed and analyzed with E flat as the keynote, though the third above that tone does not occur. The most prominent tones are E flat and B flat, the other melody tones being F and A flat. The fourth constitutes 17 of the 30 progressions. The rhythmic unit is short and unimportant. A majority of the phrases are four measures in length, though the song contains one phrase of three and another of five measures.

SONGS CONNECTED WITH CEREMONIES

DANCE IN SUPPLICATION TO THE SUN

The origin of this dance is unknown, but all the songs used at the opening of the dance were received in a dream by one person. The dance is called *Ciwiltkona*, which means "hopping," and the dance had reference to the fertility of the field, but adverse circumstances made it impossible to obtain full data concerning it. The circle of dancers might move either clockwise or contraclockwise. In the middle of the circle was a representation of the sun, toward which the dancers extended their hands during song No. 97. Many songs were sung at rehearsals, and the man giving the dance selected those to be used at the performance. One of the opening songs contained the words, "I will stand here and begin to sing. The women hear and all come. You stand here and sing with me." The next three songs were recorded by a man living near San Xavier Mission. (Pl. 13, *b*.) The following song could be sung at any time:

No. 95. "Clouds Roll Toward Me"

(Catalogue No. 1063)

Recorded by LEONARDO RIOS

TRANSLATION

At the south side is water covered with green scum. Above it clouds roll toward me. I see this and think perhaps I will be caught in the rain, so I return home.

Analysis.—This song contains six sorts of intervals in ascending and five in descending progression, which is an unusual variety. A majority of the melody lies below the keynote. Three rhythmic units occur, all beginning with the same count division. It is an interesting and lively melody, forming a notable contrast to the songs of the preceding group.

A general dancing song which was not transcribed contained the words, "A powerful eagle left his dwelling place and wandered away. He found the dwelling place of Elder Brother and went inside. He got some clouds from Elder Brother's house and wandered over the village and gave rain to the fields."

No. 96. "Great White Birds Over the Ocean"

(Catalogue No. 1064)

Recorded by LEONARDO RIOS

TRANSLATION

The great white birds that fly over the ocean came to our singing place, and over the ground they strung about.

Analysis.—The same characteristics appear in this as in the song next preceding. The tone material, compass, and first and last tones are the same, but the present song contains a much larger proportion of whole tone progressions. Attention is directed to the accented tones followed by descending fourths.

During the next song the dancers extended their hands toward the representation of the sun.

No. 97. "The Dwelling Place of the Sun"

(Catalogue No. 1065)

Recorded by LEONARDO RIOS

TRANSLATION

In the east is the dwelling place of the sun.
On top of this dwelling place the sun comes up and travels over our heads.
Below we travel.
I raise my right hand to the sun and then stroke my body in the ceremonial manner.

Analysis.—The change of tempo is the chief characteristic of this song, which has the same range and tone material as the two next preceding. The most frequent interval is a semitone and the song contains no unit of rhythm.

At the close of the ceremony a song with these words was sung (free translation): "Sadly we will go home. We have danced and been happy. We have seen our friends. Now we go to our distant homes wondering when we will come together again."

THE VIIKITA

The purpose of this ceremony was the securing of rain and good crops. The manner of its observance differed in the northern and southern parts of the reservation and information on the subject was obtained in each of these localities.[29]

The two observances are alike in the presence of "navico" or clowns, and in the carrying of representations of whatever was desired in abundance. A representation of the sun was also carried in both ceremonies. One difference between the customs was the drinking of *tiswin*, which formed part of the southern ceremony and was absent in the northern. Tiswin is the term commonly applied to a native wine made from the fruit of the saguaro cactus.

---

[29] Cf. "New Trails in Mexico," by Carl Lumholtz, pp. 92-98; "The Papago Harvest Festival," by J. Alden Mason, in the American Anthropologist, vol. 22, no. 1, pp. 13-25; "The Papago Ceremony of Víkita," by Edward H. Davis, Indian Notes and Monographs, vol. III, no. 4, Museum of the American Indian, New York, 1920.

In former times the Viikita ceremony was held every four years, that in the north being in November and that in the south being in the latter part of August or in September. Two derivations of the word *viikita* were given, the most reliable informants stating it came from a word meaning "to fast," while others said it came from *viiki*, meaning white downy eagle plumes. Fasting was part of the observance, and white eagle plumes were worn by the dancers. In the northern part of the reservation this ceremony was held near the "children's burying ground." A tradition states that a spring overflowed and threatened the country with inundation, so two children were buried alive in it to stop the flow of water. Because of this tradition it is customary for either two or four girls and boys to take part in the ceremony, representing the children who were thus sacrificed. This is peculiar to the northern observances of the ceremony. The origin of the ceremony is, in this region, attributed to a deity called Navico, who is said to have given the gourd to the Indians.

Stones are heaped above the spring in which the children were buried, and the place is surrounded with branches of ocatillo cactus stuck in the ground. (Pl. 18, *a*.) These are renewed every year and heaps of discarded branches can be seen in the background. After this spring had been choked a smaller spring issued from the ground a few rods away. This was covered with stones, and there the Indians place offerings of various trinkets or valuables. (Pl. 18, *b*.) Around this heap of stones is a well-worn path, and straight paths extend from this to the cardinal points. It was said that a person bringing a gift to the place should enter by one of the radial paths, run around the heap of stones, and run out by the path on which he had entered. The location was a few miles from Santa Rosa village. (Cf. Lumholtz, op. cit., p. 105.)

Four villages united in the northern ceremony, which was held for the last time in the year 1912 at Arci, located about halfway between Santa Rosa and Anakum. The other three villages taking part were Santa Rosa, Anakum, and Akcina. People living elsewhere and attending the ceremony connected themselves temporarily with one of these villages. About fifty people came from each of the four villages, and in each there were about six men who had charge of the ceremonial articles.

A ceremonial inclosure was made with an opening toward the east and at some distance was a similar inclosure where the singers rehearsed the songs. The walls of these inclosures were made of cornstalks, and the height of the wall was the length of two rows of cornstalks, the upper row overlapping the lower. This made a wall about 10 feet in height. Preparations for the ceremony included the gathering of the watermelons and the making of many tamales tied in the middle (wahpolihita), which were collected by the Navico and given to persons who remained all day in the ceremonial inclosure. More important than this was the making of representations of everything that was desired in abundance and depended on water for its existence, such as cattle, horses, birds, corn, pumpkins, beans, cane, and wheat, also representations of the cactus and of clouds. Some of these were large, the image of a cactus being 4 feet high but made of material so light that it could be carried by two men. A large representation of the sun was made of "something shiny." A certain man, expert in the making of the images, went from one village to another inspecting the work. He was the last man who knew the formal speeches that should precede the songs in the ceremony but he died in 1919 leaving no son, therefore his knowledge of the origin and traditions of this remarkable ceremony has perished.

It appears that not every person could carry one of these representations, for Mattias Encinas related a dream which, he said, entitled him to this privilege. He said that he could have made a representation of a cloud and carried it in the ceremony but so many others carried clouds that he never availed himself of this privilege. Encinas' son was the writer's interpreter and did not know of his father's dream until it was related and the song recorded for this work. It is a peculiarity of Papago music that the songs received in dreams are in groups of four. If more than four songs are received by one man he receives another entire group of four. The melody is often alike in the songs of the group but the words are different, constituting them "different songs" in the mind of the Indian.

Mattias Encinas said that when he was a child he attended a Viikita ceremony and wondered why the ceremony was held and why some of the men were dressed as clowns. As he grew older he sang the songs which he heard, being careful to observe the rule that these songs must never be whistled. By the time he was about 16 years old he had attended two or three of these ceremonies, and it was at this time that he had a series of dreams, one occurring every night for a period of four nights. In these dreams he saw spirits, heard them sing, and learned their songs. The first night they were close to him, they sang and walked backward until they disappeared. The next night they came again, singing, but farther away; the third night they were still farther away, and the fourth night they were so far away that he could scarcely hear them, but by that time he had learned the songs.

No. 98. "Clouds are Approaching"

(Catalogue No. 1074)

Recorded by MATTIAS ENCINAS

WORDS

Śiáli	thañthaŋiö	cûrcûŋgi	coco	kaĥowa
East	side	clouds	standing	approaching
mùmùko	nurkai		coko	thoähi
far	rain far away		raining here	thunder

TRANSLATION

Clouds are standing in the east, they are approaching,
It rains in the distance,
Now it is raining here and the thunder rolls.

Analysis.—This is the first of a set of four songs received in dreams by this singer and, as it is typical of the group, it is the only one which is transcribed. The others contain the same tones (with one exception) and only a slight difference in rhythm. Several renditions were recorded and are alike in every respect. The song contains only two intervals larger than a whole tone. The absence of the fifth and prominence of the sixth are interesting peculiarities.

The other songs of the group have the following words:

(2)

Green rock mountains are thundering with clouds.
With this thunder the Akim village is shaking.
The water will come down the arroyo and I will float on the water.
Afterwards the corn will ripen in the fields.

(3)

Close to the west the great ocean is singing.
The waves are rolling toward me, covered with many clouds.
Even here I catch the sound.
The earth is shaking beneath me and I hear the deep rumbling.

(4)

A cloud on top of Evergreen Trees Mountain is singing,
A cloud on top of Evergreen Trees Mountain is standing still,
It is raining and thundering up there,
It is raining here,
Under the mountain the corn tassels are shaking,
Under the mountain the horns [30] of the child corn are glistening.

The persons taking part in the ceremony were: (1) The leaders
(*Coïwada*); (2) clowns (*Navico*); (3) dancers and singers; (4) certain
singers who "started new songs" (*Kokspakam*); (5) one or two boys
and the same number of girls (*Hakiwata*), and a young man stationed
near them who sang special songs. The leaders (number not stated)
had their faces painted half one color and half another, either hori-
zontally or vertically divided. The clowns were painted in any
grotesque manner they fancied. Each wore a feather headdress and
a long tunic, and carried a crooked bow and arrow, also a pair of
eagle feathers tied together, such as a doctor carries and uses when
treating the sick. The latter insignia was not burlesque, as it was
believed that any of these persons could benefit, if not cure, the sick.
The office of clown was hereditary and there were usually one or
more of them in each village. The dancers were also the singers and
usually numbered about 40 or 50. They were the sons of singers and
their performance was obligatory. The songs had been taught them
by the old people whom they succeeded. They wore no clothing
except the breechcloth, even sandals being forbidden, and their
bodies were painted white, yellow, or red in solid color, no black
being used in this ceremony. Men with "bull roarers" were important to the conducting of the ceremony, as they gave signals for
assembling and for other events. A bull roarer consisted of a blade
of cactus connected with a handle of greasewood by means of a cord
about 3 feet in length. Holding the handle, a man swung the blade
through the air. The specimen illustrated (pl. 15, *c*) is about the
average size and has a blade 14 inches long. In former times the
cord was made of the fiber of a plant called *aöïta*. The blade was
painted in any solid color.[31] Lumholtz states that the blade was
painted with designs to represent corn. This instrument was one of
the ceremonial articles that were kept from year to year.

The ceremony was held at Arci, as already stated, and the people
from each visiting village camped by themselves. The signal for
assembling was given by the men with bull roarers, 60 or more of
these being in use by the time the people entered the inclosure. The
sound as they were swung through the air was said to be like thunder
and "sounds in the clouds." If a man were accidentally hit by one

---

[30] This refers to the slender spikes or prongs at the top of the stalks of young corn.
[31] Cf. Handbook of American Indians, pt. 1, pp. 170–171.

of these in another's man's hand he pressed his own blade to the wounded spot. Failing to do this he would have a sore in that place or would suffer a general illness.

At the time of the ceremony the people who lived at Arci went in a body and escorted the visitors to the inclosure. When the people were within about 50 feet of the inclosure they all rushed toward the entrance, but the people from Arci preceded the others in entering. During the day there were several processions in which the representations or images of things desired in abundance were carried and displayed to the people. It was required that each article be carried once, and that each dancer should take part in at least one procession. The images, after being thus exhibited, were placed in the inclosure and later were stored in a place known only to those connected with the ceremony.

No. 99. " We are Singing in the Night "

(Catalogue No. 1009)

Recorded by Jose Manuel

TRANSLATION

Now as the night is over us we are singing the songs that were given to us.
You see the clouds beginning to form on top of the mountains.
They look like little white feathers.
You will see them shake like feathers in a wind.
Soon the raindrops will fall and make our country beautiful.

Analysis.—This song is minor in tonality, yet one-third of the progressions are major thirds. It is peculiar in the prominence of B, the sixth above the keynote, while the fifth occurs only twice.

The first procession took place just before sunrise and was led by the *Coiwada*, walking slowly and scattering sacred corn meal with a motion like that of sowing grain. They were followed by a man carrying a representation of the sun, and by the dancers who carried a portion of the images. The clowns ran around the dancers and acted in an amusing manner. During the day the processions passed around the outside to the back of the inclosure where the boys and girls, representing the sacrificed children (see p. 138), were stationed. These children were required to stand in one place and dance all day. Behind them was a young man with small rasping sticks who sang special songs. The clowns went around the camp and sat down with one group after another, being unwilling to leave unless they received a gift of food, which they took to persons in the inclosure. Friends of the sick brought them to this ceremony with the belief that any of the clowns could benefit them, as all the clowns were supposed to be medicine men.

The Viikita as observed in the southern part of the reservation shows some differences from the northern custom. The following information was obtained at Vomari village, about 7 miles from the Mexican border. Mattias Hendricks, a Papago chief, said that the Viikita had its origin in the village of Kiithowak [32] in Sonora and was given to the people by Elder Brother, also called Montezuma. In the middle of this village there is a spring of water. The people once saw in this spring an animal that they knew belonged in the sea. The animal came out of the spring, lay around, and swallowed a few people. When the inhabitants of the village found that it was a dangerous animal they tried to kill it but could not do so. They sent word to Elder Brother where he lived in Baboquivari Mountain and asked him to come and see if he could save them from danger. When Elder Brother came toward the place he said, "I am going over yonder. You must watch and if you see clouds come up and stay in the sky you will know that I have killed the animal, but if there are no clouds it will mean that he has swallowed me." [32a] Elder Brother sharpened his knife very sharp and put it in his belt.

There is a little mountain on the north side of the village. He went along there and when he was about to turn at the point of the little mountain and could see where the animal lived a wind came and blew him right into the animal's mouth. When he got inside he crawled along and found the animal's heart, and cut its throat from the inside. The animal jumped up and then fell to the ground. When the animal died Elder Brother crawled out and found that the animal had fallen on the shore of the sea. Then clouds appeared where he had predicted and the people knew that he had killed the monster. Afterwards he returned to the village and told them about it. Ever afterwards the day was kept as a thanksgiving festival. Four Viikita songs were recorded at Vomari but no attempt was made to study the ceremony in detail. It was said that two inclosures were

---

[32] This village is referred to as Quitovaquita by Davis in his description of the ceremony. See "The Papago Ceremony of Víkíta," by Edward H. Davis, in Indian Notes and Monographs, vol. III, no. 4, published by the Museum of the American Indian, New York, 1920.

[32a] Cf. a similar signal on p. 52.

built near together and in one of these inclosures the "images" and other ceremonial articles were stored. Among the leading participants in the ceremony were two men, each of whom carried a wand about 3½ feet long, decorated with feathers in the middle and at the ends. These men had rattles attached to their ankles. They stood facing each other, one at the east and the other at the west. They "danced with one foot" and made motions with the wands. First the man at the east side sang and the man at the west moved his wand, then the man at the west sang and the man at the east moved his wand. Mattias Hendricks said that in the ceremony he attended the wands were moved forward and back with an even motion.

On the day preceding the Viikita ceremony the people placed four piles of sand beside each house, and beside the piles of sand they were required to place cooked food or cactus sirup. Three leaders of the dancers went among the piles of sand together with the clowns and all the people crowded around them. If the people wanted any of the food or sirup they were allowed to take it and hold it up, a clown shot it with an arrow and they were then allowed to eat it. If a young girl took up any of the food the clowns knew that she was unmarried. They hit her, and then anyone might take hold of her and marry her. The dancing continued all night.

One man was appointed to watch for the rising of the sun. When the sun arose on the morning of the ceremony this man put on a headdress made of feathers and led a procession which moved from the ceremonial inclosure to the place of the dancing. This man did not stop at the place of the dancing but walked from the east to the south, west, and north, returning to the east, after which he removed the feather headdress. Following him in the procession were the three dancers mentioned in connection with the piles of sand, also a man with rasping sticks and a woman carrying a basket which contained an "image." (According to Davis this was the heart of the monster slain by Elder Brother.) During the night the basket had been on top of a post. The woman placed the basket at a "little place fixed for it on the west side," and seated herself in front of it. The men with the rasping sticks sat in a line in front of her and sang, a pause being made after each song. The woman was not allowed to move from her place until sunset. At intervals during the day the three leading dancers went from the inclosure to a place where men with rasping sticks were singing, these men being others than the group near the basket. As they approached the group one of the leaders ran forward and threw sacred corn meal on the ground and the men behind him jumped and stood on the place where the meal had fallen; this was repeated and each man advanced in this manner, a special song being sung while this was done. After this was completed the leader walked as rapidly as possible to the inclosure. At the conclusion of the ceremony each person was given a "little branch of a certain tree" (prayer stick). The people took these to their homes in the assurance that they would have rain and consequently have good crops.

Medicine men exhibited their power during this gathering. Jose Ascencio (pl. 17, *b*) said he had attended the ceremony several times and that on one occasion he saw a medicine man come out of the inclosure and walk toward the east. It was about noon and the ground was hard and dusty. The man walked a little distance, sat down, made a cigarette, and smoked it. Then he took out his handkerchief, spread it on the ground, and put fine dirt in it; he took up the handkerchief by the corners, twisted it, finally twisting it tighter and tighter, and water came out of it. When he opened the handkerchief there was wet clay in it. The man put the clay in his pocket and walked back to the inclosure. There was no singing; he only "smoked and breathed on the handkerchief."

The following Viikita songs were sung during the dancing:

No. 100. " The Corn on Frog Mountain "

(Catalogue No. 1050)

Recorded by Jose Ascencio

TRANSLATION

Frog Mountain, on top of it the corn comes up.
Eat it, eat it.

Analysis.—This is a melody of unusual interest, consisting of two periods of six measures each, with a closing period of four measures in a slower tempo. A triple measure with practically the same slow tempo occurs near the end of each period. For convenience of observation the song is transcribed with A as the keynote, although the third above that tone does not appear.

No. 101. " We are Making Wonderful Things "

(Catalogue No. 1006)

Recorded by JOSE MANUEL

TRANSLATION

(Referring to the images of things desired)
Now we sit with feathers tied on our heads,
We make wonderful things which you have not seen,
But we will show them to you some day.

Analysis.—This song is minor in tonality, with the seventh as a particularly prominent tone. It has a compass of nine tones and lacks the sixth tone of the octave. About three-fifths of the progressions are whole tones.

No. 102. "Each Singer Wears a White Feather"

(Catalogue No. 1007)

Recorded by JOSE MANUEL

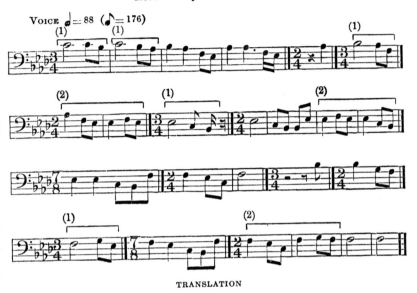

TRANSLATION

Each singer wears a white feather on his head,
Now it is nightfall,
We will sing through the night and perhaps we may do some good.

Analysis.—This is a free and pleasing melody, minor in tonality and containing the entire octave except the sixth. About four-fifths of the intervals are whole tones and minor thirds. The time in the 7–8 measures was given with clearness.

No. 103. "A Flaming Light in the East"

Recorded by JOSE MANUEL

(Catalogue No. 1008)

TRANSLATION

We see the light that brightens in the east,
It seems to turn to flame,
On the edge of it is something that looks like a white feather,
But we see that it is white clouds.

Analysis.—This particularly pleasing melody is classified with B-flat as the keynote, though the third above that tone does not occur. The tone material is that of the first five-toned scale, in which the third and seventh tones of the octave are omitted. It is interesting to note the difference of accent in measures 1 to 3 and 16 to 18. The rests and the time in the 3-8 and 5-8 measures were given with clearness.

THE RAIN CEREMONY

In the early part of August the Papago held a festival at which the medicine men made divinations for rain. This was in accordance with an ancient custom and was accompanied by the drinking of a wine made from the fruit of the saguaro cactus and commonly called "tiswin."[32b]   The principal informants on this subject were Jose Antoin, of Sells, and Mattias Hendricks, of Vomari. Practically the only difference in the two narratives was that informants at Hendricks village, in the extreme south of the reservation, said that songs were received by men while under the influence of the native wine. Information was also obtained from Sivariano Garcia, of San Xavier, but in this, as in the account of the bamboo game contest, his account was said by the informants to be the Pima version. Jose Antoin is chief of the rather large village of Pĭsĭnamak, and a small village called

---

[32b] The Papago designation is *ha'san* (saguaro cactus) *na'vai* (drink).

Harimak. He had acted as leader of the entire tiswin ceremony. His father was chief and he would have inherited the office at his father's death, as he was the oldest son, but he was so reluctant to accept the office that he left the village. He remained away several years until the people sent for him and the Government representative in charge of the reservation authorized his election as chief. The village obtained its name in the following manner: A war party killed a certain animal, brought home its head and put it in a tree. One of the early priests saw this and asked what they called it. They could not explain, and he said it was the head of a *Pisin* (Spanish word). After that time the village was called Pīsīnamak, the latter part of the word meaning "head" in the Papago language. Hendricks is chief at Vomari village.

Antoin related the following origin of the custom of making and drinking tiswin and said the incident took place at his village. There was once a woman who had a little boy. She wanted to go to another village to play *thoka* (a woman's game), so she put the child [33] to bed, placed food and water beside him, and left him alone. After a while the child awakened, ate the food, and followed his mother. He came to where they were playing the game and sat down. A woman running around in the game would see the child and say, "I found a little child;" and the mother would say, "Let him alone; he belongs to me." When the game was finished the mother took up the child, tied a cloth around his head, and stuck a feather in the cloth. Then the little boy went and played with the other children. All went well until the other children began to tease the little boy, saying he was too proud of his feather. The child stood it as long as he could, then he said that perhaps there was something inside his head of which he could be more proud than of his feather. He made a circle on the ground, stood inside it and began to sink into the ground. Some of the children said, "We had better tell his mother." One child ran and told, but when his mother got there he had sunk entirely out of sight except the feather. His mother took that out, then she went to work and called the badger, who is the best digger, and told him to catch up to the boy and bring him back. The badger dug as hard as possible but he could not overtake the boy. Then the mother called all the birds together and said, "Which of you can find a lost boy?" The crow said, "I think I can find him." The crow started and found the boy in the Kiyota Mountains. He returned and told the mother. Then the people said, "Let us go to the Kiyota Mountains and see how the boy looks." They went and found the boy standing there. The mother wanted him to go home, but the boy said, "No; I want to stay in the hills, but I will be of use to my people." Then he turned slowly into a saguaro cactus and told the people what to do. He told

[33] Throughout this narrative the term used to designate this boy is Ali, the Papago term for "child."

them to take the fruit to a house, mash it and boil it about an hour and a half, then they were told to strain it through a matting of grass, put it in an olla and seal it up. His mother said to the people, "Now you must do something in return for this." A young man said, "What can we do? We do not know about this." Then the child began to sing the following song. It was the first of many songs, probably more than a hundred, which he gave to the people, saying they were to be used in a ceremony to bring rain.

No. 104. "I Draw the Rain"   (Catalogue No. 1073)

Recorded by Jose Antoin

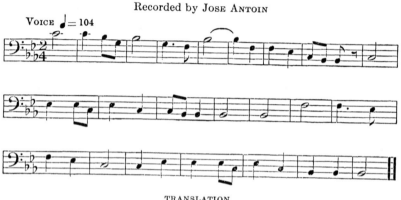

TRANSLATION

Here I am sitting and with my power I draw the south wind toward me. After the wind I draw the clouds, and after the clouds I draw the rain that makes the wild flowers grow on our home ground and look so beautiful.

Analysis.—This melody has a compass of nine tones, beginning on the highest and ending on the lowest tone of the compass. The tonality is major but half the intervals are minor thirds. No change of time occurs in the song. A quarter note followed by two eighth notes occurs three times, forming part of longer and different phrases. A reversal of these count divisions also occurs, but neither seems a rhythmic unit of the song.

Antoin said, "This is the way in which the tiswin ceremony started, and that is why we believe that if we make tiswin and go through the same action as when the custom was started we will have rain that day or very soon." [34]

The child told the people to continue this custom as long as there were any Papago living, and said that if they ever stopped this custom there would be no more rain. He said that the people must eat wild vegetables and that if they ever stopped eating wild food they would lose their vitality and not be able to stand exposure. (The informant said he will believe this as long as he lives, for he sees conditions as

---

[34] A different tradition is given by Russell, op. cit., pp. 213, 245, 256.

they were predicted. He said, "At that time men wore nothing but the G string. They rose before daylight and went out to look for Apache. See! If young men do this now they get sick and can stand nothing; they take cold and die.")

Preparations for the saguaro festival began in June when the fruit of the saguaro cactus was gathered. The fruit grows at the top of the cactus, which is a column 20 to 40 feet in height. The implement used in gathering the fruit is a long pole with a hook at the end. Much importance is attached to the shape of the hook, and the group of stars known as the Big Dipper is called the Cactus Hook because of a fancied resemblance. The work of gathering the fruit and making the sirup was done in places called cactus camps, several families combining in the work. The equipment of such a camp consisted of a thatch in a tree, on which the cactus fruit was spread to dry, and a covered fireplace. A few ollas were usually left in the camp and were not disturbed by travelers. A deserted camp south of Santa Rosa was visited and photographed. (Pl. 19, a, b.)

The cactus fruit was boiled in water, strained through a mat of grass or branches to remove seeds, etc., the juice was then boiled down to a sirup and placed in ollas, and sealed with a bit of broken pottery covered with mud. At the time of the ceremony these ollas were opened and the sirup mixed with water and allowed to ferment, making "tiswin." Smaller ollas were also filled for household use, as the sirup mixed with water and not fermented is a pleasing drink in hot weather. The sirup might be either light or heavy and could be kept for a year. If kept for a long time the color became dark. A similar drink was made from the fruit of the "organ-pipe" cactus.

The following incident was related concerning one of these camps. It was said that while the older people were busy with their work seven children strayed away from the camp and were lost. Their parents searched for them several days but could not find them. In the camp there was a man whose dreams usually came true. When the parents could not find the children they went to him. One night he "dreamed a song" and the next morning he saddled a pony and went to a place called Viïnikût. When he got to the place he found footprints of children and followed them all over the mountain. Finally he saw a boy in the bushes. He got down, tied his horse, and went toward the boy. When the boy saw the man coming he ran farther into the bushes, told the other children and they all ran away. The man chased and finally caught them and brought them home. They had been lost for eight days and would have perished without water.

The song heard by the medicine man in his dream told him that the children had not died of thirst. It had rained where they were and the water had stayed in a little "water hole." The children had found this and drunk the water. In old times Viïnikût was farm land, but the parents of the children did not remember this nor think the children might have strayed there.

No. 105. Song Concerning the Lost Children

(Catalogue No. 995)

Recorded by MATTIAS HENDRICKS

VOICE ♩ = 88

TRANSLATION

Viïnikût fields I got into.
I stayed there and my heart will be wet enough to last.

Analysis.—In this song concerning the lost children we have a wandering melody with the unusual compass of 12 tones. An ascending ninth occurs midway through the song and the ascending interval at the close suggests a query. A quarter of the intervals are fourths, which is an unusually large proportion of this interval. It is interesting to compare the rhythmic unit with measures 8 and 9 and 16 and 17, in which the note values are the same but the accent is different.

The lodge for the making of tiswin was erected near the lodge of the chief at Santa Rosa. This was visited and photographed. (Pl. 19, *c.*) It was round in shape with only one opening, a door toward the east. The lodge consisted of a framework covered with grass having tree branches or the long stems of the ocatillo cactus on the outside. Preparation for the August festival included the making of a large quantity of cigarettes for every one to use freely. These were made of native tobacco, rolled in corn husks.

The persons taking part in the ceremony comprised a leader for the entire ceremony, the men who mixed the tiswin and one man who tasted it, four men who watched the ollas in the lodge during the period of fermentation, four medicine men who made the rain divinations, and the singers, whose number was not prescribed, though 16 was the usual number, this permitting four men to be seated at and between the cardinal points during the distribution of the wine. At the four cardinal points were shallow holes with straw in them. The ollas were placed in these holes during the period of fermentation.

a, Thatch on which cactus fruit is dried

b, Place where cactus fruit is boiled

c, Lodge in which tiswin is made

The boiling of the fruit of the cactus into sirup and its storing in ollas has been mentioned on a previous page. The wine was made by mixing this sirup with water and subjecting it to heat until it fermented, when it was drunk at once. Cold water was placed in a large basket and the sirup added, the usual proportion being about half a pint of sirup to a gallon or a gallon and a half of water. A woman was never allowed to mix the tiswin, but she could bring the water if she desired. It was the belief that if a woman mixed the tiswin the people who drank it would do nothing but cry. The water and sirup were stirred with the hands, a requirement being that no implement be used. When the sirup was first put in the water one of the mixers said, "I am now mixing you up. Do me the favor to bring good wind and clouds and rain, and to keep the people from bad behavior after they have drunk the wine." This portion of the work was under the direction of an expert or "taster." From time to time the mixers took some of the sirup and water in a cup and gave it to the taster, who said "add more water," or "more sirup," according to his judgment. The entire quantity was enough to fill four ollas, each of which held 5 or 6 gallons. When the taster was satisfied with the mixture, it was poured into the ollas, which had been set in the straw at the cardinal points, and the ollas were covered tightly. This was done about the middle of the day, the door was tightly closed, and the ollas remained in the lodge that night, the next day, and the following night, the wine often being ready to use about 9 o'clock on the following morning. A fire was made outside the lodge in front of and a short distance from the door, and coals from this fire were brought and placed in the middle of the lodge to supply an even heat and induce the desired fermentation. The wood used for this fire was mesquite and ironwood, which hold the heat for a long time, giving out a gentle heat.

Four men watched the fermentation of the wine, two being on duty during the day and two during the night. These men also passed the wine to the people when it was finished. Their station in the lodge while watching the ollas was between the east and north ollas. They lay down most of the time, as it was very warm in the lodge, and they sang most of the time without accompaniment. If they were lying down when they began to sing they were required to sing four songs before rising. Either man could suggest a song or they could consult as to what song they would sing next, but there must be four songs. Among the songs of the watchers were the two next following.

No. 106. Song of the Watchers (a)

(Catalogue No. 1049.)

Recorded by JOSE ASCENCIO

TRANSLATION

The eagle is flying above in a round circle and makes a round shadow
on the ground.
I am walking around under that shadow.
The blue hawk is flying in a straight line and makes a straight
shadow.
Under that line I am running.

Analysis.—In the first phrase of this song we find the descending
fourth C to G, in the next phrase we have B flat to F, and the closing
phrase the fourth between C and G appears in both descending and
ascending progression. Although the fourth is prominent in the
framework of the melody, the interval of a minor third constitutes
about half of the progressions. The song has a compass of 11 tones
and is based on the second five-toned scale.

No. 107. Song of the Watchers (b)

(Catalogue No. 1031)

Recorded by JOSE HENDRICKS

TRANSLATION

The sun doctor with his body painted in spots.
At the edge of the earth I (the sun doctor) stand and see the
ocean with its beautiful rolling waves.
I call up the beautiful white clouds.
I am glad to see them rise.

Analysis.—A gliding and slurring of the voice characterizes this
song. The accents were light and the sixteenth notes were not
always sung distinctly. The tone material is that of the fourth
five-toned scale and the progressions are typical of that scale. The
song has a range of an octave and the keynote is near the top of the
compass.

Another song of the same class which was not transcribed contained these words: "Spotted Mountain, at the top rises a white
wind. The white wind makes the spotted mountain into a white
mountain. At the top of the white mountain rose a white eagle. I
saw it and my heart began to fail me. I scarcely knew what to do."

The watchers inspected the ollas frequently to see how the fermentation was progressing. If some fault occurred near the beginning
of the process it was possible to begin over, throwing out the wine
and making fresh. The watchers, for instance, might report that
moisture was on the outside of an olla. This indicated a slight leak
and the wine was emptied into another olla. It was expected that
the fermenting wine would rise to the top of the olla and sometimes
run over a little. This should occur four times. After it had risen
to the top of the olla the third time it was tasted and if it were not
doing well the taster and the leader of the ceremony knew what to do.
Sometimes a medicine man had interfered and used magic to spoil
the wine. In that case it would bubble up, then die down, and get
cold, and the people knew it would turn into sour water. If such a
man were detected he might be whipped or even expelled from the
village. While the wine was fermenting the medicine men were
trying to locate rain. Four men combined in this work but only two
were seated in the circle when the tiswin was drunk. These were
men who had been qualified by dreams or had "met some strange
thing at night." Their actions in trying to locate the rain were
similar to those when trying to locate the enemy, on the warpath.
The gestures were so much a matter of individuality that no action
can be said to be typical. Those who had seen the performance
said that some men used a wand, some an arrow, and others made
gestures with their hands. A man might hold up an arrow and move
it through the air as if testing the direction, or he might extend his
right hand before him and his left hand behind him, motioning to
the singers if he wanted them to sing faster or louder, as though he
felt that he had found the direction of what he sought. An informant
said that he saw a man make the rain divination at a tiswin festival
and he "made motions with a little stick with a feather on the end."
He moved the stick downward and water dripped from the end and
was caught in a bottle. The man turned and sprinkled the water
on the people. Some fell on this informant and the water felt hot.
The medicine man said, "This water is so hot that the clouds will
soon pass after a short shower, but to-morrow afternoon there will
be a cool, abundant rain." It happened as the man had predicted.
In reply to a direct inquiry the informants said that the medicine
men did not cause the rain but "located and predicted it."

The following song was sung during the rain divination:

No. 108. Song During Rain Divination

(Catalogue No. 1032)

Recorded by JOSE HENDRICKS

TRANSLATION

The eagle wing, under that I sat with the tiswin,
I drank that and I am well drunk.
The water that gathered on the blue hawk feathers at the end of the vasi,
I drank of that and was staggered.

Analysis.—This song is characterized by the frequency of the fourth which constitutes 7 of the 25 progressions. Certain simple measure divisions occur more than once, but these short phrases are so closely intertwined that it is difficult to separate one and designate it as a rhythmic unit. The emphasis upon D flat occurring midway through the song is unusual and interesting.

The people assembled to the number of 100 or more for the drinking of the tiswin. All were in gala attire but few were painted except those who were to serve the tiswin. In old times there was a special paint for use at this festival, made of white clay and a soft black mud ground together. The wine was served as soon as it was ready, which frequently was about 9 o'clock in the morning.

The circle of people were seated at the east of the lodge, opposite the door, and there was a fire in the center of the circle. One singer sat at each of the cardinal points, and there were three singers between each of these singers. Those who were seated at the cardinal points were the leaders and had their faces painted half white and half red. They were painted in pairs, the man at the north having the left half of his face painted white, and the man at the south having the right side of his face white, while the man at the east had his left cheek, and the man at the west had his right cheek white.

At the east a medicine man sat at the left of the singer and at the west a medicine man sat at the right of the singer. Each of the four men appointed to distribute the wine carried a basket filled with tiswin. (Pl. 10, *b*.) Two of these men were stationed at the eastern part of the circle and two at the western. The two at the east set their baskets in front of the singer at the east, and those at the west placed their baskets before the singer at that point. He extended his hands, side by side, hanging downward from the wrists so that the fingers almost touched the wine, then he held them up with the fingers pointed toward the sun. He repeated this four times and after the fourth time he made a sweeping gesture to include the full circle of the earth. Then the two men carrying the baskets separated, one going to the right and the other to the left. There were cups in the basket, and the wine was offered to everyone. The following song was sung while the wine was distributed.

No. 109. Song While Tiswin is Distributed

(Catalogue No. 1058)

Recorded by VICTORIA

(The words of this song were not recorded, but expressed the idea that the tiswin brought the wind and clouds.)

Analysis.—The tempo of this song is particularly slow. The song is analyzed with B as the keynote but the third above that tone does not appear. The intervals are wide, one-third being intervals of a fourth. Attention is directed to the descent of a seventh in measures 7 and 8, and the three descending thirds in the fourth and fifth measures from the close.

Many songs were sung during the distribution of the wine. The leader of the ceremony could say to the man at the east, "Start a song." He would sing it four times in a moderate voice for the others to listen, and then say louder, "All join." Then this singer at the east would say to the singer at the north, "I pass it to you," meaning that the singer at the north was to start a song. If he could not, he would say, "I pass it on," meaning that the singer at the west was to start a song. It might go around in this way, back to the man at the east, and it would be his turn to start another song. Jose Antoin said that no accompanying instrument was used in his village, but that in another village the singers walked around and shook a rattle while they were singing, although the customs connected with the songs were similar in other respects.

When the wine had been passed around once the men who distributed it stood silent and erect behind the singers while a speech was made, usually by a man dressed as if old and poor. Anyone who knew the speech could make it. His clothing was ragged, he had white clay on his hair, and walked with a cane. The speech was as follows:

"My friends and relatives, you drink the wine I have prepared expressly for you, and if any have power to draw rain from the east where stand the oldest ruins (in that old ruin lives the lightning doctor whose name is Mocking Bird) let the man ask the Mocking Bird doctor to send the best kind of wind and after that the best kind of clouds. Ask him to send the white clouds and after that the black clouds, and to make them cover the whole earth as they come toward us. The sky looks so high to us, and the clouds start from the earth and extend to the sky. In them is the thunder and the lightning which we welcome because we know they bring good to us. We hear the sound of the thunder in the mountains around us. Let us all join in our feeling to have the rain. Let us all be glad to see the water running in the little washes to moisten the fields where we plant our seed. Let us see the shape of the edges of the washes that look so beautiful to us. The plants that come up will be green and beautiful in the field, and when they have finished growing we will get the food for which we are now hoping.

"From our center turn your thoughts toward the east where stand the white ruins. In those ruins are white winds and white clouds. Have your feeling and ask for the rain to be sent to us. From those ruins come the white winds and white clouds which contain the heaviest rain. From our center turn your thoughts toward the west where stand the black ruins. In those ruins are black winds and black clouds. Have your feeling and ask for the rain to be sent to us. From those ruins come the black winds and black clouds which contain the heaviest rain. From our center turn your thoughts toward the north. There stand the green ruins. In those ruins are green winds and green clouds. Have your feeling and ask for the rain to be sent to us. From those ruins will come that which will make all green things on the earth grow faster. From our center turn your thoughts toward the south where stand the yellow ruins. In those ruins are yellow flowers. Have your feeling and ask for the rain to be sent to us. From those ruins will come the yellow clouds, that will be the finishing touch on our plants and on all things that grow on the earth. In finishing we have our feeling toward the four points of the winds and are sure we will get some help from the four ruins."

After making this speech the man was addressed by a term of relationship or as "friend." Only this one speech was made. The men with the baskets then carried the wine around the circle. If there was not enough they replenished it; if there was too much they continued to go around the circle until it was gone.

The effect of the wine was said to be a general "good feeling," and to last a night and a day. Jose Antoin said that no songs were received while under the influence of the wine, but informants at Vomari village said that songs were thus received. Rafael Mendez (pl. 16, c) said that a man who had drunk the tiswin once saw Coyote come toward him. The man began to come to his senses and Coyote sang and taught him many songs. The number was said to be about one hundred. The first of these songs was the following:

No. 110. "A Blue Wind"　　　(Catalogue No. 1026)
Recorded by RAFAEL MENDEZ

TRANSLATION

A blue wind.
I saw the tracks on the blue mountain.
Inside that mountain I found a bamboo plant growing.
From there I saw a seven-headed mountain running low from east to west.

Analysis.—The ascent of an octave at the opening of this song is unusual, and is followed by a downward gliding of the voice. The movement of the melody is free and the ascending and descending intervals are equal in number. Attention is directed to the ascent of a seventh in two progressions, at the twelfth measure from the close. Like many other Papago songs, this is distinctly different from the songs of the white race.

The man said that Coyote put his hands on him and ran them along from his head to his feet. Then he began to come to his senses. This experience was made the subject of the following song, the words of which were not recorded.

No. 111. Song After Drinking the Wine

(Catalogue No. 1025)

Recorded by RAFAEL MENDEZ

Analysis.—Two phrases in this song are designated as rhythmic units and differ only in the accent on the final tone. The song is more lively than the preceding but has the same quality of wide intervals and free progression. Both songs are rapid in tempo.

The following song is said to have been received in a similar manner.

No. 112. "You Make Me Drink Red Water"

(Catalogue No. 979)

Recorded by MATTIAS HENDRICKS

TRANSLATION

A red water you made me drink,
When I was drunk I went around as though I would fall down,
I fell on the ground face downward.

Analysis.—This song contains six sorts of ascending and four sorts of descending intervals, which is an unusual variety. It is a particularly pleasing melody and a majority of its phrases are four measures in length. The lowering of the third adds interest to the song.

A somewhat different tradition of the origin of the rain ceremony had been given by Sivariano Garcia of San Xavier village. This was read to Jose Antoin, who said that he had heard an old man relate it and that it was the Pima tradition. Garcia's narrative is as follows: Long ago, when the Papago first came to this region, there was no water and the medicine men brought rain. The custom began at Casa Grande. A medicine man living there made a long cactus, but he did not like it. He picked the fruit when it was so dry that the seeds were ready to fall. He handed it to one of his men, saying, "Take it back, I do not like it here." This man met Coyote, who wanted the seeds. The man handed them to him, and then wanted to get them back, but Coyote instead of giving them back held his hand high, and scattered them broadcast. The wind was blowing toward the north, therefore the giant cactus is everywhere growing on the south slope of the mountains and in low places. Garcia said that the medicine man made his cactus sink down in the earth, but it came up on the mountain called Kihotawak.[34a] A bird was flying over the mountain and saw the cactus. He picked some of the fruit

---

[34a] This mountain is named from its resemblance to an inverted burden basket (kiho).

and took it back to the village, and the people made it into wine. They put the wine in ollas, and the second morning it was ready to drink. Two or four villages united in making the wine. At this time the medicine men worked to get a knowledge of the rain. If their report was favorable the people planted their crops in a few days. If a medicine man could not locate the rain the first night he worked part of the next day and part or all of the next night, but if three or four men worked at the same time they could find the rain sooner. Garcia said that he had frequently been present at this ceremony and had learned many of its songs, four of which he recorded. If the people moved about the place they walked gently and slowly so as not to distract the attention of the medicine man who went around slowly, beginning at the east, then going to the north, west, and south to see if he could feel a cool breeze. In summer the rain came from the east, later from the north, and in winter or spring from the west. He felt in all directions to see if he could detect rain, and when he thought that he had the right direction he tried to bring the rain from thence. In doing this he used the means that were given him when he was made a medicine man. In the old days a man was not afraid of a test of his power. For instance, he would take in his hand the driest thing he could find and would squeeze water out of it.

The people sang to increase the power of the medicine men, this being similar to the custom of "singing for the medicine men" when they were trying to locate the enemy for a war party. (See p. 183 in which the people sang with the doctor in treating the sick, thus putting forth their power to supplement his.)

The song next following was usually sung first, as the words indicate.

No. 113. "The Songs Are Beginning" (Catalogue No. 922)
Recorded by SIVARIANO GARCIA

VOICE ♩ = 80

WORDS (NOT TRANSCRIBED)

Thaḥrai	honunĭm	kĕĕrna
Sun	going down	proper time

nûrĭnûrĭ	rzurzoŋco	yohoḥ	kaicokaci
songs	commencing	women	hearing

wowewaḥpahima	konsûŋ	thathaman
running toward	hastening	on the ground

mĕrliwa
they arrive

TRANSLATION

At sunset, the proper time for the beginning of the songs, they begin.
The women hear the song, and hasten to reach the place.
They arrive at the place.

Analysis.—It is interesting to note the varied use of a dotted eighth note in this song, especially in the latter portion where it is accented. In the sixth measure from the close it is in a double measure and in the fourth from the close it is made emphatic by being placed in a triple measure and followed by a quarter note. The two final measures of the song are pleasing in effect. The entire song is bright and cheerful with anticipation of the songs which are to be sung at the ceremony.

The other songs recorded by Garcia were not transcribed, but the words of two are interesting. His second song contains these words, "Poor old doctor, poor doctor, stringing web over the ground, and above us the clouds begin to string along like the web on the ground." The fourth song of the group contains these words, "Little Elder Brother is leading the clouds to the west. The wind comes out of every mountain, but still the clouds hang heavy over the mountain."

The Wakita

The puberty dance of the Papago was called *Wakita*. A young girl on her maturity was isolated for four days in the care of an older woman, not a relative. They prepared their own meals and ate together and the young girl occupied much of her time in making a basket which she gave to the older woman. It was part of this woman's duty to instruct the girl in the tribal ethics regarding women and also to teach her such simple household tasks as she had not already learned. During this time the girl was not allowed to taste salt and was required to use a stick in scratching her hair or body. The maturity of a young girl was regarded with awe and songs were sung to "cure her."

Soon after her isolation the parents of the girl gave a feast if they could afford it, also a dance which continued four nights, the people gathering in the evening and dancing all night. The principal songs were those received in dreams. One man led the singing, and sang each song slowly so the others could learn it, then he said, "hoi, hoi," in an encouraging manner and they all sang. In old times these songs were accompanied by the shaking of a gourd rattle. The girl for whom the ceremony was given stood next to the leading singer. She was not allowed to sit down during the entire night, though the dancers rested after each song. Her face was not painted and there was no change from her usual manner of dress. At midnight the people partook of the feast provided by her parents.

Men and women joined in the dance, standing in long lines facing each other. The men and women did not alternate but stood as they might chance to do. The dance consisted in retreating a few steps and advancing to the first position. Some old women danced around the entire group of people, singing the same song as the other dancers. The first of these songs was received in a dream by Ciko, who was one of the singers at this ceremony.

No. 114. "I Am Running Toward the Edge of the World"

(Catalogue No. 1043)

Recorded by JOSE ASCENCIO

TRANSLATION

I am on my way running,
I am on my way running,
Looking toward me is the edge of the world,
I am trying to reach it,
The edge of the world does not look far away,
To that I am on my way running.

Analysis.—This song is characterized by two ascending sevenths and a large proportion of fourths. It is freely melodic and contains all the tones of the octave except the seventh. There is no similarity between the two rhythmic units.

No. 115. " White Blossoms on Baboquivari Mountain "

(Catalogue No. 1044)

Recorded by JOSE ASCENCIO

TRANSLATION

Baboquivari is there on the east side,
It has white blossoms on it.
Toward that mountain I am on my way,
I am running to join the singer.

Analysis.—In the repeated eighth notes and simple rhythm of this song we have a graceful suggestion of the flowers on the mountain. The song begins and ends on the same tone, and the first and last intervals are fifths. About half the progressions are minor thirds.

No. 116. " Cottonwood Leaves Are Falling "

(Catalogue No. 1045)

Recorded by JOSE ASCENCIO

TRANSLATION

The cottonwood leaves are falling and flying in the air,
On top of the remaining mountain they are flying around,
And falling as though they were wet.

Analysis.—This is a particularly graceful melody containing two phrases of two measures each, followed by a phrase of five measures and a "connecting phrase" sung between the repetitions. The sequence of tones G-F-G suggests the rustle of the cottonwood leaves. The proportion of ascending intervals is larger than in a majority of these songs.

No. 117. "The Morning Is Shining Upward"

(Catalogue No. 1046)

Recorded by JOSE ASCENCIO

TRANSLATION

Poor man, did you leave me and walk away?
The morning is shining upward,
To that I am going.

Analysis.—This song is based on the fourth five-toned scale. The progressions in next to the last measures are unusual but the song contains no marked peculiarities.

No. 118. "On Top of the Mountain the Wind Blows"

(Catalogue No. 1047)

Recorded by JOSE ASCENCIO

TRANSLATION

Blackish Mountain, he stands there like a "doctor mountain."
On top the wind blows out,
On top the wind blows out,
And on top the clouds go out and cover the whole world.

Analysis.—More than half the progressions in this song are minor thirds and the song is minor in tonality. It is characterized by small divisions of the count and contains no rhythmic unit, although the rhythm of the first count in the second measure occurs several times.

No. 119. "I Go Toward the East"

(Catalogue No. 992)

Recorded by MATTIAS HENDRICKS

VOICE ♩ = 104
Irregular in tonality

TRANSLATION

I do not understand where I am going,
To Anakum I run and turn close to the village,
Going toward the east.

Analysis.—The free melodic trend of this song does not suggest a keynote with clearness, and the song is analyzed as irregular in tonality. Other songs thus analyzed are Nos. 8, 12, 14, 24, 31, 33, 36, 88, and 145. Almost a third of the intervals are fourths. Attention is directed to the opening measures of the third and fourth periods. Comparison with the rhythmic unit will show that the count divisions are the same, comprising a quarter followed by two eighths, but the time is changed from triple to double measure.

The next two songs were addressed to "*Cowaka*," this being the name given to the girl for whom the ceremony was given.

No. 120. "Cowaka, Come and Help Us Sing"

(Catalogue No. 1012)

Recorded by Jose Manuel

TRANSLATION

We stand and start the singing.
Cowaka, come out and help us sing.
We will keep you standing all night long and cure you.

Analysis.—This rather quaint melody contains three phrases which end with a descending minor third and a final phrase which ends with an ascending minor third. The song contains only four intervals larger than a minor third. It is based on the second five-toned scale and has a compass of eight tones, the melody lying between the keynote and its octave, which is an unusual melodic structure.

The melody of the following song was not transcribed.

TRANSLATION

A poor man takes the songs in his hand and drops them near the place where the sun sets.
See, Cowaka, run to them and take them in your hand and place them under the sunset.

SONGS CONNECTED WITH EXPEDITIONS TO OBTAIN SALT

The fact that the Papago made expeditions to the Gulf of California for the purpose of obtaining salt has been mentioned by several writers but the distinction is not always made between commercial expeditions and those which had for their object the securing of "medicine power" from the ocean. The commercial expeditions were made by many people and while the journey was long and hard it was not surrounded by the regulations which made the latter type of expedition a severe test of a man's physical endurance. The ocean was regarded with reverence and a man must undergo a severe ordeal in order to come into communication with it and to receive power from it. However, his journey and that of the seeker for salt had a few points in common, both being required to run four times around the bed of salt (anta) and to remain in isolation four days after their return, observing the usual customs of a fasting period.

The Papago used salt in the widespread commerce of the tribe. It was an article of barter with the Pima on the north and was also sold in Mexico, where the Sonora Mining Co. bought about 20,000 pounds annually from these Indians.[35] In 1920 an old couple was still passing through Sells, Ariz., every year with a supply of salt which was obtained from the salt deposits and carried on the backs of their burros. The salt deposit was said to be about 2 miles from the Gulf of California and about 130 miles from the southern part of the Papago reservation. Those who went for salt made their camp a little distance from the salt bed and after gathering the salt they ran to the sea and thence to their camp, but they did not go to Hiamorli (or Hiamowitcu), which was the destination of those who sought "medicine power."

An expedition to secure salt for commercial purposes had its peculiar customs. Mattias Hendricks went with his father on such a trip, the party including one man beside his father. Mattias was then a little boy, but old enough to get the horses in the morning. Those who went for salt usually took two or three pack burros or horses on which to bring back the salt. They made their camp at a distance from the salt bed and when they went to gather the salt they were required to run four times around the salt bed without stopping. The circumference of the salt bed was about a mile and a quarter. When they had done this and performed certain rites they could take the salt. There were some rocks with sharp edges near the place and these were used in scraping aside the fine substance which covered the surface of the salt and was also below it. This substance was called "salt shoes" and did not have a pleasant taste. Mattias Hendricks said he remembered that his father, after breaking through this substance, said to the salt, "Please leave your shoes because you must ride on a burro." The sharp rocks were used also in scraping up the salt. After the men had finished gathering the salt they ran to the sea without stopping and returned to their camp.

[35] Frank Russell, op. cit., p. 94.

The following song was sung in order that the men might secure a good supply of salt. It was accompanied by the rubbing of a short stick on an inverted basket. The stick was of greasewood, about 9 inches long and an inch wide, slightly flattened. The motion across the fiber of the basket was up and down, producing a soft and rather pleasant sound.

No. 121. Song Before an Expedition to Obtain Salt

(Catalogue No. 1010)

Recorded by JOSE MANUEL

TRANSLATION

We are scraping the basket and singing,
We hear the echoes in all the mountains around us,
We will make a trip to the salt and are singing to make it easy for
us to get it.

Analysis.—This song is minor in tonality but contains only one minor third. The major third occurs three times in descending progression, followed by a descending semitone which gives a peculiar and interesting effect. Almost one-third of the intervals are semitones, which is unusual in the songs under analysis. A change to a very slow tempo occurs in the closing measures.

When making the trip to obtain medicine power a man was required to walk the entire distance. If he took a pack animal he was not allowed to ride it. He carried water and pinole but was allowed to eat and drink only a very little. Beside the salt bed was a little well in which the water was salt but not so salt as the ocean. On arriving at this well he might drink a very little water. Beside the well he left whatever he was carrying and ran four times around the salt bed, going from the east to the north, west, and south. He then crossed the dunes to the sea and ran to Hiamorli. This was a sand bar extending into the sea about 50 miles beyond the salt bed and was described as the "place where the water turns and runs into the place where they get the salt." A line of hills (sand dunes) extended from the salt bed to Hiamorli and a man crossed these soon after leaving the salt bed, traveling thereafter on the sandy shore. On Hiamorli he rested a short time and "talked to the sea, asking it to make him a powerful medicine man." Then he ran back to the salt bed, drank again of the little well, and returned to his camp. He was not permitted to stop running except on Hiamorli. Only the best runners could compass this journey. An informant stated that he knew of two young men who started from the salt bed about midnight, ran to Hiamorli, and returned when the sun was at a height corresponding to about 10 o'clock in the morning. They were running almost the entire time, as the rest on Hiamorli was of short duration. The "medicine power" was usually received by a man during the period of isolation after his return home.

The following song was sung after the men arrived at the salt bed.

No. 122. "We Will Run Around the Salt Bed"

(Catalogue No. 1011)

Recorded by JOSE MANUEL

VOICE ♩ = 66

TRANSLATION

We will run around the salt bed,
We will run so fast that the stars will seem to run,
In this way perhaps one of us may secure magic power.

Analysis.—No change of measure lengths occurs in this song, which is a particularly pleasing melody. The first and second phrases begin on the unaccented part of the measure and the third phrase containing no rhythmic unit begins with a quarter note on the accented count. The song is on the second five-toned scale and contains only two intervals larger than a minor third.

The following song was sung on the expeditions to obtain salt. The melody is the same as that of the preceding song. The first word of this is "hiciä," a word whose meaning could not be ascertained. It is used at the beginning of the salt songs but in no other connection. This song is said to be very old and to have come down from some forgotten medicine man "who lived when the people first found out about medicine." On being questioned concerning the mention of rain in this and the song next following the informants said that in their opinion the sea holds everything—the clouds and the wind. The storms come from the sea and spread over the world and the clouds follow after, so they think there is some connection between the sea and the rain.   In this and the two following songs each stanza begins and ends with the word "hiciä," the meaning of which could not be ascertained.   (Cf. songs of the Limo which begin with "aliwĕrci.")

No. 123. "The Wind Blows from the Sea"

(Catalogue No. 1028)

Recorded by Jose Hendricks

TRANSLATION

By the sandy water I breathe in the odor of the sea,
From there the wind comes and blows over the world,
By the sandy water I breathe in the odor of the sea,
From there the clouds come and rain falls over the world.

Analysis.—The ascending and descending intervals in this song are almost equal in number and consist chiefly of whole tones.   The keynote is next to the highest tone in the compass and occurs only twice on an accented count.   In the opening measures a special prominence is given to the tone below the keynote.

106041°—29——13

No. 124. "The Rain on the Corn and the Squash"

(Catalogue No. 1029)

Recorded by Jose Hendricks

TRANSLATION

Under us the world spreads wide,
From that the corn comes up,
On the leaves the water moves in little drops,
Under us the mountain stands wide,
On that the squash comes up,
And the water spreads over the vines.

Analysis.—The ascending progressions in this song are more in number than the descending, which is unusual in Indian songs. Attention is directed to the ninth and tenth measures with their positive rhythm, giving stability to the rhythm of the song as a whole. The rhythmic unit occurs several times but is not an interesting phrase. The song is particularly vigorous in character.

The following song was recorded with the "seraping sticks" which are used with this class of songs.

No. 125. "The Sun Rises Over the Mountain"

(Catalogue No. 1030)

Recorded by JOSE HENDRICKS

VOICE ♩ = 54
RASPING STICKS ♩ = 54 (unaccented eighth notes)

TRANSLATION

A mountain called Hoötho, on top of it the sun rises,
It seems to waver,
A mountain called Hoötho, on top of it the sun sets.

Analysis.—The first rhythmic unit of this song occurs first with
C sharp and then with B as its initial tone. The second rhythmic
unit is an urgent little phrase, repeated on almost the same tone and
ending with an upward interval. The rhythm of the connecting
phrase resembles but does not repeat the first rhythmic unit.

WAR SONGS

The ancient tribal enemy of the Papago was the Apache. It is said
by the Papago that they never went to war against the Apache except
in retaliation for some injury done them by members of that tribe.
The following incident was said to be concerning the first war expedition of the Papago against the Apache.

A woman named Pulhaä was married and before a child was born
the food was scarce so her husband went to hunt *siras*, a small animal
that lived in the mountains. He "scared one up" and it ran into a
hole. While he was digging to obtain the animal some Apache killed
him. As he did not return in a few days his friends went out and
found him there. They gathered wood and burned his body, and
when his wife saw the flames she sang this song.

No. 126. "Yonder the Flames Leap Upward"

(Catalogue No. 918)

Recorded by SIVARIANO GARCIA

Voice ♩ = 63

WORDS

Húkiä potha	himūkai	pĕanyĕtho	jijiviä
I am	gone	I will not	return
húkiä nútha	húpaiyu	moöt	kamayu
I am	somewhere	dead	yonder
kamhomúihĭm	kúkiwa		
flames	stand up		

Analysis.—This song is analyzed with A flat as its keynote, although that tone does not occur on an accented count. In the first part of the song the sixth is flatted and appears in sequence with the fifth, this semitone progression seeming to reflect the sadness of the words. In the latter part of the song we find the sequence E flat-C of frequent occurrence. The long periods of the song are designated as rhythmic units.

After this the woman moved to another place where a child was born. When the boy was about 8 years old he learned from his mother that the Apache had killed his father and he kept thinking about going to find some Apache and taking revenge. He thought about this all the time. Once as he lay face downward on the ground a mocking bird flew above him and "gave him a long poem," telling him what to do and what to tell the people who came from war, having killed Apache. At night, when the hunters returned, he told them what the mocking bird had said. The people did not expect such things at his age and they began to see that the child had learned something wonderful. A war party was about to leave the village and they sang the following song.

No. 127 Song Before Starting on the Warpath

(Catalogue No. 919)

Recorded by SIVARIANO GARCIA

VOICE ♩ = 63 (♪ = 126)

TRANSLATION

I am going to walk far, far.
I hope to have a fine morning somewhere.
I am going to run far, far.
I hope to have a good night somewhere.

Analysis.—A comparison of the four periods in this song will show that they all end with the same phrase. The opening of the first and second differs from that of the third and fourth in rhythm but resembles it in melodic trend. Only 7 of the 49 intervals are larger than a major third. The tempo is slow and is the same as that of Nos. 126, 127, and 129, recorded by the same singer.

This boy was a "wonder child." While the warriors were away he went off night and morning to see where they were going to find the enemy. After some days fighting the Apache began to hide behind sticks and stones, then they hid behind their wives and children, and finally they were defeated. The following song was composed concerning this expedition.

No. 128. "The Apache Hid Behind Trees"

(Catalogue No. 920)

Recorded by SIVARIANO GARCIA

TRANSLATION

Yonder, near the enemy's country, stand many great trees behind which they hid.
They have retreated farther.
They act like children.
They hide behind the women or anything that will conceal them.

Analysis.—The tone material of this song consists of the first five tones of the scale of E minor, and D which appears as the tone below the keynote. Many songs contain this tone material without the peculiar effect produced by this use of the seventh. The song begins and ends on the keynote, which is the lowest tone except D. Emphasis on the keynote suggests stability and this song seems to express the confidence of the Papago in their superiority over their enemies. About four-fifths of the progressions are whole tones.

They started home victorious and at the first camp they had a general rejoicing. They prepared a drink by mixing mesquite sirup with water. This was placed in a large basket-bowl. (Pl. 10, *b*.) The warriors put the scalps on poles, called them "crow," and danced around them. They "acted crazy" and sang the following song.

No. 129. " While We Drink the Wine "

(Catalogue No. 921)

Recorded by SIVARIANO GARCIA

TRANSLATION

We make wine.
With deliberation we took our revenge.
We make the scalp poles hop like crows while we drink the wine, but
let us keep our self-control while we are rejoicing.

Analysis.—A change of tempo is a striking peculiarity of this song, reflecting the conflicting impulses expressed in the words. The change of tempo usually occurs during a rhythmic period, not between such periods. There are recurrent phrases other than those marked as rhythmic units and a comparison between the count divisions of the rhythmic unit is interesting. This song is minor in tonality and, like the song next preceding, makes an effective use of the tone below the keynote. Ascending and descending intervals are about equal in number.

It was said the Papago did not go out to make war on the Apache but followed them when they came into Papago country and stole property. The Apache raids and the campaigns of the Papago against the Apache usually took place in cold weather. A war party was well organized, and it was customary to try to have a messenger reach the Papago village every morning with news from the expedition. There were no songs at the meetings before the departure of the warriors, but long speeches were made. These were not formal, memorized speeches like those made after the expedition had started, two of which are contained in this description. It was an old belief that a war party that did not carry an eagle feather would not be successful.

In the late afternoon the warriors divided into groups and chased wild game for their evening meal. An old informant said that neither bows and arrows nor a club was allowed, and the men were required to catch the game with their hands. Another man said these were allowed but firearms forbidden. Sometimes several men chased one jack rabbit. The proper way was to catch the rabbit around the neck, but if several caught the same rabbit it was usually torn in pieces, each man keeping the part he held. A little fire was made but its light was carefully shielded lest the enemy should see it. Over this fire the meat was slightly heated, but the practice of eating meat almost raw was said to "make the men fierce." A little pinole was carried by the warriors, and San Xavier was the last place at which war parties going east could obtain this part of their equipment.

After the warriors had finished their scanty meal the leader addressed them as they sat in a great circle. The medicine men sat at a little distance toward the enemy and the singers were seated by themselves. It was the duty of the medicine men to locate the enemy, while the singers augmented their power by singing with them or "for them." Such were the only songs used by men on a war expedition. In his address the leader encouraged the warriors and, if the campaign were particularly difficult, he appointed certain men as "killers" while others were designated to protect them. Such an organized attack was different from a haphazard fight in which everyone shot. After this had been arranged the time was given over to the divinations by the medicine men, assisted by the singers. The following is the opening song which was sung by the singers for the medicine men, the purpose being to increase their power.

No. 130. Opening Song of the War Camp

(Catalogue No. 923)

Recorded by SIVARIANO GARCIA

WORDS

Hodunyĕ	gu̇sma	thahewa	gu̇tanı̆h
Night	coming down	sitting	in the night

kŭnyĕmaitha	miätha
my enemy	try to locate

Analysis.—This song is major in tonality with a special prominence of the sixth in the latter portion. It is interesting to note that if the opening of the song were in double time the third note would mark the beginning of the rhythmic unit. This shifting of accent is one of the most interesting peculiarities of Indian songs. Attention is directed to the descent of an octave in three measures and the descent of a seventh in two measures, as well as to the minor thirds at the close of this song.

It was said that one of the best medicine men was named Crow. On one occasion he was slow in taking his place with the other medicine men, so the following song was sung to call him. It is said that "when he heard this song he knew they really wanted him, so he came."

No. 131. "Help Us Locate Our Enemies"

(Catalogue No. 924)

Recorded by SIVARIANO GARCIA

TRANSLATION

Crow, hurry and come, sit down, help us locate our enemies.

Analysis.—This is a particularly interesting melody with its minor tonality and repeated whole tones at the close. The song has a compass of six tones, all of which occur in the melody. The keynote is the lowest and final tone. There is an effect of haste in the 3–8 measures which were sung in accurate time.

An interesting song which was not transcribed is that of a medicine man who was assisted by a humming bird. The words were as follows:

Ali	sicùnâŋ	gisok	makai
Little	green	humming bird	medicine man
tha	vùvùmiä	mùdùtha	kadolĕ
	together	running about	over there
nyĕmaitha	cùriŋkù	piähico	cùkithoicoä
my enemies	overtaking	nothing	in their minds

TRANSLATION

The little green bird and the medicine man together were running about over there, locating the enemy and causing their minds to have nothing in them.

Two other songs of this class were also recorded by Garcia, but were not transcribed.

SONG FOR THE WIND

Huvien.	wumia [36]	himtha	wumaci	gamuko	himtha
Wind	together	going	with him	far away	going
nyemaitha	kokopali	navukoi			
my enemies	face down	as if drunk			

TRANSLATION

A wind going with him, a wind going far away with him,
My enemies fall face downward on the ground as though drunk.

SONG FOR THE SPIRIT OWL

Komaŋ	cukona [37]	makai	thavùvùmiä	hĭmtha
Brownish gray	owl	medicine man	together	went
kadolĕ	nyĕmaitha	cùriŋakù	siöm	
over there	my enemies	overtaking	making	
kâkâsi				
sleepy				

TRANSLATION

The brown owl and the medicine man together went over there. They found my enemies, overtook them, and made them sleepy.

---

[36] In speech the terminal *ia* is omitted.
[37] The word used for owl in conversation is *cukot*.

The medicine men worked one at a time and each had his own songs. The singers knew these songs and when a man was at work they sang his songs, the purpose being to augment his power in this manner. The methods employed by the medicine men were somewhat individual. For example, one man was accustomed to set an arrow in his bow and point it first in one direction and then in another as if he intended to shoot the arrow. By this action he seemed to "test" the direction of the enemy. Some men used a wand, pointing it in the general direction of the enemy, and others extended their hands. A man might extend his right hand toward the enemy and his left hand behind him, giving signals to the singers. A certain man used a wand in this manner and it was his custom to move it up and down rapidly four times if he wanted the singers to sing faster and louder, doing this when he felt that he was finding the direction of the enemy and desired a strengthening of his power.

The idea of the next song is that the medicine man brings the enemy so near that the warriors can see them.

No. 132. Song for the Enemy's Country   (Catalogue No. 925)
Recorded by SIVARIANO GARCIA

VOICE ♩=92 (♪=184)

WORDS

Cyĕvŭt	miäwa	yuŭld	miäwa	nŭtha
The land	nearer	appears	in sight nearer	we can see

nyĕmaitha	miäwa	yuŭld
my enemies	nearer	appear in sight

Analysis.—This song is classified as major in tonality with D flat as its keynote, though it is a particularly free melody. The keynote is next to the highest tone in the song, which is unusual. There is an urging quality in the short phrases which have a descending trend. This effect is changed by the 5-8 measures and the song ends with an ascending progression which suggests a query.

One of the medicine men had power to summon a "spirit coyote" and send it forth as a spy. He sent the coyote early in the morning to see how the enemy could be attacked most effectively and said the attack should be made as soon as the coyote returned, which would be in a short time. The power of another medicine man lay in his ability to call the winds and clouds. The Apache would hear a wind, and clouds would gather with the noise of an approaching storm. This caused them to stay at home and the Papago made their attack before morning. The Chippewa and Sioux medicine man who accompanied a war party also sang songs to bring a storm so that the enemy would remain in their tents and the war party make an effective attack.

The following song of the Papago medicine men could be sung at the close of the *Limo*, as well as on the warpath.

No. 133. Song to Bring the Clouds   (Catalogue No. 926)

Recorded by SIVARIANO GARCIA

Voice ♩ = 112

WORDS

Cùwakiki	wùmiä	hĭmtha	wùmaci	gamùko
Clouds	together	going	with him	far away
hĭmtha	nyĕmaitha	zazakali	nanakĭ	
going	my enemies	staggering	as if crazy	

TRANSLATION

Heavy clouds going with him.
Clouds going far away.
Our enemies stagger as though drunk.

Analysis.—Two distinct rhythms occur in this song, one represented by the rhythmic unit and the other consisting chiefly of quarter notes. A curious interruption of rhythm occurs midway through the song. The second and third measures are duplicated in the tenth and twelfth (with a slight change in accent), while the ninth measure, with its double time, is inserted between them. The minor thirds at the close of the song are somewhat similar to those in No. 130. The song has a compass of six tones and is harmonic in structure.

When the medicine men said they had succeeded in locating the enemy it was customary for speeches to be made by the warriors. Any man who knew these speeches could rise and deliver them. After such a speech the men made a false charge, rushing forward against an imaginary enemy.

Mattias Encinas, father of the writer's interpreter, recited the two following speeches:

Speech No. 1

"Now, my relatives, you did not know that I knew this speech. It will surprise you that I stand here about to make this speech. The night has fallen. From above the top of my head comes down a great feathered bird (eagle) with noise like thunder and sits beside me. It has round leathers such as we put under the arms of our warriors. From above the top of my head a stiff-feathered bird comes down with thunder and sits at one side, with the stick that we cut for a club and put on the hip of our warriors. It was the black crow that came down from above with a great noise and sat, and by the favor of the black crow we have the bows and arrows that we hand our warriors. Oh, yes, it was Coyote that howled from his inside to give warning. It was by the favor of Coyote that we have bamboo arrows to hand to our warriors. Now, by the strength of all these I see the enemy's bows have strings of wind. We snatch them away. Now, by the strength of all these I see the sleep of our enemies like a dark cloud that we may be able to snatch them. Now, by the strength of all these I see the sandals of our enemies with the toes turned up like the end of an ear of corn, that we may be able to snatch them. Now, by the strength of all these I see the nice red painted arrows of our enemies as we grasp them. Now, as many rocks as there are and as many hills as there are and as many trees as there are, in spite of these we rush forward that we may be able to snatch the enemy. We pick them up like a ball and put it in the open palm of the medicine man and he groans and faces toward our distant home, but we will reach there soon ourselves with the scalps. There stands our ground, shaking with joy; there stands our mountain, thundering with joy; there stand our trees, shaking with joy. There any very old man wakes and walks and hears and sees as he has not done for years in joy for our victory."

After this speech the speaker sat down and anyone who knew the next speech had a chance to come forward and speak. Meantime the men, beginning at the right of the first speaker, addressed him by a term of relationship and said, "That is good," or commended him in some similar manner.

Speech No. 2

(The opening, as far as the mention of the eagle, is the same as in speech No. 1)

"It was the great white eagle, very anxious, with round leathers that he placed under his arm and the stick that we use for a club. He does not sleep but watches for the dawn. He is eager for action. He keeps acting as he will later act toward his enemies, shooting and threatening them."

After these speeches the men gathered up their belongings and went to the place where they camped. Soon after daylight they made the attack.

All the medicine men who accompanied a war party carried herbs for the care of the wounded, but used them only if singing and the exercise of "magic" power had failed. In that event a medicine man tried herbs and warm water, washing the wound or administering an herb drink. There was no singing with this treatment. When the man began to improve it was customary to apply a poultice to his wound, consisting of powdered root prepared either with or without water. The medicine man carried his herbs in a buckskin bag.

A war party returning victorious was always preceded by a herald who reached the village about daybreak. The man chosen for this duty was usually a good singer, but Hugh Norris said his father told of an instance in which the herald could not sing. This man made up a sort of song in which he said that he could not sing but the Papago were victorious, and then he began to yell, which spread the good news quite as effectively.

The song next following is concerning the man who announces the approach of a victorious war party.

No. 134. "The Voice of the Herald"

(Catalogue No. 1069)

Recorded by JUANA MARIA

TRANSLATION

When the morning starts and the sun comes up.
When the morning starts and the sun comes up.
At that time the voice of the herald sounds sweet.
It seems to be calling to me.

Analysis.—This song is transcribed with A as its keynote, although neither C sharp nor G sharp are present. This tone material is the first five-toned scale, according to Helmholtz's designation of pentatonic scales. Progression is chiefly by fourths and whole tones. The first six measures contain a downward trend of an octave. These are followed by a short rest and an ascending seventh. The rhythm changes and the last four measures have a ring of triumph, as though the herald were announcing a victory. The melody progresses chiefly by fourths and whole tones.

When the warriors approached the village the women, especially the relatives of warriors, went to meet them and receive the trophies they brought. The warriors danced on their way to the village, and on reaching the village they went to every house and danced. When this was finished they stopped until evening, when the scalp dance began. Captives, as well as scalps, were brought by the returning warriors, and the next song is concerning children taken captive among the Apache. The song has a dignity and pathos that are worthy of note.

No. 135. "The Little Captive Children"

(Catalogue No. 1062)

Recorded by VICTORIA

TRANSLATION

Men shouting "brother," men shouting "brother,"
Among the mountains they have taken little Apache children where
    the sun went down in sorrow,
All women, what shall we do to realize this?

Analysis.—The words and idea of this song are so unusual that we look for some peculiarity in the melody. We find that almost half the intervals are minor thirds, though the song is major in tonality, and that about 19 per cent of the intervals are fourths, while the major third does not occur. The last two measures, preceded by a rest and containing no progressions, are an admirable expression of the appeal contained in the final words of the song.

Warriors who had been wounded were taken to a quiet place at some distance from the camp, where they remained four days. By the end of that time it was known whether they would recover.

The warriors who killed Apache were required to undergo an ordeal of purification called lustration, during which they endured even greater hardships than on the warpath, thus expiating the crime of murder. The time of this ordeal was 16 days, divided into four periods of four days each. The entire time was called *Wowanda*, meaning "tying up." This term refers to the manner of putting the Apache scalp in a basket, which will be described. The warriors were taken to some secluded place and deprived of every comfort. They were allowed no warmth and no more bedding than when they were on the warpath. They could not even see a fire and a man who attended them was required to shield his cigarette so that they would not see its light. They wore their hair loose as though in mourning; were not allowed to scratch their bodies with their hands and were subject to many other rules. Each warrior was attended by a man of the tribe who brought him four pinches of pinole in a cup of water, morning, noon, and night, and also took him out for exercise every day. At first the attendant "walked the warrior" and then quickened the pace to a brisk run.

Four songs of this period were recorded, the second and third being transcribed. These were addressed to the warriors by old men who had charge of them during their retirement. The idea of the songs is, "You need not be proud of having killed Apache, for your hardest test is yet to come." The words of the first song are:

> Now we are going to learn something,
> You say you are brave, you say you are brave,
> Now we will learn whether you are brave,
> You will train yourself to endure hardship,
> All the tops of the mountains you will travel,
> You will have very little food or bedding,
> So we will learn whether you are brave.

A peculiar idiom occurs in the word "will travel," the word being the future tense, but the idea being that of a past action, referring to the recent experiences of the warrior.

It is said that a young man once complained of the treatment he was receiving and said to the old man in charge of the warriors, "You ought to treat us better; we are about sick." The following song contains the old man's reply.

No. 136 "You Beg for Food Like a Woman"

(Catalogue No. 1005)

Recorded by JOSE MANUEL

TRANSLATION

Now you are sitting here, acting like a woman, begging for food like a woman. You said you were brave and painted yellow spots on your head like a man, but now you talk like a woman.

Analysis.—A descent of a ninth is accomplished in the first five measures of this song, followed by a descending sixth in the next five measures, these phrases ending on the same tone. The final phrase resembles the second except for an ascending fourth at the close. The song contains no rhythmic unit and progresses chiefly by whole tones.

The third song of the group appears to continue the address of the old men.

No. 137. "I Have Gone Through This Before You"

(Catalogue No. 1004)

Recorded by JOSE MANUEL

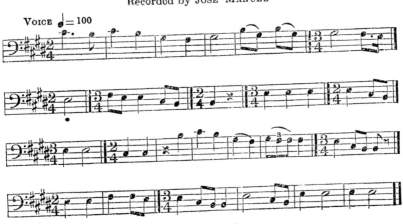

TRANSLATION

I have gone through all this before you,
I have run on the mountains and run on the plains with little food or clothing,
But I think of my shield that I use when I run up to the Apache and kill him,
I want you all to feel that way.

Analysis.—In the steady rhythm and frequent quarter notes of this song we feel the power and self-control expressed in the words. The tempo is more rapid than in a majority of songs in this group. The song is rhythmic but not thematic in character and is based on the fourth five-toned scale.

The fourth song of the group was not transcribed, but contains the following words:

> We sit here and sing, all of you feel brave, some of you
>   say that you are brave.
> Think of your club,
> Have it ready in your hand for use in danger,
> Your mind will shine ahead of you and tell you what to do.

These four songs are characterized by a repetition of a descending and ascending whole tone, and by the interval of a fourth. The songs not transcribed resemble those that are transcribed and the peculiarities of the group are not commonly noted in Papago songs.

While the wounded warriors and those who had killed Apache were in seclusion the remainder of the war party were leading a victory dance. The scalps of the Apache were placed on poles that were stuck in the ground and the people danced around them. Any member of the tribe might take one of the poles, dance with it, and return it to its place.

The two songs next following are songs of the scalp dance and were recorded by a man who had been to war against the Apache. The next song was sung by the warriors, and the last portion of the words may refer to the ordeal of purification already described.

No. 138. "Sing Louder"   (Catalogue No. 1002)

Recorded by JOSE MANUEL

TRANSLATION

Sing it so I will hear as you sing.
It is your own fault that will punish you for what you have done.

Analysis.—The tone material of this song is the fourth five-toned scale, commonly called the "major pentatonic." In the use of that scale by Gaelic peoples the sixteenth note followed by a dotted eighth is of frequent occurrence, and we find that count division in the present melody. Except for an ascending octave, the only progressions are minor thirds, whole tones, and fourths, the latter constituting about one-fourth of the intervals. It is an insistent melody with a compass of nine tones, beginning on the highest and ending on the lowest tone of the compass.

No. 139. "I Am Dancing"   (Catalogue No. 1003)

Recorded by Jose Manuel

TRANSLATION

I have jumped here and there.
While I am dancing I jump in another place.

Analysis.—The most interesting portion of this song lies in the descending quarter notes in the eighth measure. The first phrase is major in tonality, with the keynote as its highest tone, but the latter portion of the song is based on a minor third. It is interesting to note the prominence of D flat throughout the song, first in the upper and later in the lower octave. This is regarded as the keynote of the song, which contains the tones of the fourth five-toned scale.

The following song is concerning a time when the Apache pursued the Papago to a place where there were many springs.

No. 140. "A Place of Many Springs" (Catalogue No. 1019)

Recorded by RAFAEL MENDEZ

TRANSLATION

I am running on the side of the east.
The people began to push us to where the land has many springs.
There is where they left us.

Analysis.—This is one of the brightest, most attractive songs recorded among the Papago, and we seem to feel in it the joy of a desert people in the presence of water springs. They had been pursued by the enemy, but had come to a pleasant place. It is interesting to note the change of tempo occurring in the third from the last measure, followed by emphatic descending eighth notes. A dotted eighth note appears on both the accented and unaccented counts. The tone material is that of the fourth five-toned scale.

The next song was said to refer to an incident which took place in the wars with the Apache. A member of that tribe was either wounded or worn out with the long battle and was trying to escape. The Papago followed him with jeers and yells. The man repeatedly staggered and fell, then struggled to his feet and went a little farther, falling again. The Papago yelled whenever the man fell and finally killed him as he staggered, killing him before he reached the ground. Rafael Mendez asked that several sing with him when recording this song. One singer gave the "yells" which occurred at the points marked "X" in each rendition. These were shrill cries, about the duration of a quarter note of the song. It was said that the yells ought to have been given by a woman, as that was the custom of the tribe, the song growing louder as it progressed but the yells growing softer toward the end of the repetitions of the song. In this, as in numerous other instances, the musical customs of the Papago appear to have been more clearly defined than among other tribes under observation. The song had two sets of words, one of which appeared to be spoken by the Apache and the other by the pursuing Papago.

No. 141. Song Concerning a Wounded Apache

(Catalogue No. 1020)

Recorded by RAFAEL MENDEZ

WORDS

(First set of words, supposed to be spoken by the Apache)

Near sunset time I fall down,
Near sunset time I fall down,
I am going almost like a drunken man.

(Second set of words, indicating where war cries were given)

It is toward evening (yell), he falls (yell),
It is toward evening,
He falls, he staggers like a drunken man (yell).

Analysis.—This is an excellent example of a song on the first five-toned scale in which the third and seventh tones of the octave are omitted. A dotted eighth followed by a sixteenth note occurs frequently, and the song has the general effect associated with a five-toned scale. It begins and ends on the fifth, while the keynote appears only as an unaccented tone. The song is particularly vigorous except the final phrase, which is almost appealing. The triumphant yells of the warriors occur three times in the song.

The time required for the purification of Papago who had killed Apache was 16 days, the period being divided into four equal parts, as already described. On the evening of the sixteenth day the warriors bathed, braided their hair, painted their bodies, and went to the victory dance. This marked the beginning of the *Limo*, which lasted four days and was characterized by the final disposal of the Apache scalps. As the warriors advanced the people shouted and fired guns. Arrived at the place of the dance, the leader of the warriors took a shield and led the *Kapatowu* dance, jumping about and enacting scenes of the warpath.   Any one who wished could join him.   The warriors in turn took the shield and led the dance.   At this dance there were always two circles of dancers and there might be four or five different dances.   Thus a "wind dance" might be in progress during the *Limo*, four of these songs appearing as Nos. 144 to 147.

No. 142. Opening Song of the Limo

(Catalogue No. 1076)

Recorded by NUÑEZ

TRANSLATION

How did you kill?
Oh, how did you hang the scalp on the pole?

Analysis.—A sliding tone was employed throughout this song, which was the only song recorded by Nuñez.   The song is analyzed with D flat as its keynote, and the second and sixth (E flat and B flat) are strongly emphasized, a peculiarity that has been noted frequently in these songs.   Only two notes occur that are longer than a quarter note.   These are accented half notes and seem to balance the frequency of dotted eighths followed by sixteenths.   Both gourd rattles and basket drums were used with these songs.

The warriors then went to a place about 20 yards from the large dance circle, where, early the next morning, a special ceremony would be enacted.   A large fire was made and tended by the men who had waited upon the warriors during their period of fasting and who were experienced in their duties.   The men who had killed Apache sat together facing the east.   At some distance from them sat a group of men who had killed Apache on former expeditions and who sang their own dream songs.   Each man sang his song once or twice alone and then the others joined him.   These songs were Komotan and were said to be "sung for the benefit of the men who had been fasting."   The same songs were sung to cure the illnesses which were supposed to be caused by the spirits of dead Apache.   (See No. 71.) While these songs were being sung a man who had killed an Apache on a former expedition danced around the fire carrying a club and followed by four or five women. This action of the man was a severe test of his strength as he was required to keep it up until daybreak, jumping sidewise, up and down, trotting, dodging forward, falling down, and acting in every way as he had acted on the warpath. He carried whatever he had carried when on the warpath. Hugh Norris said he had seen such a man fall as though shot, then jump up and go on. The only time he stopped and walked was when he went over and put his hand on the heads of the men who had killed Apache, one after another. The singers were silent when he did this, and when it was completed he waved his hand as a signal for the singing to be resumed. When the singers were silent at other times he stood erect and danced on one foot. The women imitated his action, even trying to "jump in his tracks." They were not required to continue all night but could "change off" when they were tired.

In the early morning of the next day an Apache scalp and an effigy of an Apache was placed in a "spirit basket," to be kept and respected by each warrior who had killed an Apache. He assumed the care of this scalp as a serious responsibility, believing that sickness and evil would follow any neglect of his obligation to it. A "medicine basket" is described and illustrated by Frank Russell [39] and the writer's informant identified this as the type of basket used for containing an Apache scalp. Russell states, "Medicine baskets are the same material and style of weaving as the trinket basket." They are long, square cornered, with rounded margin, and are made in two nearly equal parts, one of which slips over the other as a lid. The effigy of the Apache was about 2 inches long, the dimensions of the basket allowing for a wrapping of cloth. It was made of a kind of mud that will not crack and the head was made of the sap that dries on greasewood. When this is soaked it becomes like glue and a face can be modeled in it. A tuft of white eagle down was put on the head. It sometimes took several men to kill an Apache and they all shared the honor, the scalp being cut into the proper number of pieces, a few hairs being sufficient to be put with the effigy. Thus the preparation for the Limo included the providing of the spirit baskets, the making of the effigies, and the count of the scalps (or portions of scalps), so there was one for each warrior who had shared in the killing of an Apache. The dividing of the scalps made it possible to provide for the spirit baskets and also have scalps for carrying in the victory dances.

An old medicine man had charge of the ceremony of placing the Apache effigies and scalps in the baskets. At the time of the ceremony he sat facing the warriors, holding the effigies and a corresponding number of Apache scalps or pieces of scalp. The warriors

[39] Op. cit., p. 145.

who had taken the scalps were seated in a row. Each had his spirit basket open before him on the ground, the cover being laid at one side of the basket with the ties spread underneath, ready to be quickly fastened. The medicine man took up a scalp and held it toward the Apache country. When an Apache spirit passed by he was aware of its presence and at once wrapped the scalp around the head of the effigy. He handed this to one of the warriors, who received it in both his hands and laid it very carefully, with both hands, in the spirit basket. In addition to the effigy, the basket contained a half-burned cigarette and "some sort of white clay made into dough." (When the Koöp songs were sung for the sick the owner of the basket took out this clay, moistened a little of it, and put it on the sick person. See p. 103.) When all the effigies had been thus placed the medicine man made a speech about the bravery of the warriors. At the conclusion of this speech he told them to take hold of the baskets, and they put on the covers simultaneously. Then the medicine man said, "I wrap one wrapping," and the men passed the cord once around the basket, all acting together. This was repeated four times and at the fourth time he said, "I tie and finish it," then they tied the last tie in the cord. Each man put his basket under his arm except the head warrior, who stood up, pointed the basket toward the sunrise, and remained standing until the sun was fully risen. It was said, "They tie the sun stripes together," referring to the streaks of light at dawn. (Cf. p. 188.)

The following song was sung at daybreak.

No. 143. Song of the Limo   (Catalogue No. 1071)
Recorded by HARRY ENCINAS

VOICE ♩ = 84

TRANSLATION

I will go inside to warm.
There we will sit a while and rub our tired legs.

Analysis.—In this song with its minor tonality and frequent semi-tones we seem to have an expression of the poignancy of the Limo, its significance and physical suffering. The two rhythmic units begin with the same count divisions. It is interesting to note that the seventh measure reverses the count divisions in the second rhythmic unit. The connective phrase shows a triplet on an unaccented count, this count division occurring on an accented count in the song.

The men who had taken care of the warriors then conducted them to a clear cold pond, breaking the ice if necessary. The men took a cold plunge, after which each man went to his own lodge, taking his spirit basket with him. It was kept in a safe place and frequently was placed in an olla. The responsibility incident to the possession of a spirit basket has been described on page 103. The *Limo* continued three more days. If the warriors who had killed Apache desired to attend these dances they wore no decorations except a horizontal line of black paint below each eye. Presents were given at these dances. The scalps that had been carried in the victory dances were taken to other villages and carried in one dance after another. Finally they were given to the warriors, who kept them.

A dance that was performed in one of the circles during the Limo was called the Wind dance. Four of its songs were recorded and are as follows.

No. 144. "I Am Going to Another Part of Elder Brother's Land"

(Catalogue No. 927)

Recorded by Sivariano Garcia

TRANSLATION

I am going to another part of Elder Brother's land,
I have reached the land,
With a handsome child (captive) I am returning.

Analysis.—The keynote of this song occurs only as the first tone and is also the highest tone of the compass. This is unique among Indian songs analyzed by the writer. The subdominant is a particularly prominent tone. Attention is directed to the third and fourth measures from the close which reverse the count divisions of the rhythmic unit.

No. 145. "A Whirlwind Is Singing"   (Catalogue No. 928)

Recorded by SIVARIANO GARCIA

VOICE ♩ = 112 (♪ = 224)
Irregular in tonality

TRANSLATION

Where is that bird going, where is that bird going?
With that bird I whirl around, whirl around higher and higher,
Just before we touch the sky, the bird faints and falls to the earth.
(This song was said to be concerning the "wind-grandson-bird")

Analysis.—This song is classified as irregular in tonality and transcribed without signature. Other songs thus transcribed and classified are Nos. 8, 12, 14, 24, 31, 33, 36, 88, and 119. The interval of a fourth which constitutes the framework of many irregular songs does not appear in this melody. The opening phrase is outlined by the interval of a fifth, the second by a fourth, and the third by a major third, each consecutive phrase being based on a smaller interval. The closing measures are on a minor third. Thus the principal melody tones are those of a minor triad and seventh but they are not used in such a manner as to suggest the lowest as the important tone. Two entirely different units of rhythm occur, the longer being in the first portion and the shorter in the latter portion of the song.

No. 146. "It Is the Woodpecker"   (Catalogue No. 929)

Recorded by SIVARIANO GARCIA

TRANSLATION

Who is that bird flying over there?
Oh, it is the woodpecker,
He does not seem to want to go anywhere,
He cries and pecks at a cactus.

Analysis.—It will be noted that the first seven measures of this song are like those of the song next preceding except for the pitch, which is a semitone higher. The preceding song is concerning a whirlwind and this is concerning a woodpecker. We might expect a wide difference in the form of the melodies but this is not present. We note, however, a succession of whole tones at the close of this song, which may suggest the monotonous tap of the woodpecker. This succession is the more interesting as the tones are the keynote and seventh. A clear distinction of time was made between the 3–8 measure and the triplet of eighth notes that follows it.

No. 147. "The Eagle Is Talking"   (Catalogue No. 930)

Recorded by SIVARIANO GARCIA

VOICE ♩ = 112

TRANSLATION

The eagle is on the highest point of rocks,
He is talking,
I was walking below and I heard the sound echo among the rocks.

Analysis.—The melodic formation of this song is unusual. The song begins with a half note on the highest tone of the compass. This tone is the keynote and it does not occur again in the song. The tone material is that of the second five-toned scale, and the interval of a whole tone between the seventh and eighth is prominent, as in several other Papago war songs.

At the last of the dances attendant upon the Limo it was made known when the races would be held. The races were the next event, and a reasonable time elapsed between the two. There was no dancing during this time.

SONGS OF THE KICKING-BALL RACES

The principal athletic contests of the Papago were the kicking-ball races in which each contestant kicked before him a wooden ball. Russell states that "the use of these balls in foot races is very widespread in the Southwest, and even yet we hear of races taking place that exceed 20 miles in length. The kicking ball, when of wood, resembles a croquet ball in size, but it is usually covered with a coating of creosote gum. These balls are made of mesquite or paloverde wood. . . . Stone balls . . . are also used, covered with the same black gum. . . . Each contestant kicks one of these balls before him, doing it so skilfully that his progress is scarcely delayed." [40]   Only two men ran at a time. Sometimes they ran

[40] Frank Russell, op. cit., pp. 172–173.

the entire distance in one direction and sometimes they ran to a given point and back again.

There is a tradition that a certain man wanted to be a good racer, so he ran every day, starting before daylight and returning when the sun rose. He worked very hard at this for a long time. One morning he met something on the road that said, "It seems as though you would never be a good runner but I will give you a song and perhaps if you sing this song you will win the race." The man learned the song, sang it, and won the race. Afterwards he used it as a dancing song in the Bat dance. He wore a feather of the blue hawk in his headband before he received this song, and believed that it assisted him in obtaining the song.

No. 148. "We Must Run"   (Catalogue No. 978)

Recorded by MATTIAS HENDRICKS

TRANSLATION

Now be ready, my poor brother, and we will start to run,
Now before us our nice ball goes far,
After it we run,
No matter what kind of ground there is,
We must run over it.

Analysis.—This song is entirely different in character from the preceding group, in accordance with its use. It is a lively melody with a simple rhythmic unit which is frequently repeated. The fourth is an interval associated with motion, and this interval constitutes 16 of the 50 intervals in this song. The compass of the song is nine tones, with the keynote about midway, and the melody moves freely between the highest and lowest tones.

It is said that medicine men were able to secure success for a racer by the use of their psychic power. The following is the song of such a man, seeking success for a friend. The words of this song were not recorded.

No. 149. Song for Success in a Race

(Catalogue No. 993)

Recorded by MATTIAS HENDRICKS

Analysis.—This song is more serious in character than the preceding. It opens with two rather wistful phrases but becomes more confident at the ninth measure. A feeling of uncertainty reappears in the last two measures. It is interesting to note the frequency with which an accented tone is approached by an ascending progression. The ninth and sixteenth measures are rendered more effective by the preceding eighth rest and ascent of a fourth. The ascending and descending intervals are about equal in number (11 and 12), which is unusual in Indian songs.

SONGS OF THE BAT DANCE

This dance is seldom held at the present time but was witnessed by the writer on the night of December 25, 1920. In order to see this, it was necessary to go about 90 miles from a town and 10 miles from Vomari village where songs were recorded. Men and women joined in this dance, moving in a circle and holding hands but not facing steadily inward. They walked behind one another, the line being led by a man who carried a gourd rattle in his right hand, shaking it in time to the music. All sang, and emphasized the song by stamping with the right foot. There was a leader of the singers as well as of the dancers.   The accompanying instrument was a basket, inverted on the ground in the middle of the circle and struck with the palm of the hand by men seated around it.   Sometimes the basket was struck with both hands, but if several men were seated around it each struck it with his right hand.

In the Bat dance the songs were sung by both men and women, the latter singing an octave higher.   During a portion of the song one or two women took a high tone and sustained it as a drone, then descended to the pitch of the other women's voices, using several intermediate tones in the descent.   It was said that only a few women could sing this drone, which appeared to be regarded as an embellishment to the song.   (See p. 14.)

According to Hugh Norris the Bat dance originated with a man who was stricken with grief at the death of his wife.   He was lying on the ground when he felt something touch him.   The visitants told him that he would have this dance and would be happy when the people were dancing with him.   They said, "Do you know what touched you?   We are the bats."   So he called it the Bat dance and he himself goes by the name of Bat.   He received the first Bat dance songs in his dream.

No. 150. Opening Song of the Bat Dance

(Catalogue No. 1051)

Recorded by JOSE ASCENCIO

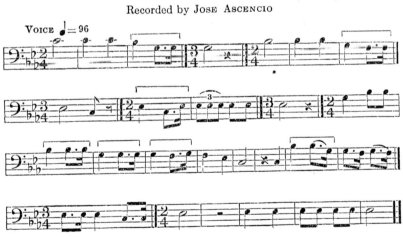

TRANSLATION

Now the songs are going to begin and I am going away.
All over the mountains and on top of the mountains I sing.
Ajo mountain, on top of it I am singing and walking around.

Analysis.—The first note of this song is the highest tone and the only occurrence of the keynote, a peculiarity noted also in No. 147. Five rests occur in the song, one being the duration of an entire measure.   The phrases, as outlined by these rests, are from three to six measures in length. The song is based on the second five-toned scale and contains only two intervals larger than a minor third.

A different origin was attributed to the dance by Mattias Hendricks, of Vomari village, who said it is associated with the foot races. According to Hendricks a certain man found that he could not be a good runner. He had a dream in which a man took him to the sea. As they walked beside the sea they saw a crowd of people dancing. The men stopped at some distance from the dancers and the escort said, "Stay here and listen to the songs they sing." When morning came the man woke and found he had been dreaming. The same dream returned four times, after which the unsuccessful runner started the Bat dance. Two songs were recorded and are the property of Kaäcok. The bats always fly in the warm evening and again in the early morning, and the songs are those of the evening and morning.

No. 151. "My Wings Make a Noise as I Fly"

(Catalogue No. 994)

Recorded by MATTIAS HENDRICKS

TRANSLATION

The evening looked red and I came out. Into all the houses I went and my wings are making a noise as I fly around in the house.

Analysis.—Almost half the intervals in this song are semitones and the minor third occurs only once. The song is harmonic in structure. Two rhythmic units occur, the second reversing the count divisions of the first unit.

The morning song was not transcribed but contained these words: "In the early morning I come out and fly all over the top of the mountain. The morning shines clear down to where the sun sets but leaves a little bit of darkness there."

DREAM SONGS

The next song was received in a dream by a Papago woman who had been taken captive by the Apache. Two women were captured by Apache warriors at a place called Big Pond. The Apache were traveling toward a mountain called Omakam. While they were camped the women escaped and afterwards one of them dreamed this song.

No. 152. Dream Song of a Captive Woman

(Catalogue No. 1048)

Recorded by JOSE ASCENCIO

TRANSLATION

When I got to the side of the mountain my heart began to give out.

Analysis.—It is interesting to note the descending series of tones in this song. There is a descending seventh in measures 6 to 10, a descending sixth in the two measures after the next rest, and a descending fifth in the next three measures. The tone material is that of the fourth five-toned scale. The song begins and ends on the fifth, occurring about midway of its compass. It is a pleasing melody with a rather appealing quality.

An old man named Victoria recorded three songs which he had received in dreams. In two songs he seems to have been wandering in the mountains while in the third he went to the "edge of the world." The second of these songs was received many years after the first song came to him.

106041°—29——15

No. 153. "I Wandered Away"   (Catalogue No. 1055)

Recorded by VICTORIA

TRANSLATION

Where the mountain crosses.
On top of the mountain, I do not myself know where.
I wandered where my mind and my heart seemed to be lost.
I wandered away.

Analysis.—The compass of this song is 12 tones, which is unusual in Papago songs. The time changes frequently and no secondary accent was given in the quadruple measure. The tempo is slow and the song is gentle and pleasing. The tone A is regarded as the keynote, though its third does not occur in the song.

No. 154. "I Am Going to the Mountain"

(Catalogue No. 1054)

Recorded by VICTORIA

TRANSLATION

Away off to the mountains where I am going.
I do not know where I am going.

Analysis.—The same tone material and extended compass which characterized the song next preceding are found in this, but the rhythm is entirely different. Two rhythmic units occur, the second reversing the note values of the first. A sliding of the voice was used in progressions from a higher to a lower tone. The phrases are short and the melody moves with a wide freedom and is particularly pleasing.

No. 155. "I Went to the Edge of the World"

(Catalogue No. 1057)

Recorded by VICTORIA

TRANSLATION

I went down to the edge of the world and from there I saw in the east where the morning was breaking. I saw white stripes.

Analysis.—This is a lively melody in the fourth five-toned scale, with a dotted eighth occurring on both accented and unaccented counts. It is interesting to note that if the opening measures were in double time we should have an additional occurrence of the rhythmic unit. The interval of a fourth occurs four times, which is not a large proportion of this interval in a song suggesting a long journey. The song consists of four periods of different lengths, the final period being more quiet than the preceding portion of the song.

The next song was received in a dream by Victoria's uncle.

No. 156. "The Thunder Sounds in the East"

(Catalogue No. 1056)

Recorded by VICTORIA

TRANSLATION

Back in the east there is a sound like thunder.
There was a great sound in the east where the thunders were sounding.

Analysis.—A sliding tone was used throughout this melody, which has a range of nine tones and is based on the fourth five-toned scale. The song contains an unusual variety of thematic material. Two phrases are designated as rhythmic units, the second reversing the note values of the first, but these contain only a small part of the rhythmic interest of the song. The final phrase, ending with an ascending fourth, has an effect of something unfulfilled, an effect noted also in Nos. 149 and 153.

The singer said that he learned the next Dream song from his mother.

No. 157. "White Mountain Birds were Singing"

(Catalogue No. 1059)

Recorded by VICTORIA

TRANSLATION

White mountain birds were singing sweetly in the east. It sounded like thunders where he was singing.

Analysis.—This song is characterized by a sixteenth note followed by a dotted eighth prolonged a quarter note value. This occurs on both accented and unaccented counts. The periods are long and the rhythm is continuous, not being broken into shorter phases. The compass is nine tones and, as in several other songs of this group, the final interval is an ascending fourth.

No. 158. "A Black Crow"   (Catalogue No. 1060)

Recorded by VICTORIA

TRANSLATION

A crow came down from above to this earth,
A black crow came down from above to this earth,
He was jumping on me.

Analysis.—This is one of the most pleasing melodies recorded among the Papago. Its movement is free and graceful, it has a compass of 10 tones, and is based on the fourth five-toned scale. The most frequent intervals are fourths and whole tones. The song is characterized by a continuous motion contrasted with the rhythmic periods into which a majority of these songs are divided.

No. 159. "I Sat Under Santa Rita Mountains"

(Catalogue No. 1061)

Recorded by VICTORIA

TRANSLATION

I was under Santa Rita Mountains.
I sat there and thought of things far away, in distant parts of the world.

Analysis.—A varied rhythm characterizes this song. The opening phrase contains only descending intervals and is three measures in length. The second phrase begins on the same high tone and is seven measures long. This is followed by a phrase of three measures, after which the rhythm is maintained without a pause to the end of the song. As in many dream songs, the final interval is an ascending fourth. The song has a compass of nine tones and is based on the fourth five-toned scale.

HUNTING SONGS

The singing of a song and smoking of an herb to attract game is a Papago custom and was noted also in the study of Chippewa and Menominee songs. Three plant substances thus used by the Chippewa are the roots of the *Arctostaphylos uva-ursi, Aster novæ angliæ* L., and *Aster puniceus* L., while the Papago use *pihol* flowers, mixed with tobacco. This is indicated in the words of a song recorded by Jose Manuel and not transcribed: "The morning is breaking. I have my bows and arrows ready. I run to a little hill. On top of it I sat down. I shot at him and wounded him. I used a little *pihol* flower which made it easy for me to catch the wounded deer."

The song next following was sung to insure success on the hunt and also to cure the illness of a child whose father had disobeyed certain rules before its birth. The father of an unborn child was restricted in conduct when on the war path and also when hunting. If he saw the motions of the deer when it was dying, or cut certain parts of the deer when preparing the meat, his child, when about 2 years old, would make the sounds and motions of a dying deer.

Observing this, the people asked the father if he had done either of these things, and if he admitted his fault they sent for a man who could sing the following song.   It was not considered necessary to send for a medicine man, as the cause of the trouble and its cure were known.   The man mixed dried *pihol* flowers with tobacco and smoked the mixture as he treated the child.

No. 160. Song for Success in Hunting

(Catalogue No. 1013)

Recorded by JOSE MANUEL

TRANSLATION

We sit here by our camp fire and start to sing our hunting song.   I can clearly see the points of the deer's ears on top of the hill.   We smoke the *pihol* flowers that make the night clear, so I can see the points of the deer's ears on the hill.

Analysis.—Two rhythmic units occur in this song, the second reversing the note values of the first.   The song is based on the fourth five-toned scale and about one-third of the intervals are fourths.

No. 161. Song of an Unsuccessful Hunter

(Catalogue No. 1018)

Recorded by JOSE MANUEL

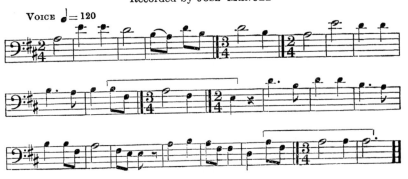

TRANSLATION

I am walking a great deal.
I am sorry I can not find any game.
I saw lots of tracks, especially on the east side of the mountain, but I
    found nothing.

Analysis.—This is a particularly pleasing melody. The keynote is D, but the most prominent tone is A. The song is major in tonality but contains only one major third; the interval of a fifth occurs four times, which is an unusual frequency for this interval. The time is more rapid than in a majority of Papago songs.

SONGS FOR THE ENTERTAINMENT OF CHILDREN

In a majority of the tribes whose songs have been recorded a lullaby has been obtained. The following is quite different from that of the other tribes. The *gisuk* was said to be "a funny little gray bird that runs on the ground." It was not identified.

No. 162. Lullaby   (Catalogue No. 1068)

Recorded by JUANA MARIA

TRANSLATION

Gisuk, black-headed gisuk.
Run and come so the baby's eyes will go to sleep.

Analysis.—This simple melody is based on the minor triad and fourth. The descending minor third G–E occurs eight times, giving a somewhat plaintive character to the song. The rhythmic unit differs slightly in its recurrences but the differences are probably due to the words. Attention is directed to the fourth and fifth measures which resemble the second and part of the third measures but show a change of accent. A similar phrase occurs near the close of the song. Thirty-four of the thirty-nine progressions are whole tones and minor thirds. Ascending and descending intervals are more nearly equal in number than in a majority of the songs under analysis.

The singer said, " An old grandmother used to sing this song when she was taking care of the baby."

No. 163. "The Squirrel and the Mesquite Beans"

(Catalogue No. 1052)

Recorded by JOSE ASCENCIO

TRANSLATION

Now the beans begin to appear on the mesquite trees. Ground squirrel does not want to wait until the beans are ripe, so he climbs the trees, gets the beans, and scatters them green under the tree.

Analysis.—The characteristic of this song is a succession of ascending and descending intervals of about the same size, giving an effect of motion and agility. The same peculiarity has been noted in songs concerning animals recorded in other tribes.[41] The song has a compass of seven tones and the tone material is that of the fourth five-toned scale.

---

41 See Bur. Amer. Ethn. Bulls. 53, p. 100; 61, p. 54; 75, p. 200.

The following song is similar to the preceding one. It should be remembered that the robin goes to southern Arizona at the beginning of their cold weather, being a harbinger of winter instead of a sign of spring, as in northern climes.

No. 164. "The Robin Brings the Cold Wind"

(Catalogue No. 1053)

Recorded by JOSE ASCENCIO

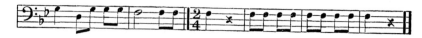

TRANSLATION

The robin spreads the green wind on us.
He spreads the coldest wind on us.
Now knock him down with a stick.

Analysis.—The tone material of this song is the fourth five-toned scale. The song begins and ends on the fifth and has a compass of seven tones. One-third of the progressions are fourths, an interval which has been found to characterize songs concerning birds and animals. The rhythm of the song is characterized by a succession of eighth notes but these appear in so many connections that they can scarcely be said to constitute a rhythmic unit. The song contains no note values except eighth and quarter notes.

MISCELLANEOUS SONGS

It is said that long ago an old woman who lived in a village back of Santa Rita Moutains received many songs. The following song came to her during a severely cold winter. "The people were so cold that they did not talk, they just sat around the fire and wondered what would happen to them. This old woman sat and thought and wondered, for old people can not stand much cold. Then this song came to her."

No. 165. "The Snow Is Falling" (Catalogue No. 1067)

Recorded by LEONARDO RIOS

TRANSLATION

No talking, no talking,
The snow is falling,
And the wind seems to be blowing backward (circling back again).

Analysis.—The structure of this song is unusually interesting. The keynote appears to be A, and the melody tones consist chiefly of the minor triad on A, with an occasional descent to F. About two-thirds of the intervals are major thirds, though the song is classified as minor in tonality. The rhythm shows a short, fluttering phrase alternating with a longer phrase which suggests calmness and self-control.

The song next following is somewhat humorous in character and is one of the few songs recorded by a woman.

No. 166. "I Met a Mexican"   (Catalogue No. 1070)

Recorded by JUANA MARIA

TRANSLATION

While I was running I met a Mexican who said,
"How do you do?"
While I was running I met a Mexican with a long beard who said,
"How do you do?"

Analysis.—This song is humorous in character and the question expressed in the words is reflected in the two final ascending intervals. No difference was found in the repetitions of the song, the 7–8 measures being given in exact time. The melody tones are those of the fourth five-toned scale. The song opens with a fifth (F sharp-C sharp) in ascending progression, followed by a descending fifth (F sharp-B), the latter occurring in descending and then in ascending progression at the close of the song. An unusual variety of intervals occurs in this melody.

The humor of the following song would appeal to adults more than to children. It was said to be "sung for fun." (Cf. the tiswin custom, p. 152.)

No. 167. "The Pigeon and His Tiswin Lodge"

(Catalogue No. 1034)

Recorded by JOSE HENDRICKS

TRANSLATION

The pigeon pretended that he was setting up a tiswin lodge. The frog doctor drank his wine, got drunk and shouted, and pulled out his cloud.

Analysis.—The intervals in this song are major and minor thirds and major and minor seconds, the first named being the most frequent. There is a taunting, teasing effect in the melody which is also humorous in character. The song is major in tonality and contains all the tones of the octave except the second.

FLUTE MELODY 1

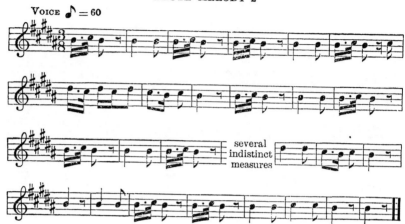

FLUTE MELODY 2

Voice ♪ = 60

several indistinct measures

MELODIC AND RHYTHMIC ANALYSIS OF SONGS BY SERIAL NUMBERS

MELODIC ANALYSIS

TABLE 1.—TONALITY

	Serial numbers of songs	Number	Per cent
Major tonality [1]	4, 6, 13, 16, 17, 23, 27, 28, 37, 48, 51, 52, 57, 58, 59, 60, 61, 71, 72, 73, 74, 75, 76, 77, 78, 79, 80, 81, 82, 83, 84, 87, 89, 91, 93, 95, 96, 97, 104, 105, 107, 108, 110, 111, 112, 113, 114, 115, 116, 117, 123, 124, 125, 126, 127, 130, 132, 133, 135, 136, 137, 138, 139, 140, 142, 148, 152, 155, 156, 157, 158, 159, 160, 161, 163, 164, 166, 167.	78	47
Minor tonality [2]	1, 7, 9, 11, 18, 19, 20, 21, 22, 25, 26, 29, 30, 32, 34, 38, 39, 40, 41, 42, 43, 44, 45, 47, 49, 50, 54, 55, 56, 62, 63, 64, 65, 66, 67, 68, 69, 70, 90, 92, 98, 99, 101, 102, 106, 118, 120, 121, 122, 128, 129, 131, 143, 144, 146, 147, 149, 150, 151, 162, 165.	61	36
Both major and minor	46, 85.	2	1
Third lacking	2, 3, 5, 10, 15, 35, 53, 86, 94, 100, 103, 109, 134, 141, 153, 154.	16	10
Irregular [3]	8, 12, 14, 24, 31, 33, 36, 88, 119, 145.	10	6
Total		167	

[1] Songs are thus classified if the third is a major third and the sixth a major sixth above the keynote.
[2] Songs are thus classified if the third is a minor third and the sixth a minor sixth above the keynote.
[3] Songs are thus classified if the tones do not have an apparent relation to a keynote. In such songs the tones appear to be arranged with reference to intervals rather than with reference to a keynote, many being based on the interval of a fourth.

TABLE 2.—FIRST NOTE OF SONG—ITS RELATION TO KEYNOTE

	Serial numbers of songs	Number	Per cent
Beginning on the—			
Tenth	71	1	
Octave	20, 48, 49, 50, 68, 103, 120, 122, 138, 147, 150	11	6
Seventh	1, 22, 67	3	1
Sixth	32, 46, 51, 52, 59, 61, 66, 99, 104, 131, 136, 137, 140, 153, 167	15	9
Fifth	3, 4, 15, 17, 18, 27, 28, 41, 44, 55, 56, 58, 60, 62, 65, 70, 72, 73, 74, 75, 77, 78, 79, 80, 81, 82, 83, 87, 89, 93, 95, 96, 97, 100, 101, 102, 105, 107, 108, 109, 111, 113, 115, 117, 121, 124, 126, 129, 133, 134, 135, 141, 142, 143, 144, 148, 152, 157, 158, 161, 163, 164, 166.	63	37
Fourth	47, 106, 154	3.	1
Third	6, 19, 23, 26, 34, 38, 39, 40, 42, 98, 118, 127, 155, 156, 159, 162	16	10
Second	10, 53, 123, 126, 132	5	3
Keynote	2, 5, 7, 9, 11, 13, 16, 21, 25, 29, 30, 35, 37, 43, 45, 54, 57, 63, 64, 69, 76, 84, 85, 86, 90, 91, 92, 94, 110, 112, 114, 116, 128, 130, 139, 146, 149, 151, 160, 165.	40	24
Irregular	8, 12, 14, 24, 31, 33, 36, 88, 119, 145	10	6
Total		167	

TABLE 3.—LAST NOTE OF SONG—ITS RELATION TO KEYNOTE

	Serial numbers of songs	Number	Per cent
Ending on the—			
Fifth	1, 3, 4, 6, 10, 19, 25, 26, 27, 28, 30, 37, 38, 46, 53, 58, 59, 60, 61, 72, 73, 74, 75, 77, 78, 79, 80, 81, 82, 83, 87, 89, 91, 93, 95, 96, 97, 100, 103, 104, 105, 107, 108, 109, 111, 112, 113, 115, 117, 121, 123, 125, 126, 127, 132, 134, 135, 138, 141, 144, 148, 152, 153, 154, 155, 156, 157, 158, 159, 161, 163, 164, 166, 167.	74	44
Third	13, 17, 22, 23, 37, 48, 49, 50, 51, 57, 68, 71, 118, 120, 122, 133, 150	15	9
Keynote	2, 5, 7, 9, 11, 15, 16, 18, 20, 21, 29, 32, 34, 35, 39, 40, 41, 42, 43, 44, 45, 47, 51, 52, 54, 55, 56, 62, 63, 64, 65, 66, 67, 69, 70, 76, 84, 85, 86, 90, 92, 94, 98, 99, 101. 102, 106, 110, 114, 116, 124, 128, 129, 130, 131, 136, 137, 139, 140, 142, 143, 146, 147, 149, 151, 160, 162, 165.	68	41
Irregular	8, 12, 14, 24, 31, 33, 36, 88, 119, 145	10	6
Total		167	

TABLE 4.—LAST NOTE OF SONG—ITS RELATION TO COMPASS OF SONG

	Serial numbers of songs	Number	Per cent
Songs in which final note is—			
Lowest tone in song	1, 6, 20, 21, 25, 26, 28, 30, 34, 38, 47, 63, 66, 104, 131, 138, 143, 162.	18	10
Immediately preceded by—			
Fourth below	29, 41, 45, 52, 64, 65, 76, 109, 153, 164	10	6
Major third below	55, 62, 71	3	2
Minor third below	7, 48, 49, 50, 51, 68, 72, 73, 74, 75, 77, 78, 79, 119	14	8
Whole tone below	53, 69	2	1
Fifth and containing two other tones below.	115, 158	2	1
Fourth and containing a fourth below.	32, 70, 80, 85, 88, 94, 151	7	4
Fourth and containing fourth and minor third below.	5, 9, 39, 58, 60, 110, 113, 121, 124, 156, 157, 159, 160	13	8
Fourth and containing one to four other tones below.	18, 27, 111, 125, 134, 135, 136, 137, 149	9	5
Major third and containing major third below.	54, 86, 90, 91, 92, 93, 165	7	4
Major third and containing other tones below.	43	1	-----
Minor third and containing minor third below.	4, 12, 22, 36, 81, 82, 83, 84, 87, 89, 107, 117, 118, 120, 122, 139, 142, 145, 150, 155.	20	17
Minor third and containing fourth and minor third below.	2, 8, 11, 13, 23, 35, 59, 61, 112, 114, 130, 132	12	7
Minor third and containing other tones below.	126, 133, 148, 152, 161, 166, 167	7	4
Whole tone and containing one to four other tones below.	3, 10, 15, 17, 31, 44, 46, 67, 101, 103, 105, 129, 144, 146, 147, 154	16	9
Half tone and containing half tone below.	19, 95, 96, 97	4	2
Songs containing tones lower than final tone.	14, 16, 24, 35, 37, 40, 42, 56, 57, 98, 99, 100, 102, 106, 108, 116, 123, 127, 128, 140, 141, 163.	22	13
Total		167	-----

TABLE 5.—NUMBER OF TONES COMPRISED IN COMPASS OF SONG

	Serial numbers of songs	Number	Per cent
Twelve tones	105, 153	2	1
Eleven tones	106, 109, 110, 138	4	2
Ten tones	13, 67, 71, 108, 139, 158	6	3
Nine tones	9, 14, 17, 32, 41, 52, 64, 101, 103, 104, 111, 112, 115, 121, 123, 125, 135, 136, 137, 147, 148, 151, 156, 157, 159, 161, 166.	27	13
Eight tones	1, 2, 4, 5, 8, 11, 15, 18, 20, 22, 23, 25, 27, 29, 30, 31, 35, 45, 48, 49, 50, 51, 58, 60, 61, 65, 68, 70, 72, 73, 74, 75, 76, 77, 80, 81, 82, 83, 85, 86, 87, 88, 89, 93, 94, 99, 100, 102, 107, 113, 114, 117, 119, 120, 122, 124, 126, 130, 132, 134, 140, 141, 142, 149, 150, 152, 155.	67	40
Seven tones	19, 24, 26, 28, 38, 39, 53, 56, 59, 62, 69, 78, 79, 84, 90, 91, 92, 95, 96, 97, 116, 118, 127, 129, 145, 154, 163, 164, 165.	29	18
Six tones	6, 7, 10, 12, 16, 33, 37, 40, 42, 43, 44, 46, 57, 66, 128, 131, 133, 143, 160, 167.	20	12
Five tones	3, 21, 47, 54, 55, 63, 98, 144, 146, 162	10	6
Four tones	36	1	-----
Three tones	34	1	-----
Total		167	-----

TABLE 6.—TONE MATERIAL

	Serial numbers of songs	Number	Per cent
First five-toned scale	2, 5, 10, 35, 86, 100, 103, 109, 134, 141, 153, 154	12	8
Second five-toned scale	18, 22, 47, 50, 56, 68, 70, 106, 118, 120, 122, 147, 150	13	8
Fourth five-toned scale	4, 6, 16, 17, 33, 48, 51, 52, 57, 58, 60, 61, 72, 73, 74, 75, 77, 78, 79, 80, 81, 84, 87, 89, 91, 93, 104, 105, 107, 113, 117, 123, 124, 130, 135, 136, 137, 138, 139, 140, 152, 155, 156, 157, 158, 159, 160, 163, 164, 166.	50	30
Major triad and sixth	82	1	-----
Minor triad and fourth	47, 149, 162	3	2
Minor triad and second	21, 29, 30, 40, 42, 44, 45, 63, 64, 90	10	6
Octave complete	1, 38, 59, 67, 125, 129, 132	7	4
Octave complete except seventh.	23, 25, 27, 28, 32, 39, 83, 95, 96, 97, 108, 110, 112, 114, 116, 126, 127, 142.	18	10
Octave complete except seventh and sixth.	7, 19, 26, 76, 131, 144, 146	7	4
Octave complete except seventh and fourth.	9, 11, 20, 41, 43, 55, 62, 65, 66, 69, 92, 99, 121, 143, 151, 165	16	9
Octave complete except seventh and third.	86	1	-----
Octave complete except seventh, fifth, and fourth.	54, 98	2	1
Octave complete except seventh, fourth, and second.	37	1	-----
Octave complete except sixth.	101, 102, 111, 128, 133	5	3
Octave complete except fourth.	13, 115	2	1
Octave complete except fourth and second.	71, 119	2	1
Octave complete except third.	15, 53, 94	3	2
Octave complete except second.	167	1	-----
Minor third and second	43	1	-----
Both major and minor in tonality.	46, 85	2	1
Irregular	8, 12, 14, 24, 31, 33, 36, 88, 119, 145	10	6
Total		167	-----

TABLE 7.—ACCIDENTALS

	Serial numbers of songs	Number	Per cent
Songs containing—			
No accidentals		147	88
Sixth raised a semitone	86, 143, 146	3	2
Fourth raised a semitone.	15, 19, 84, 133	4	3
Third raised a semitone	85	1	
Third lowered a semitone.	112, 126	2	1
Irregular	8, 12, 14, 24, 31, 33, 36, 88, 119, 145	10	6
Total		167	

TABLE 8.—STRUCTURE

	Serial numbers of songs	Number	Per cent
Melodic	3, 4, 5, 8, 9, 12, 13, 14, 15, 16, 18, 19, 22, 23, 24, 25, 28, 31, 33, 34, 35, 36, 37, 38, 39, 42, 43, 44, 46, 47, 48, 49, 50, 51, 52, 53, 54, 55, 56, 58, 59, 60, 61, 62, 64, 65, 66, 67, 72, 73, 76, 78, 80, 81, 83, 84, 85, 86, 88, 90, 92, 93, 94, 95, 96, 97, 98, 99, 100, 102, 103, 104, 105, 106, 107, 108, 109, 110, 111, 112, 114, 116, 117, 118, 119, 120, 123, 125, 126, 127, 128, 129, 130, 131, 132, 134, 135, 136, 137, 138, 139, 140, 141, 142, 144, 145, 146, 148, 149, 150, 152, 153, 154, 156, 157, 158, 159, 160, 161, 162, 163, 164.	122	73
Melodic with harmonic framework.	1, 2, 6, 10, 11, 17, 20, 21, 26, 27, 29, 30, 32, 40, 45, 57, 68, 71, 74, 75, 77, 79, 82, 89, 91, 101, 115, 121, 122, 124, 143, 147, 155, 165, 166, 167.	36	21
Harmonic	7, 41, 63, 69, 70, 87, 133, 141, 151	9	6
Total		167	

TABLE 9.—FIRST PROGRESSION—DOWNWARD AND UPWARD

	Serial numbers of songs	Number	Per cent
Downward	6, 8, 10, 15, 17, 18, 19, 20, 22, 32, 34, 37, 41, 44, 45, 48, 49, 50, 51, 52, 56, 62, 65, 66, 67, 68, 70, 71, 98, 99, 101, 102, 104, 105, 106, 108, 109, 119, 120, 122, 123, 124, 125, 127, 129, 131, 132, 133, 136, 137, 138, 139, 140, 144, 147, 150, 153, 154, 155, 156, 159.	61	37
Upward	1, 2, 3, 4, 5, 7, 9, 11, 12, 13, 14, 16, 21, 23, 24, 25, 26, 27, 28, 29, 30, 31, 33, 35, 36, 38, 39, 40, 42, 43, 46, 47, 53, 54, 55, 57, 58, 59, 60, 61, 63, 64, 69, 72, 73, 74, 75, 76, 77, 78, 79, 80, 81, 82, 83, 84, 85, 86, 87, 88, 89, 90, 91, 92, 93, 94, 95, 96, 97, 100, 103, 107, 110, 111, 112, 113, 114, 115, 116, 117, 118, 121, 126, 128, 130, 134, 135, 141, 142, 143, 145, 146, 148, 149, 151, 152, 157, 158, 160, 161, 162, 163, 164, 165, 166, 167.	106	63
Total		167	

TABLE 10.—TOTAL NUMBER OF PROGRESSIONS—DOWNWARD AND UPWARD

	Number	Per cent
Downward	2,809	59
Upward	1,929	41
Total	4,738	

TABLE 11.—INTERVALS IN DOWNWARD PROGRESSION

	Number	Per cent		Number	Per cent
Interval of a—			Interval of a—		
Fifth	10		Major second	1,362	48
Fourth	273	10	Minor second	185	6
Major third	227	7			
Minor third	752	27	Total	2,809	

TABLE 12.—INTERVALS IN UPWARD PROGRESSION

	Number	Per cent		Number	Per cent
Interval of a—			Interval of a—		
Ninth	1		Major third	149	7
Octave	2		Minor third	401	21
Seventh	12		Major second	660	35
Major sixth	32	2	Minor second	103	5
Minor sixth	7				
Fifth	148	7	Total	1,929	
Fourth	414	22			

TABLE 13.—AVERAGE NUMBER OF SEMITONES IN AN INTERVAL

Number of songs	167
Number of intervals	4,738
Number of semitones	14,222
Average number of semitones in an interval	3

RHYTHMIC ANALYSIS

TABLE 14.—PART OF MEASURE ON WHICH SONG BEGINS

	Serial numbers of songs	Number	Per cent
Beginning on unaccented part of measure.	1, 2, 4, 6, 11, 13, 14, 16, 17, 18, 23, 26, 27, 29, 30, 35, 36, 37, 45, 51, 53, 54, 55, 64, 69, 74, 76, 78, 79, 81, 82, 83, 84, 85, 87, 88, 94, 95, 97, 100, 101, 103, 112, 113, 114, 118, 121, 122, 126, 128, 130, 134, 135, 141, 145, 146, 149, 152, 157, 158, 162, 164, 165, 166, 167.	65	39
Beginning on accented part of measure.	3, 5, 7, 8, 9, 10, 12, 15, 19, 20, 21, 22, 24, 25, 28, 31, 32, 33, 34, 38, 39, 40, 41, 42, 43, 44, 46, 47, 48, 49, 50, 52, 56, 57, 58, 59, 60, 61, 62, 63, 65, 66, 67, 68, 70, 71, 72, 73, 75, 77, 80, 86, 89, 90, 91, 92, 93, 96, 98, 99, 102, 104, 105, 106, 107, 108, 109, 110, 111, 115, 116, 117, 119, 120, 123, 124, 125, 127, 129, 131, 132, 133, 136, 137, 138, 139, 140, 142, 143, 144, 147, 148, 150, 151, 153, 154, 155, 156, 159, 160, 161, 163.	102	61
Total		167	

TABLE 15.—RHYTHM (METER) OF FIRST MEASURE

	Serial numbers of songs	Number	Per cent
First measure in—			
2-4 time	2, 3, 6, 7, 9, 11, 12, 13, 17 18, 19, 21, 23, 24, 25, 27, 28, 29, 31, 32, 33, 35, 36, 37, 38, 39, 40, 42, 43, 44, 48, 50, 52, 54, 55, 56, 58, 59, 60, 61, 63, 65, 66, 67, 68, 69, 70, 71, 72, 73, 74, 75, 77, 80, 81, 83, 85, 88, 89, 90, 91, 92, 93, 94, 95, 96, 97, 99, 100, 101, 103, 104, 105, 107, 108, 110, 111, 114, 115, 116, 117, 122, 128, 129, 130, 133, 134, 135, 137, 138, 139, 140, 141, 142, 144, 145, 146, 147, 148, 149, 150, 151, 152, 154, 157, 158, 161, 162, 163, 164.	110	66
3-4 time	4, 5, 8, 10, 14, 15, 16, 22, 26, 30, 34, 45, 46, 47, 51, 53, 57, 62, 64, 76, 78, 79, 82, 85, 87, 98, 102, 106, 109, 112, 113, 118, 119, 120, 121, 123, 124, 125, 126, 127, 131, 132, 136, 143, 153, 155, 156, 159, 160, 166, 167.	51	30
3-8 time	1, 165	2	------
4-8 time	20	1	------
5-8 time	49, 86	2	1
6-8 time	41	1	------
Total		167	------

TABLE 16.—CHANGE OF TIME (MEASURE-LENGTHS)

	Serial numbers of songs	Number	Per cent
Songs containing no change of time.	3, 14, 30, 33, 38, 39, 50, 67, 104, 106, 122, 138, 139, 152	14	9
Songs containing a change of time.		153	91
Total		167	------

TABLE 17.—RHYTHMIC UNIT OF SONG

	Serial numbers of songs	Number	Per cent
Songs containing—			
No rhythmic unit	4, 6, 8, 9, 10, 11, 13, 17, 20, 22, 23, 25, 29, 31, 32, 33, 37, 45, 53, 54, 56, 57, 62, 71, 80, 81, 82, 84, 86, 90, 92, 93, 97, 104, 106, 107, 108, 109, 110, 112, 113, 115, 117, 118, 121, 123, 134, 135, 136, 137, 139, 141, 149, 158, 164, 166, 167.	57	34
One rhythmic unit	1, 2, 3, 12, 14, 16, 19, 27, 28, 30, 35, 36, 38, 41, 42, 43, 44, 47, 48, 49, 55, 60, 65, 67, 69, 70, 74, 75, 76, 77, 78, 83, 85, 87, 88, 89, 94, 100, 101, 103, 105, 116, 119, 120, 122, 124, 130, 131, 132, 133, 140, 142, 144, 146, 147, 148, 150, 152, 153, 154, 155, 157, 159, 161, 162, 165.	66	59
Two rhythmic units	5, 15, 18, 21, 24, 26, 34, 39, 40, 50, 52, 58, 63, 66, 68, 73, 79, 96, 98, 99, 102, 111, 114, 125, 126, 127, 128, 129, 138, 143, 145, 151, 156, 160, 163.	35	21
Three rhythmic units	7, 51, 59, 95	4	2
Four rhythmic units	61, 64, 72, 91	4	2
Five rhythmic units	46	1	------
Total		167	------

INDEX